MENUS FROM AN ORCHARD TABLE

MENUS FROM AN ORCHARD TABLE

Heidi Noble

whitecap

Whitecap Books

Edited by Lesley Cameron
Proofread by Ann-Marie Metten
Design by Michelle Mayne
Color photography by Chris Stearns
Black & white photography by Craig Noble

Other photography by Joie:
p. 74 – autumn; p. 80 – asparagus; p. 82 – Schubert in front of smoker;
p. 86 – bacon salad; p. 94 – garden; p. 160 – radish; p. 193 – goat;
p. 241 – Schubert shaping pasta; p. 289 – spring orchard; p. 314 – winter orchard

Printed and bound in Canada

LIBRARY AND ARCHIVES CANADA CATALOGUING IN PUBLICATION

Noble, Heidi
Menus from an orchard table : celebrating the food and wine of the
Okanagan / Heidi Noble, author.

Includes index.
ISBN 1-55285-852-9
ISBN 978-1-55285-852-3

1. Cookery, Canadian--British Columbia style. 2. Cookery--British
Columbia--Okanagan Valley (Region). 3. Wine and winemaking--British
Columbia--Okanagan Valley (Region). I. Title.
TX715.6.N63 2007   641.59711'5   C2006-904986-6

The publisher acknowledges the financial support of the Government of Canada
through the Book Publishing Industry Development Program and the Province
of British Columbia through the Book Publishing Tax Credit.

This book is dedicated, with love, to my husband Michael who embarked on this adventure with me. Joie was born out of the joy that food, wine, and travel have brought to our lives. Our business is a reflection of our desire to engage in our passions daily. What an adventure it has been and I want to thank Michael for being my "Lovely-Man Traveling Companion" on our journeys. As always, I am ready to take on whatever is next…together.

CONTENTS

In a small farmhouse cooking school nestled among a verdant grove of fruit trees, Heidi Noble and Michael Dinn have set out to explore cooking with local, seasonal ingredients. This intrepid pair, both originally from big cities, hopes to help lay the groundwork for the development of an Okanagan regional cuisine.

Is this a realistic goal? Can one develop a new cuisine? Well, broadly speaking, the term cuisine denotes a cooking style, but usually also implies a sense of tradition. The Okanagan previously boasted a local cuisine, but it differed from the great regional cuisines of Chinese and French, which stemmed from peasant agrarian societies.[1] In regions with recognized cuisines, dishes are characterized by a collection of traditional, typical recipes that have stood the test of time and are largely based on a relatively strict adherence to the use of local ingredients. A sense of belonging is also attached to the idea of cuisine, where people share a common understanding of "how and why the ingredients are put together, and the story this represents. There must also be a feeling of shared values and customs among the people, an incipient sense of belonging or wanting to belong."[2] The people of these same areas recognize the dishes and cuisine as their own, and outsiders also know them to be of that region. For dishes to become part of a regional cuisine, they must also be accepted in home kitchens. Of course, cuisines evolve, and as a matter of course, new ingredients and techniques are gradually absorbed into the cooking style alongside local ingredients.

British Columbia, however, went straight from a hunter-gatherer culture to an industrial cuisine. Earlier food styles, whether First Nations or early settlement, have largely disappeared, and today in the Okanagan we have a globalized industrial model of cuisine with some regional characteristics rather than a clearly identifiable, regional cooking style based on a sense of history, place, and community. Many people in the Okanagan rarely cook and infrequently prepare their own food from raw ingredients. They often eat in their cars and in fast food outlets, or alone in front of a television set; they often microwave food from a can, a package, or a freezer. Most of our food is manufactured in part or entirely outside our home kitchens, and takes little time to assemble or eat. Moreover, nearly half our calorie intake today comes from added fats and sugars, not from natural ingredients. Our dining is very individualized, and our cooking is conspicuous for its stylistic chaos, a sort of globalist mishmash without real relevance to the geography of our country. Meals based on ingredients from everywhere and pre-packaged food distribution are becoming increasingly the same in different parts of the world, supported by thousands of advertising messages a year paid for by global food conglomerates. Our eating patterns, from early childhood, are based not on customs, but on corporate profits and commodity pricing.

This faceless, placeless industrial cuisine is not healthy. It is characterized by increasing toxicity and lower levels of nutrients, even in industrial-scale organic food. Thomas Pawlick in *The End of Food*[3] and a CTV–*Globe and Mail* study have both chronicled a regular decrease in minerals and vitamins in conventional and organic foods from distant sources. Unripe fruits and vegetables are harvested too early, when their nutritional levels are too low, so that they can be treated for extended shipping times and supermarket shelf lives. We are also witnessing ever-increasing toxic contamination in the foods we eat.

Industrial cuisine is unsustainable in the context of global warming because it uses ingredients that travel thousands of miles, requiring the use of huge quantities of non-renewable, highly polluting fossil fuels. Even distant industrial organic food is more likely to be processed, chemically preserved, and packaged than its local equivalent. Local food production offers substantial environmental advantages over industrially produced foods since it requires far less packaging, energy-intensive refrigeration, and outside chemical inputs.

Increasingly violent storms, floods, and drought have raised public awareness of global warming. Renowned Oxford professor George Monbiot asserts that global warming is "the greatest threat the world now faces."[4] He is very alarmed about the profligate use of fuels in the transport and distribution of foods which, on average, travel over 2,000 miles to get to your supermarket. He is also concerned by the vast amounts of energy needed to fuel the average supermarket. Monbiot is strongly critical of television food personalities who promote the jet transportation of foods from across the world when so many excellent, healthy, and sustainable foods are grown locally. He opposes their use of foreign ingredients and asserts that "it is not hard to see how our diet, even for those of the most refined and demanding tastes, could in fact be improved by means of geographic restriction."[5] He urges everyone to buy locally in order to cut down on greenhouse gas emissions because our very existence urgently depends upon it.[6]

A return to a locally based food system must be an important component of a global strategy to slow global warming. Since they are less mechanized, small local farmers frequently use only half the fossil fuels per unit of food produced than that of distant, large-scale organic farms, which consume almost as much energy as conventional industrial farms. These huge organic farms and conventional farms from afar increase the pressure on small-scale farmers, particularly on organic producers who are trying to re-introduce sustainability; they are putting our local farms out of business.

If you live in Canada and your food comes from California, Mexico, or China, it is unsustainable, even if it is organic. Both food transportation over long distances and mechanized agriculture using large-scale industrial equipment and fertilizers made from petroleum products contribute substantially to global warming. Why should so many foods be transported for thousands of miles when they can be produced within a hundred? We can no longer justify being so dependent upon exotic foods which are airlifted, barged, or trucked in from far beyond our food sheds. Local is the only sustainable alternative.

Industrial cuisine also threatens sustainability through the dramatic, recent acceleration of biodiversity loss in this sixth age of species extinction. According to the UN Food and Agriculture Organization, approximately 75 percent of the world's agricultural biodiversity was lost during the 20th century, and industrial food production is the primary cause. In Michael Pollan's address to Slow Food's Terra Madre delegates in Turin in 2006, he lamented that 75 percent of the world's foods are produced from only eight species. As genetically modified organisms are allowed to proliferate in Canada, biodiversity will quickly be further eroded. Canadian biogenetics expert Brewster Kneen has found that more than 60 percent of Canada's field crops are now genetically modified—a serious threat to biodiversity throughout Canada. Today the European Communities, inspired by the precautionary principle, are less at risk than we are, because they continue to enforce a ban on most genetically modified organisms. Even industrial organic farms have become monocultures and continue to eradicate biodiversity.

Of all the sacrifices we have made for industrial convenience foods, perhaps the most significant is the sacrifice of flavor. The global media work with the planet-wide food industry to homogenize people's tastes, and the consumer is encouraged to buy roughly the same food commodities across the world. To my horror, I actually found microwaved burritos in highway convenience stores across Provence during a recent trip to southern France. Is this Provençal cuisine? The great majority of Canadian consumers are part of a food chain that is so international that very few people know where or how their food was grown, processed, or treated during its long trip to the marketplace, and it is no surprise that the end result is tasteless food.

It is imperative that we distance ourselves from this industrial food chain and the time for change is now. *Menus from an Orchard Table* proposes an encouraging, positive, and delicious alternative! The active promotion and use of regional foods and wines provides an excellent starting point and is easier to endorse and understand than the idea of a shift to a full-blown new regional cuisine. Joie Farm Cooking School is clearly on the right track.

Throughout our wider geographic region, some restaurants such as Higgins, Wildwood, and Navarre in Portland, the Raincity Grill, Aurora Bistro, and Bishop's in Vancouver have succeeded in actively showcasing foods from their immediate environs. In Seattle, the Herbfarm has done an outstanding job of educating the public and serving the best food this region has to offer with spectacular results and reviews. Here on Vancouver Island, my restaurant, Sooke Harbour House, has been growing and cooking with sustainable southern Vancouver Island ingredients successfully for nearly 30 years. Fairburn Farm, a new addition to the Vancouver Island list, is promoting the farmed foods of their immediate area. It is also encouraging that an increasing number of restaurants, such as Tojo's in Vancouver and Zambri's in Victoria, are serving more and more seasonal, regional,

clean, and ethically raised foods from their own areas and setting an example for other restaurants and home kitchens to follow.

A similar trend is beginning to establish itself little by little in the northern Okanagan Valley. Rod Butters at Fresco and Michael Allemeier at Mission Hill Winery are part of a new wave of chefs who increasingly understand the values and flavors associated with local ingredients. Many of these restaurants have helped promote regional consciousness and are building a local food movement which may eventually lead to area-based cuisines. Authors such as John Doerper with his series on Pacific Northwest cuisine, Elizabeth Levinson in *An Edible Journey*, and Anita Stewart in *The Flavours of Canada* have worked to create awareness. Several excellent, regional journalists have also contributed greatly to the understanding of this place-based approach.

We must rebuild a cooking style that is identifiable with a given area, if only to ensure that we have farmers, ranchers, and food artisans in the Okanagan Valley in the future. Canada has lost more than 80 percent of its farm population since the Second World War, and the numbers are still declining quickly. We have lost tens of thousands of agricultural workers in the last five years and the majority of our farmers are now nearing retirement age. The decline in our farm population is frequently accompanied by a loss of farm land, and in the Okanagan, cookie cutter subdivisions increasingly scar the landscape, replacing orchards and farms, particularly in the north. The knowledge and skills required to restore our farms, rural communities, fisheries, and foraged and artisanal foods are rapidly being lost. For farming to remain viable, the economics of farming need to be restored, and these food producers need our encouragement.

If we buy locally, the amount that the farmer receives will increase substantially and this is what Heidi is promoting. She understands that when she buys local, organic food in season, "much of the money that our business earns is returned directly and consistently to the hands of local farmers." Bravo!

Fifty years ago, farmers received about 75 percent of the retail price of their goods, but today they are generally paid between 5 percent and 20 percent when selling to multinational food factories and supermarkets. By eliminating distributors and middlemen who contribute to the decrease in the profit to the farmer, farmers increase their chances of survival.

Heidi regularly supports the Penticton and Naramata farmer's markets. Buying from these markets is not only fun, but it also fosters interaction and friendships between the consumer and the grower. Knowing the growers helps give nearby customers a sense of confidence in what they are buying. By focusing on the re-localization of food production and purchasing, and encouraging smaller-scale production, some cooks in the Okanagan are learning to trust the food they eat again, and this helps give people a renewed sense of belonging and commitment to a particular place, creating healthier communities and a fertile foundation on which Heidi's new regional cuisine can be built.

Menus from an Orchard Table is clearly one of the best recent books written in Canada on the direction that our new regional cuisines should take. Hopefully, it will provide a blueprint for others who want to lead their regions to a place where farmers and food artisans can thrive, a sustainable place where mouthwatering food and a healthy environment can coexist.

One of the impressive strengths of this book is that it serves as a guidebook, a catalogue of some of the best producers in the Okanagan Valley. The Valley is, after all, not only an excellent producer of vegetables and meat, but also one of Canada's best fruit producing regions,

and these marvelous ingredients should be featured on every menu in the Valley.

Regional cuisines tend to develop from local ingredients and the enjoyment that nearby populations derive from the delectable dishes. Cooks need to focus much more on their area's food supply and, ideally, on purchasing certified or non-certified organic produce from their neighborhoods when possible. The team at Joie cultivates certified organic kitchen gardens and orchards; they know when their apples and pears are ready to pick at the peak of their flavor, ripeness, and healthfulness. What they don't grow themselves, they source locally, directly from outstanding growers at farmer's markets that feature a wide array of organic products from the Valley. Joie's cooking school students accompany Heidi to these markets or on farm tours and learn how to cook with beautiful, fresh ingredients. In addition to a deeper understanding of the quality of ingredients, their reward is a delicious lunch based on their market foray.

The nature of tourism is changing rapidly in many regions of the world, and the recent development of wine culture in the Okanagan is attracting more sophisticated tourists. The wine tourist who is looking for the best in local wines for their home cellars is also looking for meals that highlight the most flavorful foods from the same region—an authentic, distinctive, local dining experience. When people go to Italy, France, or China, they expect to find the foods that epitomize the differing regions of these countries. By the same token, these same travelers expect to discover the genuine foods of the Okanagan.

Things that grow together, go together. By developing their own wines ideally suited to accompany local food creations, Michael and Heidi are advancing the understanding of how Okanagan foods and wines can complement each other. They are helping lay the groundwork for a new culture of food and wine.

Heidi and Michael's adventure, thus far, shows that they certainly have their work cut out for them. In Sooke, where I come from, we have witnessed the highest rate of removal of agricultural land in the province for quick real estate profits. A proliferation of low-grade subdivisions, fast food restaurants, and strip malls have degraded local food culture and have dramatically reduced the potential for the growth of tourism in our area. The north of the Okanagan is undergoing the same pressure, but support for local agricultural values can help obviate this outcome. It is essential to protect the Agricultural Land Reserve in the Okanagan, and Heidi and Michael's project is helping to do just that.

Heidi believes that the regions of British Columbia are the most likely place in Canada to witness the growth of authentic regional cuisines, and I am inclined to concur. Joie will certainly help to develop a sense of terroir and place. It will be interesting to see if there is a parallel evolution in the Charlevoix region of Quebec, where there are also some encouraging signs of the emergence of an exciting local food movement.

I cannot think of a region of Canada that has more potential for developing its own cuisine than the Okanagan Valley, and what better place to start than at Joie on the Naramata Bench. Amid grapevines and orchards of apples, peaches, plums, and cherries, situated in one of the very best wine producing regions in the country, they are ideally located to explore and create a cooking style that is true to place.

Equally important, they are bringing new confidence and credibility to the producers of their area who are doing their best to provide food that is good, clean, and ethical. This financial and psychological boost is needed by artisan food producers and farmers struggling for survival in an industrialized, fast food nation. Heidi and Michael are leaders of a growing local food movement in the Okanagan Valley which is helping to reassert a regional identity and create a new sense of community. We are witnessing the slow emergence of a new food culture and this book, and the example that Joie Farm Cooking School is setting, will help the people of the Okanagan build a regional cuisine of their own. Congratulations on this important book and good luck to this dynamic couple!

Sinclair Philip
Sooke Harbour House
Leader, Slow Food Canada

[1] Symons, Michael. *The Shared Table: Ideas for Australian Cuisine*. Canberra: Australian Government Publishing Service, 1997, pp. 5, 6.

[2] Santich, Barbara. *Looking for Flavour*. Wakefield Press. Kent Town, South Australia: 1996, p. 90.

[3] Pawlick, Thomas F. *The End of Food*. Vancouver: Douglas and McIntyre, 2006.

[4] Monbiot, George. *Heat: How to Stop the Planet from Burning*. Doubleday Canada, 2006, p. 212.

[5] Ibid. p. 191.

[6] Ibid. p. 212.

MENUS FROM AN ORCHARD TABLE

INTRODUCTION

This book is a book of menus. Menus can be journeys in time and season to places both near and far, and are sometimes the closest you can come to traveling without embarking on a culinary adventure yourself. The creation of Joie has been an adventure for my husband, Michael Dinn, and me, and our menus retrace our journey.

Some of my favorite cookbooks and books on food are actually books of menus, but they do more than simply list recipes, they also evoke a certain time and place. This is why I have chosen to tell the story of Joie and how it became our home, our farm, our cooking school, and our winery through a book of menus. Menus are a form of culinary escapism, but the re-telling of the creation of Joie is not escapism for me. Rather, it stirs up much emotion related to our four-year journey. For you, reading our story and reproducing some of our recipes may be an opportunity to savor the memories of a vacation in Naramata at Joie or imagining you did. People often say to us, you must be living your dream — and yes, we are lucky to live among such beauty, busily engaged in our passions, but we didn't follow a direct route to arrive at where we are now. I will use the menus from our Orchard Dinners to recount the stories of the dedicated producers I met, the wonderful guests who visited, and the incredible chefs who came to our farm to stay awhile. Moreover, I want to use our menus as a vehicle to demonstrate the birth of a new wine country cuisine in British Columbia's Okanagan Valley and to show how it is becoming a culinary destination for visitors from around the world. This book, through its menus, will examine the potential for a unique Okanagan Wine Country cuisine, placed within the larger framework of cuisine found on the West Coast of North America.

The Okanagan Valley, in the southern interior of British Columbia, is the main fruit bowl of the province. For the past 100 years, acre upon acre of this northerly tip of the Sonoran desert has been irrigated. Fruit trees and vineyards thrive in the valleys, nestled between and around a series of lakes. Predictably, being a chef, one of the first places I visited in the Okanagan from my home in Vancouver, British Columbia, was the Penticton farmer's market. As a dyed-in-the-wool urban dweller, I was accustomed to the high standards of Vancouver's Trout Lake farmer's market. I was also accustomed to high prices. However, having made a commitment to buy local, organic food in season, paying top dollar for food was not a problem for me. It was simply part of the ritual. Actually, nothing made me happier than handing over cash directly to the person who had grown the food. When I first visited the Penticton farmer's market in June of 2000, not only was the quality of the food superior, but it was also about half the price. Moreover, I was buying this food on the grower's own turf, close to its source. Many of the farmers who come to the Trout Lake market are from an area in the Similkameen Valley (just west of the Okanagan Valley) called Cawston. Those growers were at Penticton's market, all certified organic with stalls overflowing with delicious, gorgeous-looking produce. I was in love! Not only had I come to visit this wonderful burgeoning wine country with a new beau, Michael Dinn, I was now also finding myself seduced on many levels by the sheer beauty and bounty of the region.

That weekend, Michael and I became engaged. On our drive home, the first of many drives on the Hope-Princeton highway that would nurture our grand plans for "Joie," endless ideas swirled through our heads. We returned to the area a few times in the summer of 2001, first as newlyweds visiting wineries, and then later as participants in the fall harvest work on the Naramata Bench. We took many more trips to wine country in the summer of 2002, and enjoyed dinner parties, made from the bounty of the Penticton farmer's market, with new friends. As we headed home to the city, ideas and dreams danced in our minds, partnered by memories of the experiences we had had on our honeymoon at small auberges in France and agritourismos in Northern Italy in the spring of 2001 and the trips to Vin Italy I had taken as part of my job with the import wine agency I worked for between 2000 and 2004.

During my time in Italy I had been very influenced by the Italian family that I stayed with.

I found myself impressed by the strength of their family bond, their extended family unit, and, of course, their attachment to food and the pride they took in their region. I felt a similar connection to the Okanagan and its natural bounty. I wanted us to be part of the Okanagan experience, to have our own piece of this amazing area, and this realization and desire coincided with our recognition that it was time for us to embrace change and put down new roots.

A fourth trip to the Okanagan Valley, when we were staying on the Naramata Bench, saw us finally and absolutely succumb to the charms of the area. In July of 2002, we took a drive around one afternoon, called a real estate agent, and two days later made an offer on a five-acre farm on Naramata Road. After a few weeks of negotiations our offer was accepted and we took possession of our new farm with its 1,200 fruit trees and 3,000-square-foot country house. We were still feeling dazzled by the beauty of our surroundings, utterly shocked at what we had done.

I wanted us to be part of the Okanagan experience, to have our own piece of this amazing area.

That winter our lives bounced back and forth between urban and rural life as we continued to work our regular wine jobs while planning for our new life in the country. Our original plans for the property included renovating our garage into a state-of-the-art food and wine learning center, modeled on the Copia Centre in the Napa Valley. In our enthusiasm we naturally assumed that this would be a welcome addition to a burgeoning wine area and an excellent contribution to the winemaking community. However, a winter of architectural planning and bylaw reviews, plus a rude introduction to up-country politics, taught us the hard way what it was like to be city slickers with a passion for food and sustainable agriculture moving into a rural community. Naive doesn't even come close to describing us! We simply couldn't understand how people representing a community whose main job for the past 100 years had been to produce food could have no interest in adding a cooking school to that community. The Naramata Bench community that we had met initially had actually been a small group of winemakers and transplanted food enthusiasts who had created their own little enclave. The locally elected officials, on the other hand, comprised a group of people with a slightly different worldview.

Having spent the past 10 years in progressive urban environments within professional food communities in Toronto, Montreal, and Vancouver, not to mention being a graduate of a chef's school renowned for turning out more farmers than chefs, I was accustomed to being surrounded by people with positive attitudes toward buying and cooking local organic food. And because I had lived among and worked for some of the biggest promoters of this approach to food, I had convinced myself that the movement was indeed taking hold. Fast forward to my new reality where I found myself living in an area with a local governance unable to envision the idea of other people wanting to experience the foods that people ate in farm country. The notion that a local cuisine could grow alongside the new wine industry was of much interest to our local Chamber of Commerce and Tourism Office at the time but of no interest to the bureaucracy.

"Eating is an agricultural act." For me, the connection between food and agriculture was obvious, and it was an intrinsic part of my worldview. However, for the local rule makers and many of the old-time conventional farmers who sold their crops to the fruit-packing co-op, the connection appeared to be non-existent. For them, their produce was simply a commodity, a means to make ends meet, which they no longer thought about once it left their property and headed to the co-op. There was no obvious appreciation of the fact that their produce would end up on someone's dinner plate at some point. This approach to food and farming is not unusual in rural food-producing regions in Canada, and to my mind it is clearly a cultural issue.

I will never forget the moment during one bylaw meeting when I heard Wendell Berry's famous words, "Eating is an agricultural act," come flying out of my mouth in one of the many passionate tirades that erupted during these meetings. I had to explain to a room full of officious people that we grow food to eat food and that visitors to farm and wine country would certainly be interested not only in what grows here, but also in learning how to cook it in a way that would make the most of its taste and quality. The idea that food can be associated with pleasure and recreation was absolutely foreign to this group who seemed to regard food only as fuel for the body. In the winter of 2002 the notion of culinary tourism in the Okanagan was uncharted territory, and the fact that it actually already existed, not only here in Canada but also in wine country around the world, did not seem to interest them. Part of the problem was that the Okanagan has been an established destination for summertime family recreation for so long that the idea of a new kind of tourist was an uncomfortable prospect. The accepted three main interests of wine tourists—eating well, drinking well, and sleeping well—were incongruous with the fast-food restaurants, strip motels, and waterslides that already existed here. Our plan to build a center that would act as a showcase for what was happening here on the culinary and wine scene was thought of as esoteric and too city to the local powers-that-be at the time. Michael and I left that meeting in January of 2003 in shock. We were now in serious debt, and without our city jobs, city house, and "city backup." We were in deep, but we were not going back to the city.

Our licensing troubles continued to the point of us not being able to build the dream facility in our garage. We moved into our new home on the weekends of the winter of 2002/03 and lived in a constant state of incredulity as we watched the plans for our wine and food center slip away from us. March 2003 came and went, still with no permit

Why go all the way to Tuscany for a culinary vacation in wine country?

for the renovation and with thousands of dollars spent in vain. But luckily we are stubborn creatures, and, acting on sage advice from our friend and mentor Sinclair Philip of the Sooke Harbour House we did not miss our season. Sinclair told us that, even though we did not have our permit, we should think outside of the box and use what we did have. In other words, our giant farmhouse and five acres of land. After humbly asking for our jobs back in the city, we proposed a last-minute plan of us both working full-time in Vancouver and commuting to Naramata to run Gastronomic Getaways on the weekends. We completed a reno on the upstairs of our house, made three bedrooms country-chic with our art and books from our travels to wine country around the world, got a friend to develop a groovy, good-looking

website, and offered a packaged epicurean retreat. We asked, why go all the way to Tuscany for a culinary vacation in wine country? Phew. In retrospect our crazy, stubborn plan had us biting off way more than we could chew. However, our courage at that time has since been rewarded with a business that has evolved in ways that we could never have imagined when we were first starting out—and believe me, our dreams and plans for the business were grand!

During the summer of 2003 we each worked Monday through Thursday in Vancouver, cramming 50 hours' work into a four-day week. We then drove up to Naramata on Thursday evening, did prep, and received guests on Friday afternoon. On Saturday morning we made breakfast for three couples, took them to the farmer's market, returned to the farm, taught a cooking class in a makeshift kitchen in our side gardens (which I had also somehow found the time to plant with heirloom varieties of herbs and vegetables), cleaned up after the Saturday morning cooking class, prepared for dinner, and served a six-course country dinner under the stars in the middle of our orchard for up to twenty-four people. We then got up on Sunday morning, made breakfast again, taught a wine seminar, fed our guests a ploughman's lunch, sent them on their way, cleaned up, and then drove five hours back to Vancouver, only to do it all over again the next week. What lunacy! However, it was all worth it in the end as we made it through our first makeshift season and were still standing in October of 2003.

Great food doesn't happen in a vacuum.

That winter we continued to renovate the house and finished our lower floor with two more bedrooms and another bathroom, preparing for a second season of a new business concept that did not quite reflect our first conceptualized idea. If it hadn't been for Sinclair's advice, however, we never would have opened in the first place. Perhaps we would still have forged ahead with our original but very capital-intensive plan for the center, although I'm not sure now that this area could support a school of that scope. Four years later we are nearing our target destination, but the Okanagan, being five hours' drive away from Vancouver and eight hours away from Calgary, remains very seasonal, which poses its own challenges.

Who could have predicted that Michael and I would become innkeepers of a gastronomic guesthouse? Who would have thought we would be teaching cooking classes outdoors, or hosting dinners under the stars? It all taught us that small-business owners must be dynamic and always open to change, and that sometimes, just sometimes, wonderful opportunities come out of a crisis.

In retrospect, the greatest opportunity of our first year at Joie came from the necessity to cook outdoors. This had its practical benefits, of course. Who wanted to be inside when it was 104°F (40°C) in the summer? Not me. The changes we had to make to our business model in order to be open for business in 2003 resulted in a rather diversified but more solid model all round. We found ourselves offering accommodation, cooking classes, wine seminars, and the Orchard Dinners. The Orchard Dinners became my favorite part of our venture. Not only were they truly magical experiences—sitting outdoors at a linen-covered table, with proper crystal and place settings—but the menus that I was able to create allowed me not only to develop our business, but also to get to know the producers of the area which, in turn, influenced my cooking even more. The concrete act of writing those menus every week was a pleasure, but it also revealed to me the true potential of Okanagan cuisine.

Great food doesn't happen in a vacuum. As with any piece of art or creative endeavor, one is never able to fully shrug off past experiences and be untouched by their influence. When I sat down to create my menus every week, there was the issue of what I would want to cook and the matter of what was available with which to cook. Because I was new to the area, I went out on excursions to find out who was growing what and where. I also had to figure out what I was able to grow in my own gardens. I was excited by the challenge of menu planning every week because it was guided by what was available at the farmer's market that had originally sparked my interest in the area. The Okanagan was still mainly a food-producing area with a developing outside interest in its vineyards. Okanagan cuisine was in its most embryonic state at that time, but the important thing was that it was based on fantastically fresh core ingredients, as are most great world cuisines. With the Okanagan's plentiful supply of fresh ingredients at my disposal, I was thrilled to be using the market as my inspiration.

THE BIRTH OF A CUISINE

Let us take a moment to explore the notion of cuisine. For me, cuisine is the culmination of a convergence of people, places, time, and history. My definition of cuisine is one that views the food preparation of a specific place at a specific moment in time as edible culture. In this section I will examine how the influx of new people and their previous experiences to an area will inevitably influence the preparation of local foods.

When I first came to the Okanagan one element that particularly struck me, beyond the obvious natural beauty, was its awesome, edible bounty. The fundamental roots of a cuisine are a commonality of ingredients but it is the interpretations of the use of those ingredients that give definition to that cuisine as it evolves over time. As our summer Orchard Dinners at Joie were served year after year, my menus evolved under the influence of the new ingredients and producers I discovered during our farm tours with our cooking classes. My menus also continued to evolve as chef friends from my urban cooking past and new chef visitors arrived. When they saw what awesome food product was here and then applied their ideas, cooking histories, and repertoires to the ingredients to which I introduced them, our menus took an even more exciting turn. The introduction of new local ingredients and the constant stream of guest chefs bringing their personal influences to novel ingredients have actively driven the evolution of Joie's menus and the recipes used for the cooking classes. For me, the cuisine of a place happens from a consciousness of ingredients and a convergence of people. The birth of a cuisine is a form of self-awareness, an edible time and place.

THE EVOLUTION OF A CUISINE

It was almost instantly apparent to me when I arrived in the Okanagan that the convergence of local ingredients and people with a willingness to use them had not happened yet. What made this situation painfully obvious was the sheer lack of decent places to eat. Now when I say decent, I mean not only tasty, but also truly representative of what is locally good to eat. I knew that the geographical challenge of the Okanagan Valley's being far from any urban centers had a huge impact on the seasonal business of local restaurants interested in buying and serving local product—we don't have the Napa and Sonoma Valleys' proximity to savvy San Francisco here—but the overt lack of restaurants serving any local product at all was shocking. The challenge of opening a restaurant that could serve the curious tourists in the summer and the thrifty locals in the winter was also obvious. Penticton and the surrounding area are populated mainly by working-class families and retired seniors from the Prairies, not the archetypal demographics for a culinary mecca. For a variety of reasons, this group tends not to set aside significant portions of their budget for high-quality food, and the result is a plethora of restaurants that offer low-priced dinner specials and fast food, creating little demand for local meat and produce in restaurants and grocery stores. It seems that there is only a demand for local product in the summertime when the wine country tourists appear, along with journalists looking to crown the Okanagan Valley "Napa North." The seasonal nature of tourism in the Okanagan, coupled with its isolated location and the budgets of its full-time residents, makes it a hard-go for small restaurateurs and food purveyors.

I came to realize that a food culture in the Okanagan was not going to happen overnight. I had to internalize my awareness that a cuisine needs time to percolate, it needs many different voices and past experiences bringing a new perspective to new ingredients. Most of all, the local ingredients needed to proliferate and needed to get to the people in charge of purchasing and cooking food in the Okanagan Valley year round. Success depends on the willingness of people

The cuisine of a place happens from a consciousness of ingredients and a convergence of people.

in the restaurant business to lead by example, by buying direct from the growers and being committed to using local product. In my opinion, a sign of a mature and sustainable culture is a local and healthy food system. Since the local bounty was such a large part of why Michael and I came to the Okanagan, I was determined to help establish this food system by making sure our business was not only part of that economic engine, but also that it would lead by example to the others who live here. On a practical level, our business gave us the cash flow and buying power to put much cash in the hands of other local businesses, including the artisan food and wine producers. Putting money directly into the community is something I knew the local dissenters could understand and would appreciate.

Meanwhile, our business became a showcase of local bounty for visitors to the area. My weekly menu creation became driven by my curiosity and dedication to finding the best of what is grown here in the Okanagan. I was truly committed to finding new local products and making the most of them. With this book I want to share not only the menus from our journey, but also the stories of the people who grow food here. By giving you a textual lay of the land, via the products included in our seasonal menus, I can give you an insight into what was happening at Joie at the time the menus were written. In a broader sense, you can step away and see how the evolution of a local Okanagan cuisine plays a role in the continued maturation cuisine up and down the West Coast.

Okanagan product is found throughout British Columbia and is not confined to the Okanagan. However, I don't feel there is a cuisine per se quite yet. Kudos to people who have centralized the availability of local product here and have made an attempt to use it, but there is still not a critical mass of people cooking it right now. Much time and effort has certainly gone into organizing farmer's markets, restaurants showcasing local products in their menus, and small businesses putting up beautiful jars of fruit and vegetable preserves to be consumed in the winter, but for a cuisine to become fully mature, however, I think we need greater intimacy with the place.

Curiously, what is driving this intimacy with the Okanagan is the emergence of the farm-gate wine industry and the resulting wine or agritourism. A shift has occurred in people's perception of what the Okanagan Valley has to offer. Thought of for years as a family vacation destination, with much outdoor leisure and cheap accommodation or camping on offer, the age and expectations of many tourists coming to the Okanagan have changed.

Visitors' sensory experiences are moving away from the eye as they increasingly follow their taste buds, and the main draw now is the wine.

Visitors' sensory experiences are moving away from the eye as they increasingly follow their taste buds, and the main draw now is the wine. Winery tasting rooms now outnumber the orchard fruit stands and are drawing in carloads of wine tourists. Wine grapes are the new peaches, cherries, and plums. Somehow the sexy appeal of the grape brings a certain degree of esthetic expectation to all aspects of the valley experience. Grapes are bringing a cultural shift and face lift to the Okanagan. Quality wine production has added a complex new element to what the Okanagan Valley is about, not only for tourism, but for taste. Wine has brought a new species of tourist, one who demands a new type of vacation experience. Strip malls and motels are giving way to B&Bs, gastronomic guesthouses, and farm-stays. These types of accommodation provide a more personal experience and their owners also take pride in providing a stay with more intensive local immersion. Such establishments are often filled with local artworks, artifacts, books, maps, and yes, food. The wine tourist demands a more intimate knowledge of a place than is revealed by wolfing corndogs on the beach. The wine tourist insists on literally digesting the area. Agritourism gives visitors direct contact with food products, their production, and the people producing them. The distance between field and table narrows and, in turn, perspectives widen and deepen the intimacy of a place.

THE EVOLUTION OF AN OKANAGAN CUISINE AND WHERE IT FITS INTO THE MATURITY OF A WEST COAST CUISINE

You might ask how this birth of a specifically Okanagan cuisine fits into the larger picture of a specifically British Columbia cuisine. Michael, having worked since the mid-1980s as a waiter and sommelier in some of Vancouver's best restaurants, had a front-row seat for the birth and evolution of what has been deemed "Pacific Northwest" cuisine. The historian in him has a theory about its speedy maturation as a legitimate regional cuisine and the crucial role played by the BC wine industry. I would like to place his historical account in the context of a larger regional framework in order to demonstrate how what is happening in the wine country of the Okanagan Valley has become relevant to what is happening within the maturation of the cuisine of British Columbia.

As is often discussed in journalistic food circles, "Pacific Northwest" cuisine really started off in California in the late 1960s. It is often said that it was Alice Waters of Berkeley's Chez Panisse who really got the ball rolling by promoting seasonal, French-inspired country food made with locally sourced, traditional ingredients. Now you have to remember that at this time US (and Canadian) cuisine was pretty basic and, quite frankly, monotonous and myopic. It was Alice Waters's introduction of a more Mediterranean-style of eating, a cuisine shaped by an insistence on the use of fresh, seasonal ingredients, that made the most lasting impact. The temperate climate of Northern California (and all the way up the west coast through Oregon and Washington to Vancouver) translated well for this style of eating because so much is grown seasonally, almost year round. Alice Waters's voice resonated loudly up and down the West Coast and her impact has been far-reaching. Often deemed the patron saint of "California cuisine," her understanding of and commitment to the French link between people, food, and agriculture continues to influence the way thinking America eats, especially on the West Coast.

Given Alice Waters's acknowledged impact on the cuisine of the west coast it seems that the moniker of "Pacific Northwest" is both incorrect and limiting, especially for Canada. The western province British Columbia is indeed on the Pacific coast but it is located in the northwest only from a US perspective. However, the term Pacific Northwest has caught on like wild fire in food journalism and has become the accepted moniker for not only a region, but also a lifestyle and a cuisine that revolve around a high quality of life. My motives in pointing out the geographical issue and its cultural implications should not be misinterpreted here. I certainly don't want to undermine the tremendous identity that the west coast has established for itself and its regional cuisine. However, if we take a moment to pause and think about the geography of the west coast of North America, the need for a more accurate term to describe the regional cuisine actually makes sense.

The moniker of "Pacific Northwest" is both incorrect and limiting.

Despite my own reluctance to break away from the term "Pacific Northwest" the more I think in geographical terms, the more the name seems inappropriate. As we saw earlier, Pacific Northwest cuisine began in Northern California and moved its way north, toward Canada and up through to Alaska. We may share some basic ingredients, but the one thing that really binds us together is water — both the Pacific Ocean and the inland watersheds in which our salmon thrive. If we think of the Pacific Northwest more specifically from this "land-meets-water" perspective, this giant area becomes more of a biosphere in which we all share. The name Cascadia has become more accepted in ecological circles in recent years (many political separatist movements and fringe politics aside) and I think this term cuts to the core of regional food—geography.

It may seem odd to link the damp, rainy coast with the arid interior of British Columbia and Washington State, but geographically they are inextricably linked. Politically, they are also linked with large urban populations living both on the coast and inland in the interior valley. Therefore, would it not be more logical (and responsible) to take this geographical reality into consideration when we think of how we look at the way we manage our resources and local food systems? Acknowledging our mutual inhabitance of a single region and the inter-connectedness of our watersheds is key to regionally grounding our local food supply.

While California cuisine of the 1980s and early 1990s was enjoying its heyday, Sinclair and Frédérique Philip were busy developing their own interpretation of "Pacific Northwest" cuisine at the world-class destination of Sooke Harbour House, west of Victoria in the logging wilderness of southern Vancouver Island. While geographically remote, the importance of Sooke Harbour House should not be underestimated due to the longevity and sheer scope of the Philips' pursuit to evolve an absolutely pure version of local cuisine, with practically all of their ingredients coming from within a 31-mile (50-km) radius. This northern food movement had a similar respect for seasonality, but there was a distinct difference, one of identifiable regionalism, from what was happening at Chez Panisse. The movement that was happening in Canada seemed to be much more "ingredient driven" than "tradition driven." There was an absence of sentimentality for preserving a food tradition and way of life (like the Mediterranean being reproduced in California) and more of an immediacy to create, identify, and protect a local cuisine that was dictated by the availability of local product. The ingredients that were immediately available on the West Coast of Canada directly influenced the cuisine that was happening at the time. That shift changed the face of dining in British Columbia forever.

The influence of Sooke House continues to be felt at both a regional and national level, spawning an absolute diaspora of cooks from the coast, immigrating to other parts of Vancouver Island, the Interior of British Columbia, the Kootenays, and other parts of Canada, guided by the possibility of creating new cuisines upon their arrival. This movement dominated by geography has instilled confidence in the possibility (and necessity) of creating regionally based food movements all over the country.

At the same time as Sooke Harbour House was creating its own regionally based food movement, the Raintree Restaurant in Vancouver, under the direction of Janice Lotzkar and through the cooking of chefs Rebecca Dawson and Karen Barnaby, was taking a lead from California cuisine and focusing its menus around seasonal local ingredients. The Raintree, which was one of the "bridge" restaurants that moved Vancouver fine dining away from its almost exclusively European roots, proved to be a seminal restaurant in the changing status of Vancouver in the mid-1980s as it evolved from a small backwater town to an international city. Thanks to much immigration and investment from Asia, and global interest in Expo 86, the cultural landscape of the city was changing. Intentional or not, The Raintree adapted the seasonal local ingredients of British Columbia to reflect the changing population and culture of Vancouver, integrating Japanese and Chinese ingredients and techniques

Thanks to much immigration and investment from Asia, and global interest in Expo 86, the cultural landscape of the city was changing.

into their menus. Signature dishes such as wild BC salmon in a green tea butter sauce evolved. This not only conveyed a sense of the wild and indigenous products that grew in the area, it also reflected the inspiration provided by Vancouver's growing Asian community and its influence on the city's dining culture. California cuisine was the initial inspiration, but the end result was an expression of Vancouver's multicultural reality with a growing and thriving population who brought their own set of ingredients to the already bountiful West Coast and consequently changed the cultural fabric of the city.

The reclamation of Granville Island before Expo 86, transforming it from an industrial wasteland in Vancouver's False Creek to an international draw as one of the largest covered markets in the world, was certainly a beacon of change for the shopping and eating habits of Vancouverites living on the Westside and in the West End. As the 1980s gave way to the 1990s, the identity of a specifically BC cuisine was further entrenched by the green movement of that early part of the decade. Characterized by fierce, and specifically West Coast, pride the movement propelled the overwhelming support for BC-grown and -produced products. This notion of buying local extended not only to food but also to wine. The whole notion of eating locally and seasonally now seemed *de rigueur* and was truly the West Coast way by the late 1990s.

This regional pride in BC-grown products coincided with rapid expansion of the Okanagan Valley vineyards. The Free Trade Agreement with the USA in 1989 resulted in a vine-pull scheme whereby the government of British Columbia subsidized grape growers who wanted to pull out their low-quality North American grape varieties and replace them with good-quality European varietals. Further changes to the laws allowed for estate and farm-gate wineries which drove the agritourism boom that we are witness to today. Small wineries like Nichol, Kettle Valley, and Blue Mountain started to produce some fantastic wines and these small-production, boutique wines were snapped up by restaurants and visitors from the coast. The fledgling West Coast cuisine, which was beginning to find a clear identity in its ingredients and cultural influences, acquired sophistication with the addition of local BC wines to menus created with local food products. The power of those pairings on tasting menus that became popular in the late 1990s at Vancouver restaurants like Raincity Grill, Diva at the Met, Bishops, Lumière, and C Restaurant gave the province's cuisine an even greater sense of place. It seemed that BC wine sophistication further legitimized BC's version of Pacific Northwest cuisine. This sophistication was truly "Cascadian" in nature, linking the bounty of the coastal waters with the wines from the Interior.

The west coast seems to be the land of opportunity and experimentation for young cooks with its "new world" mentality and philosophy toward food.

Those chefs who were sufficiently aware and willing to support local BC product from the Fraser Valley, Vancouver Island, and the Okanagan Valley were followed by sommeliers and restaurateurs willing to support BC's new boutique wines. People like Sinclair Philip, John Bishop, Harry Kambolis, Mark Davidson, Peter Bodnar-Rod, and Brent Hayman were the leaders, promoting BC products with BC wines at restaurants like Sooke Harbour House, Bishops, The Beachside Café, C, and Raincity Grill. These restaurants showcased the best of local produce to both locals and visitors alike. Food producers and winemakers were treated with respect and were seen as celebrities in these restaurants, not faceless suppliers. Their names and the locations of their farms were added into menus and this trend became the norm around the city. These restaurant leaders and mentors went on to turn out further generations of cooks, sommeliers, and restaurateurs. It is now common in Vancouver to visit restaurants, big and small, that take great pride in their

BC wine selection, with all by-the-glass wine programs offering BC product to a greater or lesser extent. There are even a few restaurants that pour only BC wines, like Vancouver's Aurora Bistro and Pair Bistro. What a unique experience for visitors to British Columbia to enjoy.

Having completed most of my own chef's training in Montreal and Toronto, I can say that this phenomenon is truly a west coast one. The west coast seems to be the land of opportunity and experimentation for young cooks with its "new world" mentality and philosophy toward food. This liberal and modern view was one that lured me back to live and work on the west coast and has allowed many fantastic young cooks and winemakers to succeed in turning out some fine products that are well supported by the public at large. The east coast has a more ensconced and conservative attitude toward food, and is wed to older European traditions. Being geographically closer to Europe, these allegiances are probably less likely to change. I think the west coast is more willing to look to the future than to the past — new money always seems more game to take a risk than old money.

This attitude is culturally pervasive, not only in food, but in the architecture, philosophy, and music of the region. Vancouver and Victoria are cities influenced by their natural surroundings: ocean, mountains, and lush flood-plains and valleys. These natural influences are reflected in the menus of the two cities which are dominated by fish, seafood, and local lamb, poultry, cheeses, and produce from the Fraser Valley, the Interior, the Gulf Islands, and Vancouver Island. These menus, influenced by local ingredients, are now being enhanced and even validated by the quality production of local wines as well. I think the next step in the evolution of regional cuisine in BC is to turn to the place of origin of not just the food products, but also the wines. This is already happening with the emergence of the Cowichan Valley on Vancouver Island as an agritourism destination, but it is even more prevalent in the Okanagan and Similkameen Valleys, with over 100 mostly small wineries to visit.

A (VERY) SHORT HISTORY OF THE BC WINE INDUSTRY

Roman Catholic missionaries from California first planted the Okanagan Valley with grapevines over 100 years ago. The vines were prolific native North American and hybrid varietals, used mainly for the production of sacramental wines for the Roman Catholic Church and coarse jug wines for working-class people. Hybrid varieties like Ruby Cabernet, Marechal Foch, and Okanagan Riesling remained until the vine-pull scheme of the late 1980s but there were some attempts to plant quality European vinifera varieties prior to this rare but enlightened bureaucratic success story. In the mid-1970s a German research scientist named Helmut Becker was conducting fruit tree research in Summerland and communicated to his Canadian agricultural colleagues that the climate and topography of the Okanagan Valley resembled the wine-producing regions of Germany. Becker eventually facilitated the first major importation into British Columbia of aromatic vinifera varietals, like Riesling, Gewürztraminer, Pinot

Blanc, Pinot Auxerrois, and Eherenfelser. These varietals thrived in the climate of the Okanagan Valley, loving the dry heat of the northern desert and the dry, warm days and cool nights of the fall, which preserved their aromatics and acidity. Some of these original plantings can still be seen as mature vines. Uncannily, these fresh aromatic white wines match well with the food of British Columbia, namely the bountiful seafood and dishes prepared with a decidedly Asian influence. This harmony has been emphasized by such publicly supported events like Feast of Fields held both on the Lower Mainland and on Vancouver Island in mid-September, the popular annual BC Wine and Oyster Festival every January, and the wildly successful Dine Out and Dine Around Town events that have been geared toward featuring BC local food and wine mid-winter in January in Vancouver and Victoria.

The compatibility of BC wines with BC cuisine can be viewed as sheer luck or, as I prefer to see it, as a convergence of history.

The compatibility of BC wines with BC cuisine can be viewed as sheer luck or, as I prefer to see it, as a convergence of history. I believe the province as a whole was ready for change at that time. The chefs who were experimenting with a new ingredient-driven cuisine went on to taste and include BC wine in their menus, essentially treating wine like a food product, which is a very correct and European interpretation of wine. Probably the noted flavor profiles of BC wines actually validated some of their techniques, choices, and Asian influences. I don't think it's any coincidence that the use of soya for saltiness, mirin for sweetness, miso for a savory quality, and rice wine vinegar for balancing and finishing dishes is pervasive throughout Vancouver's restaurants. The harmony of these dishes lies within their components: seasonal local product prepared with a local cultural influence and paired with local wines. Go figure! This kind of human-stylistic-bias-meets-local-terroir has been happening for centuries in wine country all around the world. The natural convergence of style and wine production goes hand in hand with one influencing the other. I really don't think how well classic regional food and wine pairing works is a matter of chance. Instead, centuries of cultural influences have made these pairings harmonious and culturally entrenched. It is people, the folk who work the land, who put the culture into agriculture. Food and its preparation quite clearly define a group of people in a specific place and at a specific time.

BC WINE COUNTRY'S TIME TO SHINE (AND DINE)

Over 30 percent of wine sold through BC liquor stores originates from British Columbia. This is a unique occurrence for such a young wine-producing region. In Europe there are small regions that consume all the wine they produce. When is the last time you had a Rousette from the Savoie region of France, for example? With the entire province displaying a loyalty to BC's wine (even in its infancy), I think people's curiosity will now turn to other food products in the area. With BC wines (mainly from the Okanagan) having validated our place in the pantheon of West Coast cuisine, I believe that BC wine buyers and food enthusiasts will now make a different choice when deciding where to take their next wine tour. Instead of choosing to go to Europe, they may opt to stay closer to home. Twenty years ago, California's Napa and Sonoma Valleys, only a short plane ride away, were the only option for British Columbians to enjoy a wine tour without suffering the jet lag associated with traveling to Tuscany. Now British Columbians have a new, closer destination on their own doorstep, the Okanagan Valley.

The Okanagan, in the middle of farm country, is ripe to become the next hot destination for North American wine tourists. I think that, once here, visitors to the area who already know how well BC wines pair with the dominantly coastal cuisine of Vancouver and Victoria will want to enjoy the local bounty of the Okanagan Valley. They certainly didn't come to this land-locked valley to eat lobster!

When we established our business our goal was to share the joy that the discovery of this bountiful place brought to us. Hence the name we chose for our farm, cooking school, and wines. Joie means joy in French, and, with Joie over the past four years, it has been our genuine pleasure to share with our guests and visitors the fantastic products that are grown here. We have tailored our programs (and now the style of our wines) through the exploration of the foods that grow here in the Okanagan

Over 30 percent of wine sold through BC liquor stores originates from British Columbia.

Valley. We have come to know our guests intimately, and they have come to know the producers of the terrific products that are grown here. With visitors being drawn again and again to the tremendous beauty and bounty of the Okanagan, a wine country cuisine of its own is in demand and the raw products are all right here to support it. All great cuisines of the world are based on local, fresh ingredients, as are wine country cuisines specific to their local wines. I am confident that the exploration of the terroir of the Okanagan Valley will yield both tremendous wines and an accompanying cuisine as unique as the Valley itself. Through the menus for our Orchard Dinners from the summers of 2003, 2004, and 2005 I would like to introduce you to some of its raw treasures. Enjoy!

JOIE, YEAR ONE: THE FIRST ORCHARD DINNERS

Winter 2002 had been a challenging one for Michael and me, so at the beginning of 2003 we took a break, sought out some advice, and, acting on the excellent advice we received, began to think outside the box about our project. Powered by single-mindedness and anxious to get on with our new life, we began to plan a summer of weekend epicurean retreats. After a sudden decision to open our home as a gastronomic B&B, we threw ourselves into renovating the upper floor of the house and constructing a small outdoor "kitchen" in the vegetable garden where we could teach demonstration cooking classes on a rough-hewn table and a cast-iron propane stove.

A big advantage for us at Joie was our beautiful orchard with a view of Lake Okanagan. Our first weekend in the house was Thanksgiving weekend 2002. We invited both sides of our extended families for a harvest celebration and had our Thanksgiving dinner at a long table for 20 that we set up in the orchard. Inspired by the setting and the joy that sharing that meal among the trees brought to our families, we thought about offering set menu country dinners once a week in the orchard. In the summer of 2003 the local dining institution, the Country Squire, which offered set menu dinners in their large house in Naramata's village, was set to close. After 25 years, Ron and Pat Dyck had had enough of the restaurant business and had started The Cannery microbrewery which became an instant success. With very few dining options in this burgeoning wine country, Michael and I decided we would pick up the baton and offer what we called Saturday Night Orchard Dinners. With Lake Okanagan as a spectacular backdrop, we set a long table in the orchard with proper linen, glassware, and cutlery, and showcased local bounty

and boutique wines to visitors. We essentially set up a vacation spot that reminded us of places that we had traveled to in France and Italy.

Our Epicurean Weekend Retreat included two nights' accommodation in our newly renovated farmhouse, a trip to the farmer's market in Penticton on Saturday morning, a demonstration cooking class, and lunch. In the evening we served an Orchard Dinner and our guests would be joined by up to 20 other local epicurean travelers. All the meals plus the cooking class were based around the produce purchased from the farmer's market. The weekend finished with a wine seminar and ploughman's lunch on Sunday morning.

Michael and I spent our weekends furiously renovating and building with the help and guidance of some very talented and generous friends, and by the last week of June we were ready to go. We threw a trial dinner to test the Orchard Table with all our friends, neighbors, and local winemakers on the Bench. It was a blast. We made a few tweaks to the concept, like not serving all the dishes family style but individually plating them instead, and felt ready to open. The following week we were prepared, and welcomed our first paying guests. Little did we know what a stir our little Gastronomic B&B was about to create, especially with its Saturday Night Orchard Dinners. Over the next three years we fed hundreds of visitors to the area and people begged for a seat at our orchard table. To this day, we still receive e-mails with requests for the dinners.

It is my pleasure to share with you my menus from our orchard table and outdoor teaching kitchen from the past three years at Joie. It was a genuine delight to seek out, forage for, and serve the spring, summer, and fall bounty the Okanagan provided. Not only did I grow as a cook, a gardener, a teacher, and a host, I grew most of all as a lover of food and facilitator of the joy that good food and wine provide.

*O*ur first Orchard Dinner was attended by the couple who were staying with us that weekend as well as our new neighbors, David and Cynthia Enns (who had moved up to Naramata that year to start their winery, Laughing Stock), and their friends and family. We were also joined by Michael's mom and dad, Joe and Linda Dinn. The table was set with linen and printed menus that were held down by tiny apples that Michael had picked from the trees above. The sky had been perfectly blue that day and the air was still hot as the sun started to set. It wasn't until well after dusk when the stars magically lit up the evening sky that darkness provided some much-needed cool air and a reprieve from the burning sun.

The First Orchard Dinner

The menu I had planned included some of my favorite tried and true recipes. I had made a bright green chilled pea soup (as it was about 95°F (35°C) that weekend) and spot prawn ceviche on a bed of baby fennel that I had bought at the market that morning. It was spot prawn season, a time I wait for all year. In my excitement, I deep-fried the prawn heads tableside and made my guests eat them, an experience that not all of them had had before. I look back on that and laugh! It was a gorgeous plate that everyone enjoyed and talked about. The main course was poussin from a local meat supplier, Richard Yntema of North Okanagan Game Meats—it was only the first of many delicious local meats I would serve. I simply stuffed the baby chickens with lemons and rosemary and wrapped them in local boar bacon. This dish and the natural setting transported us all to a summer Tuscan table. The dinner finished with a delicious BC cheese board and poached apricots with lavender and honey ice cream. I had bought the honey from the market that day and the lavender, which was in bloom at the time, originated from Claybank Farm Lavender.

Nestled among the trees, we all watched the sun go down over the lake and felt the warm land breeze gently sweep down from the mountains. Michael and I looked at each other and said, "Wow, I think we've done something special here." Our first guests videotaped the scene and we used the footage, which takes my breath away to this day, on our website for a few years. I was reminded of meals I had had in Italy and France, yet all this was taking place in my own backyard! We were excited at the opportunity to create authentic experiences for our guests to remember as fondly as those they had from their previous European vacations.

A Menu to Celebrate Our First Orchard Dinner
Saturday July 12, 2003

Chilled Summer English Pea Soup
garnished with crème frâiche
Lang Vineyard Late Harvest Riesling 2001

A Seasonal Treat of BC Spot Prawn Ceviche
on a bed of shaved fennel
Blasted Church Rosé 2002

Enderby Poussin
stuffed with lemons and rosemary
wrapped in *Surprise Ranch* boar bacon
accompanied by Yukon Gold pomme purée
Cedar Creek Estate Select Pinot Noir 2001

Mixed Greens
from *Joie*'s garden

BC Cheese Board
celebrating the cheeses from
Poplar Grove (Naramata)
Natural Pastures (Cowichan Valley)
David Wood (Salt Spring Island)

"Poached" Naramata Apricots
(stolen from Gitta's tree . . .)
with *Claybank Farm* lavender and *Similkameen Apiary* honey ice cream
accompanied by the fruit wines of our neighbors, *Elephant Island*

Coffee, tea, or tisane

This dinner was attended by the guests from our weekend program. My friend and colleague Paul Watkin and his Good Drop wine group were joined by my mom, Peigi Noble, and our dear friend Paul Martin. Michael and I were exhausted, but bursting with pride at the opportunity to show off to our loved ones what we had created.

In recognition of Bastille Day, we created a menu with a Provençal theme, started the evening with a game of pétanque, and served pastis over ice. Our guests then sat down to the southern French classic *soupe au pistou*, a traditional summer vegetable soup finished with a simple garlic and basil pesto whisked in at the last minute, zucchini fritters with grilled squid, simply grilled rabbit

Bastille Day

marinated in thyme and mustard with a sauté of fresh fava beans and mushrooms, and a classic southern French almond frangipane tart studded with fresh apricots, which were still available in abundance at the market, to finish. Nature seemed to be on our side as the sky and sunset that evening anticipated the different hues of pink, coral, and salmon of the icy refreshing rosé that we would sample in the next morning's wine seminar to continue the weekend's southern French theme. The heat that weekend lifted the smells of pine needles and wild sage that the Okanagan is famous for and reminded us of our trip to Provence a few years before. More and more, the resemblance of the dry Okanagan to the Mediterranean became obvious us, and accordingly our menus and wine choices became a local reflection of classic Mediterranean menus and pairings.

A Provençal Dinner in Honor of Bastille Day
Saturday July 19, 2003

Soup au Pistou
garnished with Naramata Bench
summer garden vegetables
Lang Vineyard Late Harvest Riesling 2001

Oregano Marinated Grilled Squid
on minted zucchini fritters
Lake Breeze Rosé 2002

Fricasée of Okanagan Valley Rabbit
and fresh fava beans, baby onions, and locally gathered morels
Nichol Vineyards Syrah 2000

Mixed Greens
from *Joie*'s garden

Cheese Board
Poplar Grove Tiger Blue (Naramata, BC)
Poplar Grove Harvest Moon (Naramata, BC)
Brie de Meaux (Champagne, France)
Aged Mimolette (Burgundy, France)
Crottin de Chavignol (Loire, France)

Almond and Apricot Tart
with *Claybank Farm* lavender and *Similkameen Apiary* honey ice cream
accompanied by the fruit wines of our neighbors, *Elephant Island*

Coffee, tea, or tisane

I was absolutely beside myself with nervousness as the weekend approached. I had received a call a few weeks before from Toronto for a booking that would accommodate the director of the Toronto Symphony Orchestra/Oregon Wine Importer extraordinaire, Scott Wilson, and chef Chris MacDonald. The owner of Toronto's famous Avalon Restaurant (and now owner of the successful Cava), Chris MacDonald had been a mentor to the chef school where I trained. I couldn't believe that he was coming to stay in my house and that I would have to feed him. I was thoroughly anxious, and had endlessly thought

The first of Joie's guest chefs

and re-thought the menu for that night's dinner. The weekend finally rolled around and Scott and Chris arrived. We had a wonderful time hosting them and became fast friends (as those in the wine and restaurant businesses are apt to do), eager to send them in the right direction on their wine tours and to introduce them to a few wineries and winemakers off the beaten path. After their first night with us, Chris woke up in the morning and told me he enjoyed my linens. This comment made my day for two reasons. First of all that he had had a good sleep, and second, that someone took notice of my linen habit and admitted to enjoying good sheets. This is the sort of detail-obsessed guy that Chris MacDonald is and it's why he's such a fine chef. Although well rested, Chris was trying to quit smoking and was somewhat agitated by dinner time.

As the dinner courses were served, Chris, despite wearing his nicotine patch, could not sit still as a guest, so he decided he would get up to help me serve the rest of dinner. This was both a blessing (I was putting out food for 20 guests that night because the Orchard Dinners had caught on by August) and a curse as Chris is a bit of a tyrant in the kitchen. After giving me the gears about serving hot food on cold plates (it was 95°F [35°C], the plates were definitely not cold, not to mention the fact that I was serving dinner in the middle of the orchard and there were not a lot of options for plate warming) he then reprimanded me about not skimming the fat off the top of my rustic gratin. His comments had little effect on the dinner experience for my other guests that night, but the advice of elders (even when they are guests in your home) deserves respect. I never

(continued page 46)

A Dinner to Celebrate an Admired Chef
Saturday August 2, 2003

Naramata Garden Gazpacho
finished with Dijon crème frâiche
Blasted Church Rosé 2002

Seared BC Ling Cod
beached on crisped polenta and shaved fennel
Poplar Grove Riesling 2001

Roasted Surprise Ranch Wild Boar
accompanied by plum and rhubarb preserves
served with zucchini and Salt Spring Island chèvre gratin
Nichol Vineyards Syrah 1999

Mixed Greens
from *Joie*'s garden

Cheese Board
Poplar Grove Naramata Bench Blue (Naramata, BC)
Poplar Grove Harvest Moon (Naramata, BC)
Brie de Meaux (Champagne, France)
Langres (Champagne, France)
Crottin de Chavignol (Loire, France)

Crystalized Ginger Shortcake
with sour cherry compote and whipped crème fraîche
accompanied by the fruit wines of our neighbors, *Elephant Island*

Coffee, tea, or tisane

(continued from page 44)

served another gratin without blotting the fat off the top (even in the dark) and I never again served dinner on a cold plate. In 2004 I bought an Alto-Shaam (a warming oven that restaurants use to hold meat at a certain temperature) at a restaurant auction and ran a very long extension cord from the house to the orchard. Not only could I now keep meat warm, but I could also properly observe the rules of fine dining at my Orchard Table. Thanks for the scolding, Chris! Young cooks, even when they own their own businesses, will continue to learn throughout their careers. Chris was the first of many visiting chefs to Joie who would continue to share and teach me their tasty wisdom. Even though I had left the restaurant circuit and was cooking in an orchard, the traditions and rules of my training still ran deep.

*T*his weekend we hosted a group from Vancouver's Slow Food Convivium, as well as a few people from Kamloops and the immediate area. We spent the weekend wine touring and visiting a few local farms, including the boar farm in Oliver, the local cheese-making facility at Poplar Grove, and Claybank Farm Lavender. It was a sweltering weekend with temperatures well over 100°F (40°C) and high humidity. We had 16 people in our group which meant the entire house was full and there were even people camping out in our orchard.

Cuisine for a Forest Fire

It had been very hot and dry for the past two months and now the yellow tomatoes were ready, so for the Orchard Dinner that night I decided to make my favorite summer soup—an exercise in simplicity, containing just yellow tomatoes, salt, and rice wine vinegar. It was a perfect dinner despite the heat. That Friday evening it was so hot that Michael and I couldn't sleep. I remember we went outside at about 3:00 a.m. to find the temperature was still 86°F (30°C). The sky was also full of dry lightning, which was somewhat threatening because we hadn't had rain for 90 days. The next morning we awoke to smoke. Lots of smoke. By 3:00 p.m. on the Sunday the smoke was so thick that you couldn't see three feet in front of you and it hurt to breathe hard. Later that day, our group left and I stayed behind to pick our fast-ripening pears in the orchard. It had been so hot that they had over-ripened quicker than we could anticipate and you could hear them falling off the trees at night.

Two days later the Okanagan Mountain Park fire was burning out of control and rapidly approaching Naramata. By then I was back in Vancouver working and had to explain to my boss that I needed to take the week off to see if our home was going to burn to the ground or not. We returned immediately to Naramata and that same night we were put on a one-hour evacuation alert as the winds started to blow. Sleep was impossible. We loaded our car with our special belongings—namely, our wine cellar—then sat on the deck, watching trees explode and drinking our favorite bottles of wine that we had brought back from our honeymoon in Piedmont. What a year 2003 was turning out to be! By morning the winds had shifted and the fire spared Naramata. Unfortunately it ripped through Okanagan Mountain Park, completely obliterating it, and blew down into the Mission District of Kelowna. Other fires raged throughout BC that week, and Michael happened to witness the start of the Vaseaux Lake fire, just south of Okanagan Falls, when a bird's nest sparked off a power line and started a one-million-acre fire. What does one cook when fires rage?

**A Dinner to Celebrate
Slow Food in British Columbia**
Saturday August 16, 2003

Chilled Yellow Heirloom Tomato Soup
garnished with chive oil

Composed Fish Plate
of house-cured wild sockeye and tea-smoked white spring salmon mousse
accompanied by haricot vert vinaigrette

Roasted Surprise Ranch Wild Boar
accompanied by apricot preserves, wilted Swiss chard, and steamed Pontiac potatoes

Mixed Greens
from *Joie*'s garden

Cheese Board
Poplar Grove Tiger Blue (Naramata, BC)
Poplar Grove Camembert (Naramata, BC)
McLennan Creek Ash Chevrontina (Abbotsford, BC)
Mountain Meadow Brie (Chase, BC)
Chaumes (Périgrod, France)
Le Bois Blond (Provence, France)
Banon de Chalais (Rhône, France)

Dark Chocolate Pavlova
with *Claybank Farm* sour cherry compote and whipped crème fraîche

Coffee, tea, or tisane

All dishes accompanied by wines gathered from our tours

Almost one month later, and after three weeks of heavy smoke, signs of life began to return to the Okanagan Valley. Although we had only been on evacuation alert for one week and the fire had been almost put out in the park, the media frenzy had the whole world thinking that the entire Valley was either still on fire or had burned to the ground. This was not good for tourism. The public perception was that things were gone, or that those affected by the fire did not want to be bothered by outsiders. This was not the case. The B&Bs and small wineries were hurting for business. There was not a soul around except for the locals. It was a full month after the fire before we held the next Orchard Dinner and it

Post-fire Dinner

was a small one on our deck overlooking the orchard. We had some neighbors by and a wonderful couple who came back the next summer for one of our Joie Pratique programs. We were grateful for the company, the business, and the new friendships. Mid-September in the Okanagan is when the days are still hot, the evenings are cool, and darkness comes early. As a cook, it was the time of year when the excitement of harvest begins and summer's bounty is at its height. One has the urge to switch over to heartier flavors and cook heavier food. It is the time of year to crave rich, filled pastas, warm soups from root vegetables, and braises. Soft fruits are replaced by hard fruits and warm baking spices are a comforting way to end a meal and watch the sun go down a little earlier.

A Dinner in Honor of a Change in Seasons
Saturday September 13, 2003

A Late Summer Yellow Tomato Soup
dancing with *Joie*'s heirloom tomatoes
Blasted Church Rosé 2002

Joie's Seymour Squash Ravioli
with brown sage butter
Poplar Grove Reserve Chardonnay 2001

Braised Shuswap Beef Shortribs
accompanied by fresh broad beans, baby onions and
locally gathered chanterelles, and roasted fingerling potatoes
Black Hills Note Bene 2001

Mixed Greens
from *Joie*'s garden

Cheese Board
Poplar Grove Tiger Blue (Naramata, BC)
Poplar Grove Farmhouse Camembert (Naramata, BC)
McLennan Goat Pyramid (Abbotsford, BC)
David Wood's Truffled Chèvre (Saltspring Island, BC)
Brie de Meaux (Champagne, France)

Poached Pears
with *Claybank Lavender* shortbread and bitter chocolate mousse
accompanied by the fruit wines of our neighbors, *Elephant Island*

Coffee, tea, or tisane

I was about to enter my 29th year on September 29th, 2003. What a year it had been! The summer heat had waned, it was now officially fall, and our apples were ready to be picked. For dinner that week I cleaned out the garden and made the final tomato dish of the season and squash ravioli, and created what would become the signature Orchard Dinner dish of the 2004 Orchard Dinner season, the Pheasant Ballottine with du Puy Lentils (see page xx). It is a wonderful dish and one that I could prepare in advance to finish tableside and slice at the orchard table to easily serve 20 or more guests. As the season drew to a close I was proud of what we had accomplished that year — our house reno,

Fall Welcomed In

a crash course in orcharding and running a five-acre farm, starting a new business while managing the stresses of a five-hour commute, making new friends in Naramata, and creating wonderful menus from the produce of all the local growers I continued to meet. My mind whirled with plans for next year's season. I definitely wanted to teach more and to continue with our magical dinners under the stars. Michael and I made plans to end our regular jobs (for real this time) in early 2004 after my last trip to Vin Italy. That winter we continued to commute and to renovate our farmhouse, and we finished the lower floor of the house so that we could expand the guesthouse for the coming year's cooking programs.

A Dinner in Honor of Friends
Saturday September 20, 2003

Heirloom Tomato Tartar
with chive oil and croûtons
Lake Breeze Rosé 2002

Butternut Squash Ravioli
with brown sage butter
Poplar Grove Reserve Chardonnay 2001

Truffled Pheasant Ballottine
with *Claybank Farms* sour cherries and pistachios
garnished with du Puy lentils, chanterelles, and roasted fingerling potatoes
Nichol Vineyards Syrah 2000

Mixed Greens
from *Joie*'s garden

Cheese Board
Poplar Grove Tiger Blue (Naramata, BC)
Poplar Grove Farmhouse (Naramata, BC)
McLennan Goat Pyramid (Abbotsford, BC)
Moonstruck Baby Blue (Saltspring Island, BC)
Brie de Meaux (Champagne, France)
Morbier (Jura, France)

Joie Orchard Pear Tarte Tatin
with cardamom ice cream
accompanied by the fruit wines of our neighbors, *Elephant Island*

Coffee, tea, or tisane

October Wine Festival Time: The Visitors Return

*T*his was the final Orchard Dinner of our first season. I was thrilled that we were booked out with 24 people because it was the Okanagan Fall Wine Festival. We had much to celebrate at the end of our first season, especially since at the beginning of 2003 we weren't certain that the season was even going to happen. With a strong start and then a big pause just as we were gathering momentum, the season finished with a bang. The dinner was attended by our dear friends Graham and Jenny Peers who had become engaged that weekend, and our friend and colleague Tim Pawsey who writes for the *Vancouver Courier* and *Northwest Palate*. That weekend, Tim wrote a fantastically complimentary article about Joie and took beautiful photos of our orchard table. I was just as nervous cooking for Tim as I had been for Chris MacDonald earlier that year. Tim was the first journalist who had come to check out what we were doing and I really respected his writing. Tim truly knows and loves good food and wine. I had cured a giant side of salmon caught earlier that summer by our neighbor Aaron Anderson and Tim showed me a trick to freeze the side slightly first and then slice it with my salmon slicer. Always grateful for new tricks, I served it up on some blini to start the meal. I bought the first Jerusalem artichokes of the season and made my favorite fall soup with them. I also had access to some beautiful chanterelles so I sautéed them with fresh chestnuts and stuffed them into a local lamb leg. It was delicious! I was happy to serve up a truly local and seasonal meal to someone whose opinion I respected and to my friends who were celebrating their love. I gave Michael a kiss and we drove back to our apartment in Vancouver to settle down for a long winter's nap in preparation for the crazy 2004 season ahead. Luckily for us, we had no idea what we were in for.

A Dinner in Honor of the Okanagan Wine Festival
Saturday October 4, 2003

Cured Wild Spring Salmon
served on buckwheat and apple blini
with roasted beets, rocket, and horseradish crème fraîche
Lake Breeze Blancs de Noir 2002

Purée Palestine
Jerusalem artichoke soup finished with white truffle oil
Adora Pinot Blanc 2002

Roasted Naramata Bench Leg of Lamb
stuffed with chestnuts, currants, and chanterelles
accompanied by du Puy lentils, baby onions, and *Surprise Ranch* boar lardons
Poplar Grove Merlot 2001

Mixed Greens
from *Joie*'s garden

Cheese Board
Poplar Grove Tiger Blue (Naramata, BC)
Poplar Grove Farmhouse Camembert (Naramata, BC)
McLennan Goat Pyramid (Abbotsford, BC)
David Wood's Fresh Goat (Salt Spring Island, BC)
Brie de Nangis (Marne, France)
Epoisse (Burgundy, France)

Italian Prune Plum and Almond Tart
with *Claybank Farm* lavender-scented whipped mascarpone
accompanied by the fruit wines of our neighbors, *Elephant Island*

Coffee, tea, or tisane

JOIE, YEAR TWO: SOLD OUT!

As crazy and topsy-turvy as our first year was, the second year turned out to be even crazier. We opened up several more rooms of our house and expanded our offerings to include B&B rooms, our dinner and weekend packages, Monday cooking classes, and five-day intensive cooking programs throughout the summer, complete with three days of farm touring. We changed our name from Joie Gastronomic B&B to Joie Gastronomic Guesthouse and Farm Cooking School. The new outdoor orchard kitchen was serious. It's situated on top of a poured concrete pad overlooking our orchard and Okanagan Lake and is equipped with two Garland commercial stoves running off a big propane tank, three custom, stainless-steel–topped work islands with running water and electricity (the islands had been hauled out of a retail space in Gastown in Vancouver and given some much-needed love and attention), and a large stainless-steel sink for washing the garden vegetables. Of course, the kitchen had gone way over budget by the time we had finished it, but it was undeniably spectacular and we finished it off with a stone-walled herb garden and 16 raised potager garden beds. I could hardly wait to use the new kitchen.

*W*e opened our newly refurbished farmhouse door in the first weekend in May of 2004. Those staying for that first weekend program were taken mushroom foraging, and we certainly found mushrooms. During those first two weeks of May, Michael and I picked over 100 lb (45 kg) of fresh morels. We used them in our dinners and our classes, served them for breakfasts, and dried them. We had enough dried morels for Joie for the next two years! The abundance of the morels was one of the few positive outcomes of that horrible fire in 2003. For that first weekend Orchard Dinner I used some of my favorite spring recipes: a pea and sorrel soup, smoked Kootenay trout my brother Alex caught in Nelson, a classic lamb navarin using all the first spring vegetables in the garden with the added bonus of fresh morels, and the first rhubarb from the garden.

May Is Morel Month at Joie!

Morels, 2004"
Joie,
Naramata B.C
Judy Crumlin

A Dinner in Honor of Spring
Saturday May 8, 2004

English Pea and Sorrel Soup
Wild Goose Stoney Slope Riesling 2002

Smoked Kootenay Speckled Trout
with horseradish crème fraîche and chervil oil
Lake Breeze Rosé 2002

Jay Springs Ranch Navarin Printanier
with Okanagan Mountain Fire morels
Black Hills Note Bene 2001

Mixed Greens
from *Joie*'s garden

Cheese Board
Poplar Grove Tiger Blue (Naramata, BC)
Poplar Grove Naramata Bench Blue (Naramata, BC)
Hilary's Camembert (Cowichan Valley, BC)
McLennan Creek Ash Chevrontina (Abbotsford, BC)
10-year-old Cheddar (Quebec)
Brie de Meaux (Champagne, France)
Aged Mimolette (Burgundy, France)

Roasted Rhubarb and Lemon Curd
with *Claybank Farm* lavender sablée
Elephant Island Apricot Wine 2003

Coffee, tea, or tisane

*T*his weekend we had many of the same Slow Food gang from Vancouver who had been our guests on the weekend of the fire, plus the food and beverage management from the Metropolitan Hotel in Vancouver. Many who had slept in the orchard on the night the fire started came back to reap some rewards from their experience. Our large foraging crew had an excellent day, collecting about 33 lb (15 kg) of morels that day, followed by a wonderful picnic. That night our menu featured morels in every course, and wine pairing particular to mushrooms—lots of pinot noir and gamay amassed from that day's late-afternoon wine touring.

Slow Food Returns

A Dinner in Honor of Okanagan Mountain Fire Morels
Slow Food Vancouver Convivial Forage
Saturday May 15, 2004

Spring Asparagus and Sorrel Soup
with sautéed morels

Handmade Ravioli
filled with morels and chive mascarpone

Jay Springs Ranch Lamb Leg
stuffed with morels and accompanied by du Puy lentils
and spring garlic

Mixed Greens
from *Joie*'s garden

Cheese Board
Poplar Grove Tiger Blue (Naramata, BC)
Poplar Grove Naramata Bench Blue (Naramata, BC)
Hilary's Camembert (Cowichan Valley, BC)
McLennan Creek Ash Chevrontina (Abbotsford, BC)
10-year-old Cheddar (Quebec)
Brie de Meaux (Champagne, France)
Aged Mimolette (Burgundy, France)

Almond Tart
perfumed with *Claybank Farm* lavender and accompanied by rhubarb compote

Coffee, tea, or tisane

"Foraged" wines from neighboring Naramata Bench farm-gate wineries
will accompany each course

Guest Chef at Joie

I had been invited to speak at the Cascadia Culinary Conference on Whidbey Island which would mean being away from Michael and the farm for the first time. I was loath to leave a sold-out long weekend at the farm but I had asked my chef friend Andrey Durbach and his wife, Sian, of Vancouver's Parkside restaurant, to come up and cook that weekend's Orchard Dinner. I also enrolled my mom to help Michael run the guesthouse that weekend. All went well at the conference, which was a fabulous experience for me. However, in Naramata that weekend it was cold and poured with rain, and a full-house of a strange mix of guests drove my helper crew around the bend with their special

needs (a birder who wanted a hot breakfast a 6 a.m., a marathoner who wouldn't eat anything, and dinner guests who didn't like the art in our dining room). I felt badly for my crew upon my return. When I saw the menu that Andrey had prepared I thought my guests were privileged to have had the Parkside experience prepared with delicious Naramata ingredients on their Okanagan holiday. I wish I could have eaten the meal! Having said that, I did find a rogue dolce de leche pannacotta in the fridge when I returned . . .

**A Special Evening with
Chef Andrey Durbach of Parkside Restaurant**
Saturday May 22, 2004

Zebroff Family Tomato and Vegetable Gazpacho
with Digby scallop ceviche
La Frenz Semillon 2003

Joie Garden Arugula Caesar Salad
with grilled white asparagus
Lake Breeze Rosé 2002

Halibut in Cartoccio
with fresh artichokes, fava beans, and
Okanagan Mountain Fire morels in red wine vinaigrette
Poplar Grove Gamay Nouveau 2003

Cheese Board
Poplar Grove Tiger Blue (Naramata, BC)
Poplar Grove Naramata Bench Blue (Naramata, BC)
Hilary's Camembert (Cowichan Valley, BC)
McLennan Creek Ash Chevrontina (Abbotsford, BC)
10-year-old Cheddar (Quebec)
Brie de Meaux (Champagne, France)
Aged Mimolette (Burgundy, France)

Dulce de Leche Pannacotta
Elephant Island Apricot Wine 2003

Coffee, tea, or tisane

The Orchard Table Grows Longer

*T*his weekend really epitomized the style of the menus that our guests were served over the course of the 2004 Saturday Night Orchard Dinners. As the dinners became more popular I had to figure out how to feed up to 28 people by myself. I wanted the menus to be fresh, local, classic wine country cuisine, but also not too fussy. That weekend featured a cold fish course of ceviche and herb oil, followed by a salad I created to showcase the fresh honeycomb that the Similkameen Apiary had begun to sell at the market. The combination of the sweet chewy honeycomb, the salty Tiger Blue cheese from

Poplar Grove, toasted hazelnuts, and bitter greens from our garden was a harmony of local tastes and textures. It was a dream to pair up with local wines as well. We served this dish at almost every Orchard Dinner because it was such a great showcase for my favorite local products from the market, and also because not very many people had ever tried fresh honeycomb. If you haven't tried it, visit your local farmer's market that has an attending apiary and ask to try it out. Honeycomb is a unique and healthy eating experience with all the bee propolis it contains. I also began to serve pheasant ballottine regularly as local pheasant was a real treat for our guests and the ballottines, with an impressive sliced and stuffed roll presentation, were a dream to serve to a large group of people. Chocolate and candied orange tart is a delicious way to showcase Okanagan summer apricots. It is also easy to slice and portion for a large group as the chocolate filling is quite sturdy.

A Dinner in Honor of the Sun
Saturday June 12, 2004

Scallop and Joie Garden Radish Ceviche
Wild Goose Stoney Slope Riesling 2003

Composed Salad
of *Joie* garden greens, *Poplar Grove* Tiger Blue Cheese, and
Similkameen Apiary honeycomb
with roasted Naramata hazelnuts
La Frenz Semillon 2003

North Okanagan Pheasant Breast
stuffed with foie gras terrine and dried plums
accompanied by a ragout of Okanagan Mountain Fire morels and baby garlic
Poplar Grove Benchmark Merlot 2002

Cheese Board
Poplar Grove Farmhouse Camembert (Naramata, BC)
Poplar Grove Naramata Bench Blue (Naramata, BC)
10-year-old Cheddar (Quebec)
L'Empereur (Quebec)
Chenal du Moine (Quebec)

Valrhona Manjari Chocolate and Candied Orange Tart
with apricot compote
Elephant Island Apricot Wine 2003

Coffee, tea, or tisane

*M*id-July signals full summer, the time of year when the garden starts producing like mad. Our phone was also ringing constantly. To another full table of 28, I served a cold gazpacho with ceviche, the winning honeycomb composed salad, braised rabbit legs with grilled loins wrapped in bacon accompanied by the first carrots out of the garden

Cooking, Cooking Every Day

that I made into delicate carrot and mascarpone ravioli, and light apricot and almond galettes to finish the meal. That week was a full one, with a weekend program and a Joie Pratique, book-ended with an Orchard Dinner on the other side. It was a pleasure for me to cook for my Joie Pratique students who had been learning all week long. A few of the couples from the course joined us again for the Orchard Dinner after they had worked so hard cooking for each other all week. I guess they just couldn't get enough.

A Dinner to Celebrate Summer
Saturday July 17, 2004

Aperitif
Hawthorne Mountain Brut

Naramata Garden Gazpacho
with BC spot prawn ceviche
Lake Breeze Semillon 2002

Composed Salad
of *Joie* garden greens, *Poplar Grove* Tiger Blue cheese, and
Similkameen Apiary honeycomb with roasted hazelnuts
La Frenz Alexandria 2002

North Okanagan Rabbit Two Ways
with carrot mascarpone ravioli,
Okanagan Mountain Fire morels, and fresh fava beans
Nichol Vineyards Syrah 2000

Cheese Board
Poplar Grove Farmhouse Camembert (Naramata, BC)
Carmelis Grapeleaf Flute Chevre (Kelowna, BC)
McLennan Creek Ash Chevrontina (Abbotsford, BC)
Chenal du Moine (Quebec)
Aged Mimolette (Burgundy, France)

Apricot and Toasted Almond Galette
with cinnamon ice cream
Elephant Island Apricot Wine 2003

Coffee, tea, or tisane

By the end of the month it was still hot and we had seen over 100 people come through the farm and guesthouse. However, just as we were starting to flag, some welcome visitors arrived at our farm and changed the rest of our summer. Cameron (Cam) Smith and Dana Ewart rolled down the driveway one Tuesday afternoon while I was teaching a Provençal class. Cam and Dana were on a break from cooking for tree planting camps in northern Alberta that summer. They had worked for Chris MacDonald at Avalon in Toronto years before

The Angels of Joie

and Chris had told them to stop by and check us out if they were in the area that summer. We put them up for a week in a king-sized bed, fed them, and treated them to hot showers. They were so grateful that, in their very hard-working-Cam-and-Dana-way, they proceeded to clean up our gardens, do chores, cook, clean, and generally be more helpful than we could have ever imagined after having worked 90 days in a row without a day off. Michael and I did things like go for a swim, lie on the beach, and drink beer in the orchard while watching the full moon rise. They truly were a blessing and we didn't want them to leave. After Dana ate her first warm peach right off the tree, she didn't want to leave either.

A Dinner to Celebrate Naramata Days Festival
Saturday July 31, 2004

Aperitif
Hawthorne Mountain Brut

Chilled Carrot Soup
with orange and coriander
Wild Goose Stoney Slope Dry Riesling 2002

Composed Salad
of *Joie* garden greens, *Poplar Grove* Tiger Blue Cheese, and
Similkameen Apiary honeycomb with roasted hazelnuts
Hester Creek Trebbiano 2002

Crispy Enderby Pheasant Breast with Sage and Pancetta
finished with lemon and black pepper jus and
served with cipolinni onion and rosemary gratinée
Poplar Grove Gamay Nouveau 2003

Cheese Board
Poplar Grove Farmhouse Camembert (Naramata, BC)
Carmelis Grapeleaf Flute Chèvre (Kelowna, BC)
McLennan Creek Ash Chevrontina (Abbotsford, BC)
Brie de Meaux (Champagne, France)
Aged Mimolette (Burgundy, France)

Poached Naramata White-fleshed Peaches
accompanied by *Claybank Farm* lavender sablée and crème fraîche
Elephant Island Apricot Wine 2003

Coffee, tea, or tisane

Kindred Spirits

A week later, Cam and Dana were still with us. They were taking both a physical break and some time out from their careers to think about their next move and had no firm plans for the rest of the summer. It was a pleasure to cook with them all week. Dana had attended the Stratford Chef School at the same time as I did, and both Dana and Cameron had worked at Montreal's Toqué! after I had. Having them around was like having the clones that I had wished for all summer magically appear. What a treat it was to have company in the form of hardworking, kindred spirits who were just as inspired by fresh, local products and classic techniques as I was.

That week we made a classic vichyssoise with the first leeks of the season from our garden and good-looking potatoes from the Similkameen. That was followed by a lovely cold composed salad of green beans served with a confit of the first heirloom tomatoes of the season and a slice of local goat cheese. For the main course we served a boned-out boar leg, stuffed with a southern-French-inspired mix of black olives, basil, and orange zest. For dessert we made a galette from the new crop of Claybank Farms' meaty Balaton sour cherries that Cam and Dana had help pit that week. Together they had efficiently pitted over 50 lb (23 kg) of sour cherries by hand without a peep. God bless the cooks with no fixed address who had made their way to Joie for a rest!

A Dinner to Celebrate the Heat of Summer
Saturday August 7, 2004

Aperitif
Hawthorne Mountain Brut

Vichyssoise
with *Poplar Grove* Tiger Blue croûtes
Hillside Muscat Ottonel 2003

Zebroff Family Farm Haricot Vert Salad
with tomato and thyme confit garnished with
Carmelis Grapeleaf Flute Chèvre
Kettle Valley Semillon/Sauvignon Blanc 2003

Roasted Enderby Wild Boar Leg
stuffed with orange, basil, and black olives
accompanied by polenta, white beans,
and sage brown butter
Poplar Grove Benchmark Cabernet Franc 2001

Cheese Board
Poplar Grove Farmhouse Camembert (Naramata, BC)
Poplar Grove Naramata Bench Blue (Naramata, BC)
Mountain Meadow Brie (Chase, BC)
McLennan Creek Ash Chevrontina (Abbotsford, BC)
10-year-old Cheddar (Quebec)
Brie de Meaux (Champagne, France)
Aged Mimolette (Burgundy, France)

Balaton Sour Cherry Galette
accompanied by scented geranium cream
Elephant Island Apricot Wine 2003

Coffee, tea, or tisane

Cam and Dana felt unnecessarily guilty for having soaked up the hospitality at Joie for so long. Either they had itchy feet or their pioneering spirits were getting the better of them, but mid-August saw them push off to explore the West a little more. As they set off on a tour of Whistler, Vancouver Island, and Alaska, Michael and I reminisced about their efficient spirits as we finished up our fourth month of the 2004 season, seating another 100 people at our orchard table, in our cooking classes, and two more Joie Pratique sessions.

Pressing On

As the end of August grew near, I longed for a change of seasons and flavors. It was still hot, but I craved darker game meat, red wines, and chocolate. That week I chose to use venison for our main course and continued my love affair with the ballottine. I lined butterflied venison loins with Swiss chard and stuffed them with chanterelles. Our pear harvest was bountiful again, so I prepared a delicious classic flourless chocolate cake with very dark chocolate and served it with some poached pears. The last weekend in August is always a poignant time in the Okanagan, as it is still summery and smoking hot despite the fact that the days are growing shorter, there are fewer people on our beautiful beaches, and the kids return to school.

A Dinner to Celebrate the Beginning of Harvest
Saturday August 28, 2004

Aperitif
Township 7 Seven Star Brut

Chilled Heirloom 'Dixie Gold' Yellow Tomato Soup
Lake Breeze Semillon 2003

Prosciutto-wrapped Fairhaven Peaches
stuffed with *Carmelis* fresh goat cheese
and served with *Joie* garden mizuna
Blasted Church Hatfield's Fusé 2003

Enderby Venison Ballottine
stuffed with chanterelles and Swiss chard
served with potato and thyme gratin and roasted shallots
Lake Breeze Pinot Noir 2002

Cheese Board
Poplar Grove Farmhouse Camembert (Naramata, BC)
Salt Spring Island Blue Juliette (Saltspring Island, BC)
Moonstruck Savoury Moon (Saltspring Island, BC)
McLennan Creek Blue Chevrontina (Abbotsford, BC)
Hilary's Waxed Goat Cheddar (Cobble Hill, BC)
Hilary's Red Dawn (Cobble Hill, BC)
Le Gamin (New Brunswick)
Queso Romero (Catalonia, Spain)

Gâteau Victoire
with pears poached in red wine
Elephant Island Apricot Wine 2003

Coffee, tea, or tisane

*S*eptember was packed with shoulder-season wine tourists who filled our Epicurean Weekend Retreats and my last Italian-themed Joie Pratique, Tour d'Italia, was sold out. Michael and I put on our track shoes and pushed through to the end of a long season. On the eve of my 30th birthday there was a lot going on at Joie. I had crushed my first grapes (Muscat—my favorite!) that would go into our first vintage of our Noble Blend 2004. That same day, I also had 28 paying guests

Cuisine Canada's Northern Bounty Conference

from Cuisine Canada's Northern Bounty pre-conference tour coming for lunch. I had a head cold and I was exhausted from having worked the past five months without a day off. Despite my physical discomfort and exhaustion, I was excited about the lunch because Cuisine Canada had special meaning to me. One of the directors of the Stratford Chefs School where I trained, Eleanor Kane, was also one of the inaugural board members of Cuisine Canada. Eleanor had instilled in each and every graduate the importance of our role as young chefs to establish our own version of Canadian cuisine as we went out into the world. Our training at Stratford had encouraged us young chefs to make regional adaptations of the seasonal bounty wherever we lived in Canada by applying our family and cultural influences to the preparation of those local ingredients.

Eight years after Eleanor's instruction, with the guests of the 2004 Northern Bounty Conference sitting on our deck, including my first boss from my first kitchen job in Edmonton in 1989, I was happy to showcase the finest our region had to offer in the manner that I had been taught all those years ago. I had carried that philosophy with me to all the different places in which I had lived and worked until that day. It was a real moment of pride to

(continued page 76)

A Luncheon for Northern Bounty VI
Naramata Bench Visit
Thursday September 23, 2004

This menu has been composed to showcase both
the bountiful food and remarkable wines of the Naramata Bench
in the spirit of the September 2004 harvest

Joie Hubbard Squash and Anjou Pear Soup
garnished with crème fraîche and chervil oil
La Frenz Alexandria 2003

Composed Salad
of *Joie* garden greens, *Poplar Grove* Tiger Blue cheese, and
Similkameen Apiary honeycomb with roasted hazelnuts
Red Rooster Pinot Gris 2003
Lake Breeze Blanc de Noirs Rosé 2003

Enderby Pheasant Ballotine
stuffed with *Claybank Farm* Balaton sour cherries
wrapped in *Surprise Ranch* boar prosciutto
served with du Puy lentils and finished with sage brown butter
Poplar Grove Benchmark Merlot 2001

BC Cheese Board
Poplar Grove Farmhouse Camembert (Naramata)
Poplar Grove Naramata Bench Blue (Naramata)
Carmelis Goat Flute (Kelowna)
McLennan Creek Ash Chevrontina (Abbotsford)
Moonstruck Beddis Blue (Saltspring Island)
Hilary's Red Dawn (Cowichan Valley)
Mountain Meadow Sheep Camembert (Chase)

Petits Fours
Dark Chocolate-dipped Dried *Joie* Pears, *Claybank Farm* Lavender Sablée,
Ambercot Acres Dried Plum Biscotti, and Langues de Chat
Elephant Island Apricot Wine 2003

Coffee, tea, or tisane

(continued from page 74)

show them what I had grown at our farm and to showcase my favorite local products in the afternoon's lunch.

At the end of the event I was presented with a special lavender plant from the pre-lunch tour that had been arranged for the group at Claybank Farm Lavender. The plant was a wild cultivar of culinary lavender that had appeared in Pati Hill's field. When that happens, you are allowed to name the cultivar. Pati named it *Chef Heidi Noble* lavender. Everyone on that tour was given a Chef Heidi clone to take home with them. Pati sent one over for me with the tour and the plant was presented by a woman for whom I had worked 16 years earlier when I was just 14 years old. What a birthday! What a year! As harvest wore on, we saw 2004 come and go. We were excited to have now added wine production to Joie's offerings and 2005 looked like it would shape up to be yet another busy year.

The fall and winter of 2004 passed in a blur of winemaking that bombarded our overwhelmed bodies and minds. By the time the spring of 2005 arrived we had made 840 cases of our own wines: our Noble Blend, which is an aromatic Alsatian-style blend of Gewürztraminer, Muscat, and Kerner, our Un-oaked Chardonnay, and a Pinot Noir Rosé. We made the wines on a shoestring, a prayer, and eight credit cards. Nervous as hell and rather over-extended by March, we announced to the world and the 140 restaurant clients from our wine agency days that not only was Joie open for its third season, but now we also had wine to sell. Suddenly we were not only tweaking Joie for its third season, offering B&B rooms and an Orchard Dinner to the guests of our cooking school weekend programs, but we also found ourselves having to put on our old wine-sales hats.

Thank goodness the wines were well received! They sold out in only eight weeks, just in time for us to open up in the last week of April for our third season of Joie. The wines caused a huge flurry of interest in our cooking school and the cooking school was causing a huge flurry of interest in our wines. It seems the whole connectedness of the joyful harmony of food and wine that we had tried to discover and reinforce with our previous two seasons was really striking a chord with the public and the media. People had internalized that there truly was a burgeoning food and wine culture in their own backyard. Our marketing slogan, "Why go all the way to Tuscany for cooking school in wine country?" had planted a seed in the collective consciousness of BC, and now it seemed as if the whole country was being affected, as we received hundreds more guests from Vancouver, Vancouver Island, Alberta, Ontario, and even from as far away as Yellowknife, San Diego, and Ireland. Some guests were, of course, returning guests, which was extremely flattering, especially as a number of them were actually returning for their third season of learning, indulging, relaxation, and fun. We were overwhelmed by gratitude to clients who booked well in advance that year for our programs, and to our wine restaurant clients who welcomed us back into the fold of Vancouver's restaurant and wine community—this time as producers. We hunkered down not only to host a new season, but also to manage our wine business and keep an eye on our rapidly approaching 2005 harvest.

May Is not Morel Month at Joie!

I was happy to get back out into the outdoor kitchen that May. Fueled by memories of the previous year's spring morel forage, at its height in the second week of May, we planned a whole month of weekend retreats around morel foraging on the still burned-out mountain. The first week of May yielded little in the way of morels, so for the first Saturday Night Orchard Dinner I used our stash of dried morels from the year before to supplement the few fresh ones that we found with our guests. I remained confident that the sacred second week of May would deliver us our bounty, but that weekend came and went and we had still very little in our baskets. On the May long weekend we were totally skunked and only found one lone morel. We were mortified, but we learned our lesson about the bounty and famine cycle of nature: appreciate the glory of the bounty when it comes but don't expect such wonders on a consistent basis. It was an excellent lesson for us to learn as we moved into a second year of winemaking. Fresh morels or not, we enjoyed beautiful spring menus through the month of May, and focused on the sorrel and rhubarb from our garden, asparagus from the Similkameen Valley and the wispy asparagus growing wild in our orchard, and the first local chickens of the season, poached in a morel broth and light reduction sauce.

A Dinner to Celebrate Morels
Saturday May 14, 2005

Aperitif
Hawthorne Mountain Brut

Joie Sorrel and Claybank Farm Asparagus Soup
with Dungeness crab
Joie A Noble Blend 2004

Morel, Mascarpone, and Mint Ravioli
napped with sage-blossom brown butter
Poplar Grove Reserve Chardonnay 2003

Poached Spring Chicken and Fiddleheads
in Okanagan Mountain Fire morel cream
Cedar Creek Platinum Reserve Pinot Noir 2002
Quail's Gate Family Reserve Pinot Noir 2002
Blue Mountain Striped Label Pinot Noir 2002

Cheese Board
Tomme de Savoie (Savoie, France)
Chevre en Ashe (Loire, France)
Époisses (Burgundy, France)
Little Qualicum Cheesework Rathtrevor (Qualicum Beach, BC)
Chèvre Noir (Quebec)

Ginger Pound cake Filled with Orange Curd
with *Joie* garden rhubarb granité
Elephant Island Apricot Wine 2004

Coffee, tea, or tisane

*A*s elated as we were by the past two years of cooking and teaching, I found myself feeling a little tired and uninspired by my own repertoire. As I was struggling with these feelings, a miracle visitor arrived just like the year before. During one of our one-day cooking classes, again teaching the Provençal class (an eerie coincidence), chef Jason Schubert rolled down our driveway on his motorcycle. Schubert, as he is affectionately known by his friends, had been cooking for my friend Andrey Durbach on and off for the past six years. Andrey had taught

Jason Schubert Rolls in on His Motorbike

Schubert everything he knew, and Schubert had also gone on to do stages at a few Michelin-starred restaurants in the UK. Moreover, Schubert just plain loved to cook and work. Hard. Like Cam and Dana, he was an incredibly industrious, inspired cook with a grave reverence for classic technique and, in Schubert's case, classic dishes with an old-school 1970s French presentation. Schubert arrived at Joie on his way back to Ontario with plans to visit his mom and perhaps help his buddy Mike in Arva, Ontario, to open up a restaurant in an historic, still-functioning flour mill. About three hours into his cross-Canada journey, Schubert's old Honda motorcycle broke down in Princeton. He called us from there, wondering if he could stay with us for a few days while his bike got fixed in Penticton. The bike made it as far as our place, and those few days turned into weeks and then months, and, like Cam and Dana, Schubert gradually became part of our Joie family. He began helping me cook for the Saturday Night Orchard Dinners, and was usually in charge of the composed salads and main courses while I made the soups and the dessert. I learned so much from Schubert that summer, especially from his talents and fascination with classic charcuterie. He loved to take animals apart so I immediately ordered a whole boar and a crazy array of organ meats from Richard Yntema of Okanagan Game Meats in Enderby. At the first dinner, Schubert busted out his ironic 1970s food styling with a consommé and braised boar cheek tortellini complete with Savoy cabbage timbales. It was going to be a summer of classic cuisine at Joie — just what I needed to break away from my own classics.

A Dinner to Celebrate Early Summer
Friday June 3, 2005

Aperitif
Hawthorne Mountain Brut

*Joie celebrates the cooking of visiting chef
Jason Schubert this weekend!*

Scallop Ceviche
topped with *Joie* garden radishes
La Frenz Viognier 2004

A Composed Salad
of *Carmelis* Moonstruck goat cheese, *Similkameen Apiary* honeycomb, and
Naramata Bench hazelnuts topped with
Joie's garden greens
Joie A Noble Blend 2004

Enderby Boar Consommé
with braised boar cheek tortellini, Savoy cabbage timbale, and truffle essence
Herder Estate Pinot Noir 2003

Okanagan Cheese Board
Poplar Grove Tiger Blue (Naramata)
Poplar Grove Harvest Moon (Naramata)
Carmelis Chabichou (Kelowna)
Carmelis Lior (Kelowna)

Crannòg Blackcurrant Preserves Tart
with Chantilly cream
Elephant Island Cassis 2004

Coffee, tea, or tisane

Schubert stayed on another week as his bike was still not fixed. Life in the Okanagan runs at a slower, more relaxed pace. Unfortunately for Jason that meant phone calls remained unreturned and no one was moving fast. That week Schubert made a coppa, which hung in our basement drying all summer, and zamponi from a pig's trotter.

Cooking Up a Storm with Schubert

He then took apart a boar's hindquarter. That week he also declared that he was going to start to build our farm a small stone smoker. We trotted off to a landscaping place in town to find some sand, stone-working tools, and bags of concrete. Jason started digging and began to lay the flat foundation stones for the smoker. The project took all summer.

Excited by the prospect of having our own hot-smoked fish soon, I made a simple cold starter dish with smoked albacore and greens drizzled with chive crème fraîche. That week Jason shared his delicious marinade recipe for duck with soy and maple with me. It is classic practice to marinate duck in rock salt and thyme before it is confited. I loved Jason's salty/sweet mix of flavors and his spin on a soy and maple marinade, which replaced the classic ingredients. Jason confited the legs and crisped them up before serving them with the seared marinated breasts cooked rare. We served the dish with more of the delicious Savoy cabbage that was in season at the market.

A Dinner to Celebrate Early Summer
Friday June 10, 2005

*Joie celebrates the cooking of visiting chef
Jason Schubert this weekend!*

Aperitif
Elephant Island Little King Brut 2003

BC Smoked Tuna with Chive Crème Fraîche
served with *Joie* garden French breakfast radishes and herb salad
Joie Un-oaked Chardonnay 2004

Ricotta and Spring Pea Ravioli
napped with rosé beurre blanc
Poplar Grove Reserve Chardonnay 2004

Duck Two Ways
confited leg and seared marinated breast
served with buttered Savoy cabbage
Herder Estate Pinot Noir 2003

Okanagan Cheese Board
Poplar Grove Tiger Blue (Naramata)
Poplar Grove Harvest Moon (Naramata)
Carmelis Goatgonzola (Kelowna)
Carmelis Goat Lior Special Edition (Kelowna)

Claybank Farm Balaton Sour Cherry Clafouti
Elephant Island Stella Port 2002

Coffee, tea, or tisane

Having Fun with the Classics

*S*chubert wanted to make the delicious Tuscan classic vitello tonnato to start the Friday Dinner. With smoked tuna still stuck in my mind from the week before, I suggested that Schubert make his version of the classic tuna, caper, and anchovy dressing (he fondly referred to it as tuna gravy) and that we should serve this tuna gravy on top of cold, thinly sliced smoked tuna instead of cold thinly sliced roasted veal shin. I laughed as I told him that this very Italy-meets-BC dish could be now known as "tonnato, tonnato" instead of vitello tonnato. The combination of smoked tuna with the tuna mayonnaise was delicious and the name stuck. We ended up eating quite a lot of tuna gravy as a regular part of our family meal that summer, topping oil-soaked croutons with greens. To continue with our Italy-meets-BC theme that week, I made my version of a soup from chickpeas and fontina that I had enjoyed immensely at Peter Zambri's restaurant in Victoria a few years prior. It is a rich, silky soup, surprisingly light and healthy as it is finished with olive oil and Parmesan instead of butter. For the main course we wrapped fresh halibut in prosciutto and simply seared it off in salty little packages, finishing it with a light tomato and orange sauce and brown butter. We made a gooseberry crostata (a rustic open-faced pie) for dessert with mascarpone sorbetto. "Viva Toscana" in the Okanagan Valley!

A Dinner to Celebrate Early Summer
Friday June 17 , 2005

Joie celebrates the cooking of visiting chef
Jason Schubert this weekend!

Aperitif
Elephant Island Little King Brut 2003

Tonnato, Tonnato
BC smoked tuna served with tuna and caper mayonnaise and fresh nasturtium buds
Joie Pinot Noir Rosé 2004

Chickpea Soup with Fontina
Poplar Grove Reserve Chardonnay 2004

BC Halibut Cheek Wrapped in Prosciutto
served with a tomato and orange, asparagus, and Sieglinde potatoes,
finished with sage brown butter
Herder Estate Pinot Noir 2003

Okanagan Cheese Board
Poplar Grove Tiger Blue (Naramata)
Poplar Grove Harvest Moon (Naramata)
Carmelis Goatgonzola (Kelowna)
Carmelis Goat Lior Special Edition (Kelowna)

Gooseberry Crostata
with mascarpone sorbetto
Pentâge Late Harvest Sauvignon Blanc 2002

Coffee, tea, or tisane

Schubert and I continued on our Italian theme and, as there was starting to be an abundance of zucchini in the garden, I made a delicious and indulgent zucchini soup that week with rich chicken broth and finished con panna. That course was followed by a gorgeous carpaccio of Enderby venison that Schubert put together, finished with a little salad made with pickled beets and parsley (he loved the intensity of the parsley that grew on the farm and often made parsley salad). Imagine the color of deep-garnet–colored venison tenderloin and

Bring Out the Stunt-stomach

jewel-like beets with bright green parsley on the plate, the whole works glistening

with olive oil. It was a beautiful plate. For the main course, Schubert made a delicious risotto with Swiss chard and a marsala jus out of pheasant bones, topped with a crispy, juicy breast of pheasant and crispy sweetbreads. I would have liked to have been a guest myself that weekend!

Our special guests that weekend were winemakers Lawrence and Sharon Herder of Herder Family Estate Winery of Cawston in the Similkameen Valley and their Pinot Noir was delicious with the pheasant dish. To finish we had an intense chocolate tart studded with cherries and Stella Port from Elephant Island. If you have never tasted their beautifully made port-style wine (they even have a solera) made from their farm's Stella cherries, you're missing a real treat. It's also a killer with chocolate and fresh cherries.

A Dinner to Celebrate the Arrival of Summer
Friday June 24, 2005

*Joie celebrates the cooking of visiting chef
Jason Schubert this weekend!*

Aperitif
Elephant Island Little King Brut 2003

First of the Season Zucchini Soup
Poplar Grove Reserve Chardonnay 2004

Venison Carpaccio with Pickled Beet and Parsley and Onion Salad
finished with *San Giuliano* primer olive oil
Joie Pinot Noir Rosé 2004

Roast Breast of Enderby Pheasant and Veal Sweetbreads
on Swiss chard and chaneterelle risotto
finished with Marsala jus
Herder Estate Pinot Noir 2003

Okanagan Cheese Board
Poplar Grove Tiger Blue (Naramata)
Poplar Grove Naramata Bench Blue (Naramata)
Carmelis Goat Lior Special Edition (Kelowna)
Pentâge Late Harvest Sauvignon Blanc 2002

Bittersweet Chocolate Tart
with *Claybank Farm* Balaton sour cherries
Elephant Island Stella Port

Coffee, tea, or tisane

Canada Day was upon us again and the weather was slowly starting to resemble summer. It had been a rainy spring and a fairly cool start to the summer. That evening it was reasonably hot, so a refreshing ceviche was a perfect way to start our Friday Dinner, with the crispy thin radishes laid out like the strips of scallops. It was a pretty dish. For the second course that week, Jason made a country terrine from all parts of a local lamb with a classic celery root remoulade (shredded raw celeriac tossed in a creamy mayonnaise) and a savory tangy

Groovin' to the "Oldies"

pear and shallot compote made from the dried pears from our orchard. Schubert continued the whole animal theme by braising boar cheeks all afternoon and making a delicious farce to put into filled mezzalunas, pasta like half-moon raviolis. We served a small piece of rich boar belly that he had braised all afternoon and then crisped the fat side, which produced a wonderful contrast of textures within the same dish. It sounds like a savage dish to eat in the summer, but the portions were manageable and were accompanied by a sauté of fresh fava beans and Swiss chard—a small nod to the vegetable kingdom. For dessert we made an incredible lemon tart from the Roux brothers' cookbook (a classic tome from which we had been having fun cooking all summer). We studded the tart with local raspberries from just down Naramata Road and then Schubert caramelized the top. Again, this was a dish with awesome textural contrasts. The freshness of the lemon and tangy berries was an excellent way to end a protein-heavy meal.

A Dinner to Celebrate Summer in Canada
Friday July 1, 2005

*Joie celebrates the cooking of visiting chef
Jason Schubert!*

Aperitif
Elephant Island Little King Brut 2003

BC Spot Prawn Ceviche
with *Joie* garden nasturtiums and radishes
La Frenz Alexandria 2004

Terrine de Campagne
with watercress, celeriac remoulade, and *Joie* dried pear and shallot compote
Joie Pinot Noir Rosé 2004

Crisp Enderby Boar Belly
with braised boar cheek mezzaluna,
served with a sauté of fresh fava beans and Swiss chard
Lake Breeze Seven Poplars Pinot Noir 2003

Okanagan Cheese Board
Poplar Grove Tiger Blue (Naramata)
Carmelis Goat Lior Special Edition (Kelowna)
Carmelis Heavenly (Kelowna)
Pentâge Late Harvest Sauvignon Blanc 2002

Caramelized Tarte au Citron
with first of the season Naramata Bench raspberries
Elephant Island Framboise Wine 2004

Coffee, tea, or tisane

I made a carrot soup from the purple dragon carrots fresh out of our garden. The soup itself was a deep orange and was garnished with curly strips of the purple skin of the carrots. Purple carrots are actually orange inside, but the skin will stay purple if you fry them in hot oil. They make delicious chips for eating or garnishing. At the bottom of the bowl was a little treasure of BC spot prawn ceviche. The orange soup, coral-colored prawns, and purple carrots were a pretty start to the meal. Schubert made a traditional Alsatian onion tart with a quenelle of homemade boar rillette on the side. Rillette is shredded confited meat combined with duck or pork fat to form a delicious spread. Schubert had taken the remainder of the boar leg from the week previous and confited it in duck fat. The onion tart and boar rillette was a marriage made in heaven when paired with our 2004 Noble Blend. It was that specific type of food that inspired us to make the wine in its aromatic, spicy style. Pork, onions, and nutmeg are the hallmark of country food eaten in Alsace and they pair

Classic Dishes Made Under Summer's Influence

well with the aromatic grape varietals of that region like Gewürztraminer, Muscat, and Riesling. We simply roasted a pheasant two ways that night and served it with the fabulous fava beans that were still found in abundance at the Penticton farmer's market. I made a galette with plums and pistachio nuts and served it with an orange blossom ice cream. This is a dessert with a bit of a Middle-Eastern flair. Orange blossom water is a lovely way to accent high-acid summer fruit and is somewhat exotic, transporting you to yet another hot-weather place.

JOIE

A Dinner to Celebrate the Late Arrival of Hot Weather
Friday July 22, 2005

*Joie celebrates the cooking of visiting chef
Jason Schubert this weekend!*

Aperitif
Elephant Island Little King Brut 2003

Heirloom Dragon Carrot Soup
with BC spot prawn ceviche
La Frenz Semillon 2004

Alsatian Onion Tart
with boar rillette
Joie A Noble Blend 2004

Roast Breast of Enderby Pheasant and Ballotine of Leg
served with fresh fava bean ragout
Blasted Church The Dam Flood 2004

Okanagan Cheese Board
Poplar Grove Tiger Blue (Naramata)
Poplar Grove Camembert (Naramata)
Carmelis Goatgonzola (Kelowna)
Carmelis Lior Special Edition (Kelowna)

Joie Golden Plum and Pistachio Galette
with orange blossom ice cream
Elephant Island Apricot Wine 2004

Coffee, tea, or tisane

At the end of July every year, we experience an overflow of zucchini and beets in our garden. To celebrate the ever-expanding patch, Schubert picked a few zucchini blossoms (possibly in the hope of preventing more zucchinis from reaching maturity) and stuffed them with a mushroom duxelle (a classic farce of mushrooms and shallots), deep-fried these stuffed blossoms, and served them with a simple lemon aioli. We also had beets like mad in the garden so I roasted some beautiful yellow beets and we made Schubert's recipe for goat cheese pannacotta (see page 191), using local goat's milk and goat cheese lebneh from Carmelis' Goat Cheese Artisan in Kelowna. Tangy goat's cheese and earthy beets are another marriage made in heaven and they are even better when paired up with spicy arugula to contrast the creamy, mellow pannacotta. Schubert roasted duck breasts and served them with a sauté of yellow plums from our garden. The plums were a traditional tangy accompaniment to the rich duck breasts. We also made individual lemon curd and blueberry tarts for dessert with blueberries that were grown just up the road from us.

Cooking from the Garden's Overflow

A Dinner to Celebrate the Heat of Summer
Friday July 29, 2005

*Joie celebrates the cooking of visiting chef
Jason Schubert this weekend!*

Aperitif
Elephant Island Little King Brut 2003

Zucchini Blossom Stuffed with Mushroom Duxelles
served with lemon aioli
Joie Un-oaked Chardonnay 2004

Roasted Yellow Beets
with goat cheese pannacotta and arugula
La Frenz Semillon 2004

Roasted Wentzel Duck Breast
served with Lyonnaise potatoes, green beans, and golden plums
Herder Gamay Noir 2004

Okanagan Cheese Board
Poplar Grove Tiger Blue (Naramata)
Poplar Grove Camembert (Naramata)
Poplar Grove Harvest Moon (Naramata)
Carmelis Goatgonzola (Kelowna)
Carmelis Lior Special Edition (Kelowna)

Lemon Curd and Naramata Blueberry Tartlets
Elephant Island Apricot Wine 2004

Coffee, tea, or tisane

*C*rispy sweetbreads were served up this week along with a delicious split pea purée that Schubert made with dried split peas cooked in ham hock stock and lots of olive oil to emulsify them. It was a beautiful, textured dish with the crispy sweetbread paired with the earthy purée and finished with a sage brown butter emulsion. To balance the rich flavors of the first course, I made a light and cold sockeye salmon tartar. After our guests' palates were refreshed, Schubert made a classic Tuscan cacciatore with pheasant and served it with potato and Parmigiano Reggiano ravioli. A cacciatore is the Italian version of the French chasseur, or hunter's stew. As we had made a substantial meal, we stuck to another lemon tart for dessert, this time studded with the new crop of Claybank Farms' Balaton sour cherries.

Balancing Heavy Dishes by Applying New Techniques

A Dinner to Celebrate the Bounty of Summer
Friday August 12, 2005

Aperitif
Elephant Island Little King Brut 2003

Crispy Sweetbreads
with split pea purée and sage brown butter emulsion
La Frenz Semillon 2004

Wild Sockeye Salmon Tartar
with *Joie*'s garden greens and crème fraîche
Joie Pinot Noir Rosé 2004

Enderby Pheasant Cacciatore
served with potato and Parmigiano Reggiano ravioli
Lake Breeze Seven Poplars Pinot Noir 2003

Okanagan Cheese Board
Poplar Grove Tiger Blue (Naramata)
Poplar Grove Camembert (Naramata)
Carmelis Goatgonzola (Kelowna)
Carmelis Lior Special Edition (Kelowna)

Caramelized Lemon Tart
with new crop *Claybank Farm* Balaton sour cherries
Elephant Island Apricot Wine 2004

Coffee, tea, or tisane

*B*ecause of an unusually cool summer, I wasn't able to make my favorite yellow tomato soup until the third week of August. That week in our cooking classes we did an all-tomato class, so I continued with the theme through the first course of the Orchard Dinner. We cured a sockeye salmon that week and, for the second course, we created a

Summer Weather Finally Reveals Itself

dish that featured a duality of temperatures by thickly cutting the salmon and searing only one side of it so that one side was warm and crispy and the other side was cold and cured. We served the cured salmon with

steamed, heirloom yellow-fleshed potatoes and tangy crème fraîche. Schubert had confited the legs from the whole ducks the week before and we shredded the meat, sautéed some Swiss chard, and made a delicious creamy risotto with the confit and chard stirred in and then drizzled over a smoked-bacon jus that Schubert had made from the duck carcasses. That week I made up a different custard for our favorite tart, using fresh orange juice instead of lemon and adding some fresh ginger. The combination was just as refreshing as our parade of classic lemon tarts had been all summer.

A Dinner to Celebrate Returning Friends
Friday August 19, 2005

*Joie celebrates the cooking of visiting chef
Jason Schubert this weekend*

Aperitif
Elephant Island Little King Brut 2003

Chilled Yellow Heirloom Tomato Soup
Herder Pinot Gris 2004

Warm Salad of Cured Sockeye Salmon
and Sieglinde potatoes finished with horseradish crème fraîche
La Frenz Alexandria 2004

Wentzel Duck and Swiss Chard Risotto
finished with sherry vinegar and double-smoked bacon jus
Lake Breeze Seven Poplars Pinot Noir 2003

Cheese Board
Poplar Grove Tiger Blue (Naramata, BC)
McLennan Creek Goat Flute (Abbotsford, BC)
Carmelis Lior Special Edition (Kelowna, BC)
Époisse (Burgundy, France)

Orange and Ginger Tart
with Kootenay huckleberry compote
Elephant Island Apricot Wine 2004

Coffee, tea, or tisane

*T*he final week of Schubert's summer at Joie coincided with Cam and Dana's return to Joie. Just as Cam and Dana finished up another summer of cooking for tree planters, Schubert decided it was finally time to pay that visit to his mom in Arva. Schubert's bike never did get fixed (and is still in our garage as a testament to his visit). However, the smoker was finished with the help of my brother Craig Noble. More regal than Schubert's bike, the hand-built stone smoker stands as a reminder of the hard-working, true artisan that Jason Schubert is. What a gift to leave to the farm. Thank you, Schubert!

The Smoker Remains

During our last weekend of cooking together, Schubert and I made the last yellow tomato soup of the season, a savory red onion and thyme tart Tatin served with a slice of Carmelis's goat piccolo (a Loire valley–style goat cheese similar to a St. Maure, with the ash on the outside), a crispy skinned pheasant with sage and pancetta slipped under the skin, and sautéed spaetzle and gorgeous Vancouver Island chanterelles that Cam and Dana had brought back with them. We sat Cam and Dana at the table as usual, fed them, and gave them a bed and a hot shower. They then moved back into Joie for the rest of the fall season. They would soon make Naramata their fixed address. Schubert made it back to London, Ontario, safely (on the plane) and spent the winter and spring/summer 2006 at his buddy Mike's flour mill. He happily went back to working shifts at "The Mill" and became the official live-in chef.

Schubert has now gone on to open his own restaurant in London and we wish him all the luck in the world. Schubert, like many chefs, lives to feed people. His time with us at Joie made a deep impact on my cooking and I made a friend for life. We look forward to his next visit to Joie.

A Dinner to Celebrate the Waning of Summer
Friday August 26, 2005

*Joie celebrates the cooking of visiting chef
Jason Schubert this weekend and the return of our
chef friends, Cameron Smith and Dana Ewart!*

Aperitif
Sumac Ridge Brut NV

Chilled Yellow Heirloom Tomato Soup
La Frenz Semillon 2004

Red Onion and Thyme Savory Tarte Tatin
with *Carmelis* Piccollo Goat Cheese
Herder Pinot Gris 2004

Crispy Skinned Pheasant
served with spaetzle, braised purple cabbage, and Vancouver Island chanterelles finished with a Riesling jus
Lake Breeze Seven Poplars Pinot Noir 2003

Okanagan Cheese Board
Poplar Grove Tiger Blue (Naramata)
Poplar Grove Naramata Bench Blue (Naramata)
Carmelis Lior Special Edition (Kelowna)
Carmelis Chabichou (Kelowna)

Caramelized Tarte au Citron
with new crop *Claybank Farm* Balaton sour cherries
Elephant Island Apricot Wine 2004

Coffee, tea, or tisane

Cooking with Cam and Dana Again

Michael and I were thrilled to have Cam and Dana with us again at Joie. Just as in the previous year, they moved straight into helpful mode and got the gardens cleaned up for fall. Cam was also stoked about the new smoker and we took it for a few serious test drives those first few weeks of September, smoking everything from whole hindquarters of lamb, to bacon, fresh sausages, pork shoulders, nuts, salmon, tuna, almonds, and even a round of hard cheese. In the menu in the second week of September we used a smoked albacore tuna loin, cured in the Joie smoker, to make that summer's signature dish, Tonnato, Tonnato. Dana made a delicious soup out of a giant hubbard squash from our garden and some of the abundant pears that were very ripe in our orchard. Cam braised lamb shanks and made a delicious stuffing for large cappelletti out of the meat. For dessert I made pots de crème flavored with cardamom and espresso, and Dana made honey madeleines to be paired with an interesting bottle of homemade Sauternes that one of our customers had traded us for a bottle of rosé. The 10-year-old dessert wine was a wonderful pairing with the rich caramelized flavors of the pots de crème and the brown butter in the madeleines.

A Dinner to Celebrate the Impending Grape Harvest
Saturday September 10, 2005

*Joie celebrates the cooking of visiting chefs
Cameron Smith and Dana Ewart this weekend!*

Aperitif
Sumac Ridge Brut NV

Tonnato, Tonnato
BC smoked tuna with tuna and caper aioli
Pentâge Semillon/Sauvignon Blanc 2004

Hubbard Squash and Bartlett Pear Soup
with pear butter and chèvre croutons
Dirty Laundry Woo Woo Vines Gewürztraminer 2004

Braised Enderby Lamb and Porcini Cappelletti
served with Swiss chard and finished with truffled lamb jus
Fairview Cellars Cabernet Sauvignon/Merlot 2003

Cheese Board
Poplar Grove Tiger Blue (Naramata, BC)
Poplar Grove Naramata Bench Blue (Naramata, BC)
Carmelis Lior Special Edition (Kelowna, BC)
Carmelis Heavenly (Kelowna, BC)
Mimolette (Burgundy, France)

Cardamom and Espresso Pots de Crème
with brown butter and *Similkameen Apiary* honey madeleines
Kurt Aydin's North Vancouver Sauterne 1997

Coffee, tea, or tisane

The last tomatoes of the year went into a delicious roasted tomato soup to begin our final Saturday Night Orchard Dinner of 2005. Cam and I braised a pork belly in apple juice from the orchard and served the belly pieces crispy on top of braised purple cabbage with a side of apple and sage compote. It was a dish designed to signal the beginning of harvest. We braised more lamb that week, but this time it was cheek meat which we served as a ragù on top of soft polenta. For dessert we used dark chocolate to make a classic chocolate tart which we studded with the last Naramata fall raspberries. Once we wrapped up our last Orchard Dinner, Michael and I shifted back into winemaking mode and began our second vintage, working the 2005 harvest at Pentâge Winery with our friend and mentor Paul Gardner. Cam and Dana moved into a small picker's cabin at Claybank Farm and began working as consultants and head cooks at a small grocery store that had just opened on Vancouver Hill in Penticton, called the Bench Artisan

Food for the Beginning of Harvest

Market. The following spring Cam and Dana bought their first ever home on a mountain above Penticton and opened a much-needed catering company called Joy Road Catering which they run from a wonderful workspace in their home on Joy Road. A coincidence of names? I think not. They're wonderful additions to the area and the Okanagan is lucky to have them. Cam and Dana are now putting their own mark on the Okanagan and are adding to the critical mass of chefs staking out a place amid the bounty of this Valley.

A Dinner to Celebrate the Harvest Season
Friday September 16, 2005

Joie celebrates the cooking of visiting chefs
Cameron Smith and Dana Ewart this weekend!

Aperitif
Elephant Island Little King Brut 2003

Roasted Heirloom Tomato Soup
Herder Pinot Gris 2004

Crispy Pork Belly
with *Joie* apple compote and braised purple cabbage
Dirty Laundry 'Madame's Vines' Gewürztraminer 2004

Braised Enderby Lamb Cheeks and Porcini
with soft Parmeggiano Reggiano polenta
finished with truffled lamb jus
La Frenz Reserve Cabernet Sauvignon/Merlot 2001

Okanagan Cheese Board
Poplar Grove Camembert (Naramata)
Poplar Grove Naramata Bench Blue (Naramata)
Poplar Grove Harvest Moon (Naramata)
Carmelis Lior Special Edition (Kelowna)
Carmelis Goatgonzola (Kelowna)

Bittersweet Chocolate Tart
with Naramata Bench fall raspberries
Elephant Island Framboise Wine 2004

Coffee, tea, or tisane

|MARKET|

- cippolini
- meloni
- watercress
- cucumbers
- honeycomb
- potatoes

|DRUG STORE|

- crutches

|SAFEWAY|

- garbage bags
- paper towel

|IL VECCHIO|

- capers
- anchovy
- prosciutto

Going into our fourth season with the cooking school in 2006, Michael and I decided to close our guesthouse as our wine production and its accompanying sales needs grew. For the 2006 season, we continued with our outdoor cooking classes on the weekends, offered our Saturday Morning Farmer's Market Class, and taught regional cooking classes each Sunday throughout the summer. The summer of 2006 also brought more guest chefs to Joie's kitchen through two-day weekend workshops. We had Park Heffelfinger and George Siu of Vancouver's Memphis Blues BBQ do a serious smoking and southern BBQ session with our new stone smoker. Chef Dana Ewart conducted an artisan baking workshop, sharing much of the wisdom that she gleaned from working with James MacGuire of Le Passe Partout in Montreal. Chef John Taboada of the acclaimed Portland, Oregon, restaurant Navarre taught regional Spanish cooking and introduced our guests to the culture of true Spanish tapas. The talented and charismatic Chris Stearns (who also took the stunning photos for this book) taught a classic and seasonal cocktail class. Chef Cameron Smith led us through an intensive two-day charcuterie workshop with his amazing butchery skills, also gleaned from Montreal's Le Passe Partout, and his intuitive way with meat. We finished up our 2006 season with Chef Vikram Vij of Vancouver's Vij's and Rangoli restaurants. Vikram shared the beauty and inspiration of his modern Indian cuisine, using seasonal BC ingredients. The kitchen never smelled more delicious than during Vikram's class.

When I look back on this most recent summer, as well as the previous three summers, I feel very blessed to have this farm and kitchen to host the wonderful people I have met along the way. Like me, they are obsessed with and inspired by real, fresh, local seasonal food, prepared with a reverence for classic techniques. Their varied backgrounds and experiences all converged at different times here, and using the best the Okanagan had to offer, they cooked the most beautiful country food here in our burgeoning wine country.

The evolution of Joie's cuisine has really been an edible discovery. I am 10 times the cook I was when I arrived here. My boundaries have been pushed by access to new ingredients and I have been truly inspired by the respect I have for those chefs who came to Joie for a rest. I thank all the wonderful souls who have passed through my kitchen and my heart. I leave you with a collection of my recipes and those that were passed on to me by those special guests. Enjoy and bon appetit! May these recipes inspire you and may your local market be your true guide when you cook.

IN ACKNOWLEDGEMENT OF OUR PRODUCERS

I feel a great deal of pride about the success of our four years of Orchard Dinners and cooking classes. However, I cannot claim sole responsibility for this success. Much of the pride that I feel can be attributed to the food I was privileged to buy from my local producers at the Penticton farmer's market or directly from their farms. The producers remain the true stars of the show.

Yes, the dishes I turned out for our dinners were beautiful and tasty, but the great dishes I made were only as good as the quality of the raw product with which I worked. My pride originates not only from providing my guests with a good time, a fine meal, and a local, authen-

tic experience, but also from knowing that I was able to directly support a wide network of farmers each of the 25 weeks of the growing season by purchasing food for my breakfasts, lunches, cooking classes, dinners, and farm tours. Much of the money that our business earned was returned directly to the hands of local farmers. The success of our business therefore enhanced the success of our local farmers. Every week I looked forward to seeing them, visiting with them, and proudly introducing our guests to them and their wares at market trips or on farm visits.

I enjoyed getting to know our producers personally and hearing the stories of how they came to farm or

had returned to farming. They all have different, crazy stories and their own reasons for doing what they do now with passion. Farming in a sustainable manner is a thankless task and my hat goes off to each and every one of them. It is one thing to run a sustainable farm, but it is an entirely different matter to run a sustainable business. All my producers are characters in their own right, and I think it is those magnetic personalities and their love of people and food that keeps them going and helps them succeed. Self-promotion is not necessarily synonymous with farmers, but the successful ones know they are farming food for people to eat, not just farming for the sake of it. There is something about growing and producing food that is specifically human. Even the shiest among them holds close the link between growing food and eating food. Food is grown to be eaten, and when eaten, food is generally shared. Good, healthy, sound local food is the basis of our society. Farmers are the keepers not only of our food but also of our health and well-being. I have deep respect for the growers we work with. I admire their passion and commitment to farming itself as well as the work involved in getting their products to market. It is my pleasure to introduce you to a few of them, their products, and their properties.

Backyard Beans
Liz and Richard Haverkamp

RICHARD HAVERKAMP was once our Volkswagen mechanic. He and his wife, Liz, also supplied our guesthouse with delicious locally roasted coffee beans. They are a micro-roastery committed to using premium organic, farmer-friendly, shade-grown coffees. They sell their beans at the Penticton farmer's market, Naramata's coffee shop, Village Grounds, and in a few of the better grocery stores in Penticton. They feel that by drinking organic, farmer-friendly, shade-grown coffees, their customers can help provide for the earth and its peoples rather than constantly taking away. Backyard Beans urges their customers to drink coffee with a conscience. They are a home-based business, open between "the hours of waking up and going to sleep" should you need to call in your order for a few pounds of their Dancing Goat blend or my personal morning-time favorite, the Smooth Operator blend.

Carmelis Goat Cheese Artisan
Ofer and Ofri Barmor

OFER AND OFRI Barmor are two of the most inspiring people I have ever met. They moved to Canada from Israel in 2002 after living through a horrific car accident that put Ofri in a coma and Ofer in a wheelchair, 100 percent disabled. They found their alpine property in Kelowna's Mission District over the Internet and purchased it from the previous owner in Kelowna in the spring of 2002. That year they moved their lives and two daughters, Lior and Carmel, to the Okanagan Valley. Ofri was raised on a farm in the Jisrael Valley, but neither Ofer nor Ofri had any experience in making cheese—only eating it, as they like to joke. They embarked on an extended trip to France where they spent time with cheesemakers and learned their craft. Upon arrival in Kelowna, they immediately set up their goat barn, a herd of 90 alpine goats, and a cheese production facility. Shortly after the goat barn was completed and filled with goats in mid-August of 2003, the horrific Okanagan Mountain Park forest fire burned down the barn and the dairy, and burned right up to the door of their house. Being the brave, capable people that they are, they moved the goats off the property as the fire approached and rebuilt the barn and dairy when the worst had past. By early 2004, they were back in business having established the production of their cheeses. Ofer and Ofri make 20 varieties of goat cheeses in a number of different styles. When most people think of goat cheese, they think of fresh cheese, but Ofer also makes a few bloomy

styles, as well as brine-washed cheese. The part that impresses me the most is that they have a cheese ripening cave, which means they have invested time and inventory in making matured goat cheeses. Their cheeses are wonderful, some of the most flavorful in BC, and are true to their historical and regional inspiration. Whenever I visit their farm I am in awe of Ofri's energy, and Ofer's adaptability simply amazes me. They are kind, talented people with strong opinions and high standards. They also love to eat. Just the kind of folk that the Okanagan needs, in fact.

Crannóg Ales and Left Field Farm
Rebecca Kneen and Brian MacIsaac

AS LUCKY as I am to have Richard Yntema's product from North Okanagan Game Meats, I am even luckier to receive the very delicious and limited editions of chickens and Tamworth and Durroc pigs (as well as awesome beer!) from Crannóg Ales in Sorrento in the Shuswap area of the North Okanagan Valley. Rebecca and Brian run Canada's only certified organic farmhouse microbrewery, one of only a handful of such breweries in the world. They brew unfiltered, unpasteurized ales using only organic ingredients, some of which come right from their own farm, Left Fields. The farm and brewery are fully integrated, with the brewery providing food for the livestock, and the farm providing hops and fruit for the brewery. All the brewery by-products are used on the farm for compost, irrigation, or feed. Water for the brewery comes from a well in the center of their farm which is fed by springs on the farm as well as streams from the mountains that surround them. Brian and Rebecca's ale is amazing and their chickens and pigs are the luckiest animals in the world for being able to eat the spent mash from the brewery every day.

The brewery is the marriage of their two dreams: to farm organically, and to have their own brewery. As well as being a talented brewmaster, Brian is a fabulous artist who specializes in original Celtic designs, and the brewery building and surrounding structures are adorned with his Celtic art. Brian is motivated by what he refers to as a cultural agenda. The Gaelic culture is paramount to his identity. The brewery benefits from this as the styles of ales that Gaels traditionally enjoy are exactly what he likes to brew. Rebecca, having lived on farms for most of her life, is a tireless food activist, farmer, and food enthusiast. I am lucky to be able to share their animals with our guests and to enjoy Brian and Rebecca's generous friendship.

Dumplingdale Organic Farm
Gabi and Dave Cursons

GABI AND DAVE grow the most beautiful vegetables I have ever seen. Their farm is located in Cawston in the Similkameen Valley, and their stall at the farmer's market is a thing of beauty that stands as an inspiration to market gardeners everywhere. Gabi is originally from Germany and came to Canada as a trained pediatric nurse. Unable to work without being fully retrained she traveled to the Similkameen Valley and worked as a volunteer on an organic farm for 10 years. She met Dave there and the couple bought their own farm in 2003. They both work the beautiful, small farm in Cawston, and have turned it into a totally sustainable and intensive property with the help of a conservation grant from the Land Reserve. Gabi works the market gardens full-time and Dave is still actively employed as a social worker. Gabi prefers to plant her beds as diversely as she can, growing many varieties of beautiful vegetables from heirloom seeds that have long gone out of commercial production. She prefers growing many things for the market instead of only four crops for a limited number of wholesale clients.

I am so glad she has chosen to plant in this manner as the vegetables at Dumplingdale's stall are always laid out like treasures and merchandised in a manner that makes any chef want to take it all home. Gabi and Dave sell gorgeous, crinkly Savoy cabbages — they're the size of my head and I can never say no to them! — old conical-shaped German varieties of firm green cabbage, intended for sauerkraut, the tiniest haricot verts ever seen (it must take Gabi hours to pick a pound of them), jewel-like red and white cippolini onions, and perfect little Bambini eggplants. Every week without fail their stall inspires my last-minute menu changes and impulse buys.

Similkameen Apiary
Blair and Cheryl Tarves

BLAIR AND CHERYL Tarves have one of the busiest stands at the Penticton farmer's market. Their honey is intensely flavored, coming mainly from beehives located on their property and other outyards, many of which are organic orchards in the arid Similkameen Valley. Their honey is flavored by a diverse variety of plants that they cultivate or that grow wild on their property in Cawston (they live right across the street from Gabi and Dave Cursons at Dumplingdale Farm) and the Similkameen honey plants like white clematis, sweet clover, alfalfa, chokecherry, sumac, elderberry, goldenrod, oregano, mint, and Oregon grape lend their honey unique flavors and a rare quality. The Similkameen Apiary property is stunningly beautiful and their honey house, where the extraction is done, is one of the best-smelling places I have ever been. It is fragrant with the ambient smells of indigenous plants, honeycomb, wax, pinecone smoke (Blair uses Ponderosa pinecones as fuel for his smoker to calm the bees), and Blair's Drum tobacco.

In August of 2005 I spent three days at the Apiary during an intense nectar flow with my chef friends Cameron Smith and Dana Ewart. Mid-August is when the pollinating plants are at the height of their nectar production and the bees fill the honey supers in the hives. We spent several days with Blair and Cheryl, helping them pull honey (remove the full combs from the bee hives). This is a rather harrowing process for the uninitiated as you must smoke out or literally blow out the bees from their home to pull out the full combs. During that stay we learned more than we ever thought possible about bee life, pollination, color spectrums, and honey extraction. Blair and Cheryl have cleverly organized their business to give them a year-round income—pollinating orchards in the spring, selling honey and breeding queens in the summer, harvesting in the fall, and processing honey and wax in the winter—and we have wonderful memories of an afternoon spent catching queens with Blair. The three days I spent with them at the apiary was a life-changing and unforgettable experience. I have a new reverence for honey and enjoy coming up with new ways to incorporate their products into my dishes and desserts.

Claybank Farm Lavender
Pati Hill

PATI HILL is an encyclopedia of knowledge about farming and gardening. Pati was one of the first people I met when I moved to Naramata and she has become a great neighbor and cherished friend. Pati is also one of my most-frequented suppliers. On a trip to France six years ago, Pati visited the south of France and was taken with the fragrant rows of stunning lavender found there. With an interest in one day making soap and other products, Pati took a perfumer's course in Grasse. Once home Pati planted the field in front of her farmhouse with five different cultivars of lavender, and set up one of the best examples of agri-tourism that the Okanagan Valley has ever seen with her soap-making facility and farm-gate shop, complete with an outdoor sink for test-driving her products along with a pink lavender lemonade stand. Pati's farm, Claybank, also supplies us annually with a gorgeous meaty variety of Hungarian sour cherry, called Balaton, as well as with culinary lavender, her *herbes de Provence* mix, and mini-soaps and lavender water for our guesthouse. Pati's farm-gate shop has temporarily closed, but you can still find her down at the Naramata farmer's market on Wednesdays, selling her soap, live lavender plants, and lavender products of all kinds. Pati is the best-smelling person in town!

The Fruit Guy—Farmer at Large
Michael Welsh

MICHAEL WELSH is the very quiet, shy man who runs our orchard at Joie. I met Michael, who has been with us almost from the beginning, at our local farmer's market when I was trying to find someone who would actively farm our five-acre orchard organically (a thankless task, especially for apples!). Our orchard, planted with Spartan and Red and Golden Delicious apples and Bartlett pears, had been farmed conventionally for 50 years before we arrived. Over the course of three years, Michael took our farm from the sorry state it was in to a transitional state, to being certified organic in the spring of 2006. Michael and his crews have picked fruit in the dense smoke of forest fires, removed countless pounds of damaged apples from the trees, and made large chainsaw cuts throughout our entire orchard to bring the trees down to a more workable height. Our orchard is now healthy and Michael does a booming business selling our fruit, and other people's

fruit, as juice, soft dried pears, and apple chips at the Penticton and Naramata farmer's markets and Trout Lake and Granville Island under the banner of "The Fruit Guy." If you are ever lucky enough to meet Michael, ask him about his time spent at Sweet Pit, a commune where he lived for almost 20 years. It is not every day you meet someone who has been involved in agriculture for 20 years and who has also been versed in the art of living communally! We are fortunate to have Michael farming our orchard and are very grateful for all his help over the years.

Elephant Island Orchard Wines
Del and Miranda Halladay

I COULD write a whole book on the talented winemakers of the Okanagan Valley, but I particularly wanted to mention my friends and neighbors at Elephant Island Orchard Wines. Del and Miranda and their children, Finn and Maya, live next door to us and our orchards form a 10-acre block. The winery itself is nestled in a Stella Cherry block that belongs to Miranda's grandmother, Catherine Wisnicki. Catherine was one of the first women to become an architect in Canada and bought the property in the early 1970s as an investment and retirement property. Everyone thought she was crazy, including her engineer husband, Paul, who called the investment a white elephant. Catherine and Paul had esthetic versus structural arguments about the house they constructed on the property. Catherine designed for what she called the pleasure of her eye and so Paul came to refer to the property as Catherine's "eyeland." Hence the name that it has morphed into today—Elephant Island.

Paul Wisnicki's heritage is Polish and most of the fruit wine recipes that Del and Miranda use today were his inspiration (cleaned up and tweaked originally by consulting winemaker Christine Leroux). Today, Del makes the wines, and what I respect the most about Del and Miranda's approach to their products is their respect for not only the product (they use almost all locally grown fruit), but also the process. Their soft fruits and apples are treated like white wines and the dark berries like red wine. Their sparkling wine, Little King (named after their late first son, Rex), is produced méthode champagnoise and they use an in-house–made framboise liqueur for its dosage. They also make a port-style wine through a solera system. Their fruit wines are indeed serious wines, made with the best fruit in season and with a reverence for the great and classic winemaking techniques of the world of wine. Not only do I enjoy using Elephant Island's wines in our menus, I also enjoy telling their story. I think their winery is one of the most appropriate examples of a regional product that shows respect for the history of the fruit-growing industry of the Naramata Bench, the new industry of quality wine production, and the authentic and intimate agritourism that farm-gate wineries can offer.

North Okanagan Game Meats
Richard Yntema

I ALWAYS look forward to phoning Richard to place my meat order. He is passionate about what he does and is always keen to hear about what I intend to cook with his product. He has a farm, RiversBend Fallow Deer Farm, in Enderby, north of Vernon. There he raises lamb, venison, boar, and a few wild turkeys; he also has a small abattoir and butcher shop. Richard is a purveyor of some of his neighbors' farmed animals like rabbit and pheasant, and also free-range eggs. He was originally a home-builder in Abbotsford, BC, but he wanted to escape the hectic life in the Lower Mainland to raise his family in a slower-paced environment, and so he moved to Enderby 16 years ago. A self-taught farmer and butcher, Richard has one of the few small abattoirs in the Valley. As large-scale farms and agri-business consume the meat and poultry business, it is increasingly difficult to find locally raised meat. There are not many people on small farms anymore and there are very few local abattoirs left in the province. Also, Health Canada has cracked down on those small abattoirs with new regulations that are more suited to larger-scale operations, necessitating expensive stainless-steel work areas and large loading docks that might not be appropriate to the scale or budget of some existing operations. I am fortunate, and always grateful, to have access to Richard and his wonderful products which are always delivered with a smile and great conversation.

Okanagan Grocery
Rhys Pender and Alishan Driediger

RHYS AND ALISHAN work out of their home in Peachland, with their bakery, a wonderful custom bakeshop, located in an outbuilding in their backyard. They sell their breads wholesale to restaurants and shops throughout the Okanagan Valley as well as running a small store-front venue in the Guisachan Village in Kelowna. Rhys and Alishan's breads are delicious and gorgeously crafted on a small scale in a rustic, Levain-style, made with unbleached organic white flour and no unnecessary additives. They make a core selection of staple breads like baguette, a

seven-grain rye, foccacia, Callebaut chocolate bread, and a fig and anise loaf. They also produce many seasonal breads on a rotational basis throughout the week and season. Rhys and Alishan make all the bread I use for our cooking classes and supplied the sweet loaves that I would order for our breakfasts when we ran our guesthouse. I also know Rhys and Alishan from another life, in the Vancouver wine business. Rhys and Alishan are both trained chefs who worked in Vancouver and then returned to the Okanagan to where Alishan grew up. Rhys was involved in the wine trade in Vancouver as a buyer for a private wine shop and is now a Master of Wine Candidate (there are only about 250 of those in the world) and a wine educator with Okanagan College. He is now part of a new wine education school in the Okanagan called Fine Vintage Ltd. that offers the prestigious courses of the Wine and Spirit Education Trust and consulting services to local wineries and restaurants. Much like Michael and me, Rhys and Alishan have worn many hats throughout their transition to the Okanagan and through the growth of their business. I wish we saw more of each other, but despite that, there is considerable comfort in just knowing that there are more young couples out there in the Okanagan cutting an edible swath into the culinary landscape.

Pentâge Winery
Paul Gardner and Julie Rennie

I MUST mention Paul Gardner and Julie Rennie here as they have been patient and generous mentors to Michael and me during our new careers as winemakers. Paul is a marine engineer who worked for 20 years on the tug boats of Vancouver and the fuel ships that travel the Great Lakes and St. Lawrence Seaway and he is affectionately known to us as "Captain." Paul is infinitely curious; an engineer to the death, as he can be found in the winery, constantly fixing, modifying, and upgrading our equipment and the equipment belonging to Pentâge. Paul has a bit of a stainless steel fetish that has become contagious. Our new winery purchases have become much shinier (and more expensive!) in the past couple of years.

Pentâge winery is located on the Skaha Bluffs along East Lake Road, just south of Penticton. Michael and I feel blessed to work there through the fall during crush and into the winter months as we continue to work on our wines. The customized winery itself is perched high on a cliff, with a stunning view of both Skaha Lake and Lake Okanagan. Paul and Julie's vineyard, Vista Ridge, is seven planted acres that they planted together in 1997. It is one of the most lovingly tended and hardest pruned vineyards in the valley. With its resident winter bighorn sheep and Paul's indispensable and infinitely patient assistant winemaker, Dwight Sick, Pentâge is a place where our Joie wine magic happens, under the watchful (and sometimes wandering) eye of Paul and his eager apprentices. Without Paul, Julie, and Dwight, Michael and I would not be where we are today with our wines.

RECIPES

COLD SOUPS

CHILLED DRAGON CARROT AND CORIANDER SOUP

Serves 6

FOR THE SOUP

¼ cup (60 mL) unsalted butter

1 Tbsp (15 mL) coriander seeds, lightly toasted and then ground

½ cup (125 mL) sliced onion

4 cups (1 L) peeled and sliced heirloom carrots

4 cups (1 L) filtered water (chlorine gives carrots a funny taste)

4 cups (1 L) fresh orange juice

2 sprigs of fresh thyme

salt

freshly ground pepper

zest of 1 orange

FOR THE CARROT CHIPS

4 cups (1 L) vegetable or peanut oil for deep-frying

2 heirloom carrots

I like to make this soup in the summer when I have purple dragon carrots in my garden. You can often find purple carrots at the farmer's market as well. Dragon carrots are purple on the outside, but deep orange on the inside. They lose their purple color when you cook them, unless you quickly deep-fry them in their skins. I often save some of the peelings to make crispy chips for garnish when I make this soup. The purple and orange of this soup are a beautiful presentation.

Melt the butter in a pot. Add the coriander seeds and the onion and cook until the onion is soft but not brown. Add the carrots and cook for a few minutes, stirring to coat the carrots with the coriander and butter. Add the filtered water and orange juice to just barely cover the carrots. Add the thyme and season to taste with salt and pepper. Cook the soup over medium heat, uncovered, for about half an hour, until the carrots are very tender.

Once the carrots are soft, place the vegetables and some of the liquid in a blender and process until smooth. Do not add too much liquid initially or the finished soup will be too thin. The final purée should have a slightly thickened consistency. If it seems too thick, add a little more liquid. Return the purée to the pot and gently heat through. Check the consistency and seasoning. Adjust the seasoning with salt if necessary. Process the purée in the blender a second time and strain the soup through a fine mesh sieve into a clean bowl. Finish the soup by stirring in the orange zest.

If you are garnishing with purple carrot chips, heat the oil in a wok or heavy-bottomed saucepan to 325°F (160°C). Using a mandoline (see page 133), slice the carrots lengthwise into fine strips. When the oil has come to temperature, plunge a handful of the carrot strips into the oil. Stir to separate the strips and cook until crisp and slightly golden. Remove from the oil and drain on paper towels. Season to taste and set aside until needed.

To serve, ladle the soup into chilled shallow soup bowls. Garnish with purple carrot chips or croutons. Do not add the croutons or chips too far in advance as they are best if they have some crunch and are not soggy.

SUGGESTED WINE PAIRING

BC: Wild Goose Riesling, Okanagan Falls

International: Lingenfelder "Bird Label" Riesling, Germany

VICHYSSOISE

Serves 6

FOR THE SOUP

1 Tbsp (15 mL) unsalted butter

3 leeks, the dark green tops discarded
   and the leek whites split lengthwise,
   washed well of all dirt and sand, and
   chopped coarsely

1 cup (250 mL) chopped white onion

2 medium white-fleshed potatoes, like
   Russets, peeled and cut into 2-inch
   (5-cm) dice

2 cups (500 mL) light chicken stock,
   warmed

1 tsp (5 mL) salt

1 cup (250 mL) whole (3.25%) milk

1 cup (250 mL) half-and-half (10%)
   cream

freshly ground white pepper

½ cup (125 mL) whipping (35%) cream

FOR THE GARNISH

4 slices white bread or stale baguette, cut
   into ½-inch (1-cm) cubes

2 Tbsp (30 mL) unsalted butter

1 bunch fresh chives, finely chopped
   (with blossoms if possible)

I love serving vichyssoise in the summertime to start a meal. I can buy fantastic leeks at the farmer's market and look forward to making this soup when they appear in the late summer. When I was a kid, one of the first fancy restaurant experiences I remember was being served vichyssoise with purple rosemary blossoms floating in it at Janet Lynn's in Waterloo, Ontario. In retrospect Waterloo seems like a strange place to have a fine dining experience, but whenever I eat vichyssoise it still makes me feel grown-up.

Heat a large heavy-bottomed pot on medium heat and melt the butter. Add the leeks and the onion and cook, covered, over low heat, stirring occasionally, until softened. Add the potatoes, warmed chicken stock, and salt. Simmer the mixture, covered, for 30–40 minutes, or until the potatoes are soft. Add the milk and the half-and-half and bring the mixture just to a boil, stirring all the time.

Using a blender, purée the mixture in batches and strain it through a very fine mesh sieve into a bowl. Make sure the soup is not too thick or stodgy. Adjust the consistency with more stock if necessary, and adjust the seasoning with salt and white pepper to taste. With a cold soup, you have to increase the amount of salt that you use as the chill will dull your perception of saltiness. Stir the cream into the soup and chill for at least two hours.

Serve the soup in a chilled bowl and garnish with small cubes of bread fried in butter for croutons and finely chopped chives and a few torn up chive blossoms if you have them.

SUGGESTED WINE PAIRING

BC: Lake Breeze Pinot Blanc, Naramata
International: Cameron "Giovanni" Pinot Blanc,
Willamette Valley, Oregon

CHILLED ENGLISH PEA SOUP

Serves 6

(see page 133)

FOR THE PESTO

½ cup (125 mL) chervil or tarragon
  leaves
½ cup (125 mL) bunch flat-leaf parsley
  leaves
½ cup (125 mL) basil leaves
1 shallot, finely minced
½ cup (125 mL) olive oil
juice and zest of 1 lemon
1 tsp (5 mL) salt
1 tsp (5 mL) freshly ground pepper

FOR THE SOUP

2 L (8 cups) chicken stock (or vegetable
  stock for a vegetarian soup)
1 lb (500 g) fresh and then frozen English
  peas
2 Tbsp (30 mL) rice wine vinegar
2 Tbsp (30 mL) fresh lemon juice
1 tsp (5 mL) lemon zest
salt
freshly ground pepper
crème fraîche for garnish

This soup is like the essence of pea in a bowl. The technique used to make it yields a bright, almost sonic green color. Since this is supposed to be a chilled soup I replaced the classic cooked mirepoix (see page 133) with an uncooked, fresh pesto. I look forward to the first English peas of the season every year so that I can make this soup.

Prepare the pesto by blending all of the ingredients together in a blender until the mixture can be drizzled. Store the pesto in a jar and reserve.

For the soup, put the stock in a large pot, bring to a boil, and maintain a gentle boil. Meanwhile, set up a large bowl over an ice-water bath to cool the soup once it is blended. Set a blender next to the ice-water bath with a fine mesh sieve and a ladle close to hand—timing is everything with this soup if you hope to achieve its bright green color.

Plunge half of the frozen peas into the boiling stock and cook until the peas float and turn bright green (this should take 1–2 minutes). Do not cover the pot while the peas are cooking. Once the peas have turned bright green, remove half of them from the stock with a slotted spoon and place them in the blender. Fill the blender three-quarters full with stock and add 2 Tbsp (30 mL) of the pesto. Blend at high speed for 2 minutes. The liquid in the blender will turn bright green. To maintain this bright green color, pour the soup out of the blender and through the mesh sieve. Use a ladle to push the pea pulp through the sieve. By straining the soup straight into a bowl set over ice water you allow the soup to cool and stop the cooking process immediately. Repeat this process with the remaining peas and liquid until all the peas have been blended. Add the rice wine vinegar, lemon juice, and zest. Season the soup with salt and pepper to taste. The soup should have a fresh, bright flavor.

Cool the soup in the refrigerator until ready to serve. Serve in a chilled bowl and garnish with crème fraîche.

SUGGESTED WINE PAIRING

BC: Pentâge Sauvignon Blanc, Penticton
International: Henri Bourgeois Sancerre, Loire Valley, France

MIREPOIX (from the French town of the same name) is the French name for a combination of onions, carrots, and celery or celeriac. Mirepoix, either raw, roasted, or sautéed, is the flavor base for a wide number of dishes, such as soups, stocks, stews, and sauces. Traditionally, the ratio for mirepoix is 2:1:1 of onions, celery, and carrots. In Italy a mirepoix is called a "soffrito" and often uses fennel stocks instead of celery.

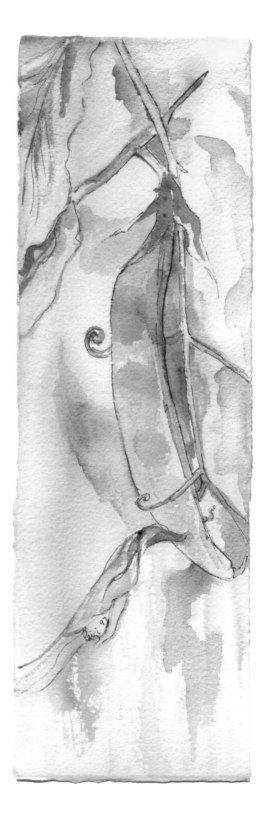

CHILLED YELLOW TOMATO SOUP

Serves 6

5 lb (2.2 kg) yellow tomatoes (preferably large heirloom like Dixie Gold), washed and quartered
2 Tbsp (30 mL) extra virgin olive oil
¼ cup (60 mL) rice wine vinegar
1 tsp (5 mL) salt

freshly ground pepper
1 bunch fresh chives, finely chopped for garnish
small colorful heirloom tomatoes cut into interesting shapes for garnish
extra virgin olive oil for garnish

I make this soup about three weeks a year when the yellow tomatoes in the garden and at the market are at the peak of their ripeness. Yellow tomatoes have the most amazing creamy texture when puréed. This soup is an exercise in summer simplicity, containing only five ingredients. It can be garnished with other small heirloom tomatoes that are in season at the same time or with a single ceviched spot prawn or scallop.

Place the tomato quarters in a blender and blend until smooth. Drizzle in the olive oil while the blender is still running. Add the rice wine vinegar, salt, and pepper. Blend again. Taste the soup and adjust the seasoning, remembering that the soup is going to be chilled, so any taste of saltiness will be dulled.

Strain the soup through a fine mesh sieve to remove the tomato skins and to give the soup an even creamier texture.

Chill both the soup and serving dishes until ready to serve. Cold soup should always be served in a cold bowl. To serve, ladle the soup into the chilled bowls and garnish with freshly chopped chives, the small cut-up tomatoes, and a drizzle of extra virgin olive oil.

SUGGESTED WINE PAIRING
BC: La Frenz Semillon, Naramata
International: Chateau Tours de Mirambeau Entre-Deux-Mers, Bordeaux, France

NARAMATA GARDEN GAZPACHO

Serves 6

2 cups (500 mL) chopped field or
  beefsteak tomatoes
½ cup (125 mL) roughly chopped
  English cucumber
½ cup (125 mL) roughly chopped green
  bell pepper
1 small clove garlic, finely chopped
½ cup (125 mL) roughly chopped red
  onion
1 cup (250 mL) tomato juice
1 tsp (5 mL) salt

2 Tbsp (30 mL) sherry vinegar
½ tsp (2 mL) freshly ground pepper
1 Tbsp (15 mL) fresh jalapeño chili,
  finely chopped
1 cup (250 mL) cold water
½ cup (125 mL) freshly chopped parsley
½ cup (125 mL) freshly chopped cilantro
juice and zest of 1 lemon
2 Tbsp (30 mL) extra virgin olive oil,
  plus more for garnish
croutons for garnish

Gazpacho is a wonderful way to cool yourself down in the summertime and you will instantaneously feel like you are dining in Andalusia, Spain. Gazpacho should not be a purée of summer vegetables; rather, it should have crunch. I add back some of the vegetables into the purée for textural interest. The more olive oil–drenched croutons the better.

Mix the tomatoes, cucumber, bell pepper, garlic, and onion with the tomato juice in a bowl. In two batches, put the ingredients into a food processor and pulse until they are finely chopped, but not puréed. The soup should have some texture. Add the salt, vinegar, pepper, chili, water, herbs, lemon zest and juice, and olive oil. Stir well and set aside in the refrigerator for 1 hour or overnight until chilled.

Make croutons by drizzling a baking sheet with olive oil and salt. Add small pieces of stale bread and lightly coat. Bake for 10 minutes at 350°F (180°C).

To serve, divide the soup among 6 chilled bowls and sprinkle with croutons. Garnish with a drizzle of good-quality extra virgin olive oil.

SUGGESTED WINE PAIRING
BC: Le Vieux Pin Pinot Noir Rosé, Oliver
International: Segura Viudas "Lavit" Rosado Cava, Penedes, Spain

HOT SOUPS

SPRING ASPARAGUS AND SORREL SOUP

Serves 6

1 onion, diced
1 carrot, diced
3 celery ribs
1 Tbsp (15 mL) unsalted butter
1 bay leaf
salt
freshly ground pepper
8 cups (2 L) chicken stock (or vegetable
   stock for a vegetarian soup)

1 lb (500 g) fresh asparagus
1 bunch of fresh sorrel leaves
2 Tbsp (30 mL) rice wine vinegar
zest of 1 lemon
finely chopped chives, for garnish and
   torn up chive blossoms if you have
   them

This soup can be served for a treat with a bit of fresh Dungeness crab meat or a piece of seared salmon in the center of the bowl.

Prepare a mirepoix (see page 133) by sautéing the onion, carrot, and celery in the butter with the bay leaf until soft. Season to taste with salt and pepper. Meanwhile, put the stock in a large pot and bring to a boil.

While the stock is boiling, prepare to blanch the asparagus. Timing is everything with this soup in order to achieve its bright green color, so set up a blender and a bowl of ice water to cool the asparagus after it is blanched. Plunge half of the asparagus into the boiling stock and cook until it turns bright green, about 2–3 minutes. Remove the asparagus from the boiling stock with a slotted spoon and plunge into the ice-water bath to cool.

Add the mirepoix and asparagus to the stock and bring back to a boil. Reduce the heat and simmer, uncovered, for 2 minutes. In batches, blend the sorrel with the stock mixture until very smooth. Pour through a fine mesh sieve straight into a bowl set over ice water to cool quickly, stop the cooking process, and maintain the bright green color.

Add the rice wine vinegar and lemon zest and season to taste with salt and pepper. The soup should have a fresh, bright flavor.

To serve, gently heat the soup and ladle into warm soup bowls. Garnish with finely chopped chives and chive blossom.

SUGGESTED WINE PAIRING
BC: Stag's Hollow Sauvignon Blanc, Okanagan Falls
International: Matua Sauvignon Blanc, Hawkes Bay, New Zealand

ZUPPA DI ZUCCHINE

Serves 6

2 lb (1 kg) zucchini (about 4 medium)
2 Tbsp (30 mL) olive oil
3 cloves garlic, peeled and thinly sliced
sea salt
freshly ground pepper
¼ tsp (1 mL) chili flakes or a small
    peperoncino
2 cups (500 mL) light chicken stock,
    vegetable stock, or water, hot

¼ cup (60 mL) whipping (35%) cream
½ cup (125 mL) grated Parmigiano
    Reggiano cheese
8 leaves fresh basil, finely chopped or
    chiffonade (see page 250)
1 large handful flat-leafed parsley, finely
    chopped
juice and zest of 1 lemon

This is one of my favorite recipes from the *River Café Cook Book*. It's a perfect soup to make when you have far too many zucchini in your garden! Its creaminess can be attributed to cooking the zucchini down until they are very silky.

Cut the unpeeled zucchini in half. Lay the zucchini on its flat side and then cut into ½-inch (1-cm) half-moon slices. Heat the olive oil in a large heavy saucepan and slowly cook the zucchini. Cook for 5 minutes on low, and then add the garlic slices. Cook until the zucchini has "melted" and turned golden and very soft, about 20 minutes. Add a pinch of salt, some freshly ground pepper, and the chili flakes.

Pour the hot stock over the soft zucchini and simmer, uncovered, for 15 minutes. Transfer the soup in batches to a blender and purée until smooth. Taste each batch for seasoning, and add more salt, if necessary. Put the blended soup into a clean pot and keep warm until serving time. Right before serving add the cream, grated Parmigiano Reggiano, and fresh herbs and finish off with the lemon juice and zest.

Serve with crusty bread.

CHEF'S TIP

If you have zucchini plants, pick one of the blossoms and chiffonade (see page 250) that too, for a garnish.

SUGGESTED WINE PAIRING
BC: Golden Mile Chardonnay, Oliver
International: Tamellini Soave, Veneto, Italy

SOUP AU PISTOU

Serves 6

FOR THE PISTOU

2 garlic cloves

1 tsp (5 mL) salt

1 cup (250 mL) basil leaves, packed

½ cup (125 mL) grated Parmigiano
   Reggiano

½ cup (125 mL) extra virgin olive oil

freshly ground pepper

FOR THE SOUP

½ lb (250 g) tender young fava beans,
   shelled

1 onion, peeled and stuck with 2 cloves

8 cups (2 L) flavorful chicken stock

1 leek, white scrubbed free of sand and
   thinly sliced

6 young carrots, peeled and cut into very
   thin rounds

¼ lb (125 g) baby turnips, peeled,
   and cut in half, if small, or ¼-inch
   (0.5-cm) dice

½ lb (250 g) baby nugget potatoes, skins
   on and cut into half-moons

1 lb (500 g) small zucchini, topped,
   tailed, and cut into ¼-inch (0.5-cm)
   dice

½ lb (250 g) French green beans, topped,
   tailed, and cut into ¼-inch (0.5-cm)
   lengths if larger

½ lb (250 g) English peas, shelled

4 tomatoes, concassé (see page 141)

salt

freshly ground pepper

This soup is best made in the height of summer when the vegetables are at their peak of flavor. It will fill your house with the scents of Provence. "Pistou" is Provençal dialect for a pesto or garlicky herb paste, whisked in to this soup at the last moment. This soup's origins are truly Mediterranean, as it is said to have originally come from Genoa, Italy (the home of pesto), up the Ligurian coast.

To prepare the pistou, peel the garlic, put it in a blender or mortar and pestle with a pinch of salt, and crush to a purée. Add the basil and crush until smooth. Add half of the Parmigiano Reggiano and then pour in the oil in a steady trickle with the blender still running, or while stirring continuously with a mortar. Season generously with salt and pepper. Reserve the pistou at room temperature until needed.

Prepare an ice-water bath. Bring a pot of salted water to the boil and blanch the shelled fava beans for 2 minutes. Remove the beans with a slotted spoon and plunge into the ice-water bath. Once cooled, peel the tough jackets from the fava beans.

Prepare the broth for the soup by putting the

clove-stuck onion in a pot with the chicken stock. Bring to a boil and cook for half hour. Add the leek, carrots, and turnip and simmer gently, uncovered, for 15 minutes. Add the potatoes, and as soon as the liquid returns to a boil, add the zucchini. Add salt and pepper to taste and cook for about 15 minutes, until the potatoes are tender. Discard the onion and add the fava beans, green beans, peas, and tomatoes. Cook just until the peas and fava beans have turned bright green, float on the soup, and are warmed through.

Whisk in most of the pistou right before serving, but make sure to reserve some pistou for each individual bowl as well. This will make the soup extra rich.

Serve the soup in hot soup bowls, making sure the different vegetables are evenly distributed. Drizzle the remaining pistou into each bowl. Serve the remaining Parmigiano Reggiano separately.

SUGGESTED WINE PAIRING

BC: Joie Pinot Noir Rosé, Naramata
International: Domaine Ott Rosé Bandol,
Provence, France

CONCASSÉ ('con-cass-eh') means to roughly chop and is generally used in reference to tomatoes. To make a tomato concassé, remove the core from the tomato, score an X in the skin, and place into boiling water for 10 seconds; remove from the water and place under cold running water or plunge into an ice-water bath. The peel should now just slip off. If it doesn't, pop the tomato back in the boiling water for a few more seconds. Cut in quarters and remove the seeds and rinse out. These quarters are now referred to as "filets." Neatly chop the tomato quarters into a small ½-inch (1-cm) dice.

CHICKPEA SOUP WITH FONTINA FINISHED WITH LOVAGE PESTO

Serves 6

FOR THE LOVAGE PESTO

1 large bunch flat-leaf parsley

1 large bunch lovage leaves (or substitute more parsley if you don't have lovage)

1 small bunch chervil (or basil or tarragon – something with an anise flavor)

½ cup (125 mL) extra virgin olive oil

juice and zest of 1 lemon

½ tsp (2 mL) salt

freshly ground pepper

FOR THE SOUP

1 medium onion, chopped into ½-inch (1-cm) dice

2 carrots, chopped into ½-inch (1-cm) dice

2 ribs celery (or lovage stalks), chopped into ½-inch (1-cm) dice

¼ cup plus 1 Tbsp (75 mL) extra virgin olive oil

3 cloves garlic, finely chopped

pinch of chili flakes

1 bay leaf

2 19-oz (540-mL) cans chickpeas, well rinsed and husked (you can also use dried chickpeas, if they have been soaked and then cooked the day before)

8 cups (2 L) water, vegetable stock, or chicken stock, warm

salt

freshly ground pepper

zest of 1 orange

7 oz (200 g) fontina cheese, cut into 6 1-inch (2.5-cm) cubes (1 for each bowl)

I made this soup after an inspiring trip to Zambri's restaurant in Victoria, BC. I love Peter Zambri's regional Italian cooking, which is solely driven by fresh product. Michael and I have been known to take a ferry just to eat at Zambri's. Peter made this soup to begin a long lunch one day. I enjoyed it so much I went home to see if I could recreate it. I added the lovage pesto one spring morning when there was not much up in the garden except mint, parsley, and our giant lovage plant!

Prepare the pesto by blending all the ingredients together. Store in a tightly sealed jar in the refrigerator until needed, or for up to 2 weeks.

Prepare a soffrito (see page 133) by sautéing the chopped onions, carrots, and celery in 1 Tbsp (15 mL) of the olive oil until soft and slightly caramelized. Add the chopped garlic, chili, and bay leaf.

While the soffrito is sautéing, rinse the chickpeas, pat them dry, and begin to husk them by rubbing them between your hands. Their shells will lift off and you can then pick them off. Getting every single shell is not necessary, but by removing most of them the chickpeas will cause less flatulence (as the shells are pure cellulose and indigestible). Removing the shells will also give the soup a silkier texture when puréed. Add the shelled chickpeas to the seasoned soffrito and sauté for about another 3 minutes to give the chickpeas a little color.

Add the warm liquid to the pot to cover and float the chickpeas. Simmer the soup, uncovered, for about 20 minutes to blend the flavors. Season to taste with salt and pepper.

Remove the bay leaf and then place the soup in a blender. Blend until you have a thick, silky liquid, not a stodgy stew. Adjust the consistency of the soup with more of the remaining warm liquid if necessary. When the correct consistency has been achieved, blend in the remaining extra virgin olive oil, adding it in a slow steady stream as the blender is running. This will give the soup an even silkier texture. Once blended, put the soup back into the pot to keep warm.

To serve, place a cube of fontina cheese on the bottom of 6 warmed bowls. Pour the hot soup over the cheese to melt it, and drizzle each bowl with some lovage pesto and a fine grating of orange zest. The fontina will be a gooey treasure at the bottom of the bowl.

SUGGESTED WINE PAIRING
BC: Kettle Valley Semillon/Sauvignon Blanc, Naramata
International: Regaleali "Leoni," Sicily, Italy

BC BOUILLABAISSE FINISHED WITH PISTOU

Serves 8

FOR THE BROTH

5 lb (2.2 kg) halibut or other firm
    white-fleshed fish, fillet or whole
2 lb (1 kg) mussels
2 Tbsp (30 mL) olive oil
⅔ cup (150 mL) dry white wine
3 carrots, peeled and finely diced
2 stalks celery, finely diced
2 yellow onions, peeled and finely diced
3 sprigs parsley
3 sprigs fresh thyme
2 bay leaves
8 cups (2 L) cold water
½ tsp (2 mL) sea salt
¼ cup (60 mL) Pernod

FOR THE SOUP

3 Tbsp (45 mL) olive oil
4 onions, thinly sliced into half-moons
3 bay leaves
1 sprig thyme
pinch of saffron (about 15 threads)
½ tsp (2 mL) salt
freshly ground pepper

6 cups (1.5 L) water
1 tsp (5 mL) sea salt
½ lb (250 g) small red-skinned potatoes,
    peeled and cut into thin half-moons

PISTOU FOR FINISHING

3 cloves garlic
½ cup (125 mL) finely chopped flat-leaf
    parsley
½ cup (125 mL) fresh basil
1 cup (250 mL) extra virgin olive oil
1 tsp (5 mL) sea salt
juice and zest of 2 lemons

FISH FOR THE SOUP

2 lb (1 kg) small halibut cheeks
16 spot prawns, peeled, de-veined, and
    tails left on, or langoustines
4 squid, cleaned and separated into
    tentacles and bodies chopped into fine
    rings
1 lb (500 g) clams
1 lb (500 g) swimming scallops or honey
    mussels

We made this bouillabaisse countless times during our Provençal one-day cooking classes and our Joie Pratique five-day program. I have adapted the Fish Soup with Onions Stewed in Saffron recipe from the *Chez Panisse Cooking* book to incorporate BC fish and seafood and make more of a traditional bouillabaisse that demands to be enjoyed with a cold glass of rosé. Classic bouillabaisse is made with fish like sea bass or dorade and the oceans of crustaceans found in the Mediterranean. I have also incorporated the halibut cheeks, spot prawns, swimming scallops, and honey mussels that BC is famous for.

If you are using whole fish to prepare the broth remove the gills from the fish, and then cut the carcass into three or four large pieces. Rinse the head and carcass under cold water. Make cuts on either side of the pin bones running vertically down the fillet and remove the strip of fish containing the bones. Reserve these scraps for the broth. Cut the fillets into 1-inch (2.5-cm) pieces and set aside on a plate. Scrub the mussels thoroughly. Warm the olive oil in an 8-quart (8-L) stainless-steel pot. Add the pieces of fish carcass and cook, turning them over to expose all surfaces to the heat, until their color changes to white and the fragrance of the fish is released. Add the wine and scrape up any bits of fish stuck to the bottom of the pot. Add the mussels, vegetables, herbs, bay leaves, water, and salt. Make certain all the fish is submerged under the water. Bring to a simmer, skim off any white froth that rises to the surface, and cook slowly, uncovered, for half an hour. Meanwhile, prepare the onions and potatoes for the soup.

Warm the 3 Tbsp (45 mL) olive oil in a heavy-bottomed casserole (at least 5 quarts/5 L). Add the onions, bay leaves, thyme, saffron, salt, and pepper. Combine well and cook over low heat, until the onion just begins to caramelize and is very soft, about 25 minutes. Stir the onions often to prevent sticking. Reserve until needed.

In a 5-quart (5-L) pot, bring the water to a boil, add the salt and potato slices, and cook for 5–6 minutes or until the potato slices are just tender. Drain.

Prepare the pistou by pounding the garlic to a paste in a mortar. Add the parsley and basil and pound them to a similar consistency. Stir in the olive oil, salt, and lemon juice and zest.

To serve the soup, strain the broth over the onion mixture and simmer for 5 minutes. Discard the fish bones and mussel shells from the broth pot. Add the potatoes and onion mixture to the broth and simmer for 3 minutes. Add the halibut cheeks, prawns, and shellfish and cook at a bare simmer, covered, for 2–3 minutes, until the shells of mussels, swimming scallops, and clams open up. Discard any that do not open. Stir in half of the pistou. With a slotted spoon, transfer all the fish and shellfish to a bowl and divide into warm soup bowls. Spoon some potatoes, onions, and broth overtop. Drizzle each bowl with a bit of the remaining pistou and serve immediately.

Traditionally bouillabaisse is served with a rouille-soaked crouton. Rouille is an aioli that is flavored with roasted red pepper and thickened with bread. This soup is rich on its own, but try drizzling rouille into it as well!

PURÉE PALESTINE

Serves 6

FOR THE PURÉE

1.5 lb (750 g) Jerusalem artichokes,
  peeled, sliced, and cut into 2-inch
  (5-cm) pieces
1 head of cauliflower, cut into 2-inch
  (5-cm) pieces
2 Tbsp (30 mL) vegetable oil
salt
freshly ground pepper
¾ cup (175 mL) unsalted butter
½ cup (125 mL) sliced onion

½ cup (125 mL) celery root, cut into
  ½-inch (1-cm) dice
6 cups (1.5 L) light chicken stock, warm

FOR THE PARSNIP CHIPS

4 cups (1 L) vegetable oil
1 lb (500 g) parsnips, trimmed and
  peeled

FOR THE GARNISH

chopped chives

This is a recipe I adapted from my time at the Stratford Chefs School. I prefer to roast the Jerusalem artichokes with some cauliflower in the oven first to give the soup an even greater depth of flavor. This silky soup is also delicious if you roast a head of garlic with the artichokes and cauliflower.

Preheat oven to 375°F (190°C).

Toss the J-chokes and the cauliflower in the vegetable oil and season with salt and pepper. Put them in a roasting pan and roast for about 40 minutes until the vegetables are slightly golden and the artichokes are fork-tender.

While the artichokes and cauliflower are roasting, melt ¼ cup (60 mL) of the butter in a large pot. Add the onion and celery root and cook, covered, on low heat until soft but not brown. Add the roasted artichokes and cauliflower, cover the vegetables with about 4 cups (1 L) of the warm chicken stock and season to taste with salt and pepper. Bring to a simmer. Gently simmer for about half an hour.

When the artichokes are tender, pour the contents of the pot into a blender. Blend until very smooth and strain through a fine mesh sieve into a clean saucepan. If necessary, adjust the consistency of the soup with the remaining stock.

To prepare the parsnip chips, heat the oil in a wok to 325°F (160°C). Using a mandoline, slice the parsnips lengthwise into fine strips. When the oil has come to temperature, plunge a handful of the parsnip strips into the oil. Stir to separate the strips and cook until golden. Remove from the oil and drain on paper towels. Season and set aside until needed.

Gently heat through the soup just before serving. Check the seasoning. Whisk in the remaining butter, bit by bit, to glaze and enrich the soup.

Ladle the purée into warm shallow soup bowls. Top with a few parsnip chips and snipped chives and serve.

SUGGESTED WINE PAIRING

BC: Blue Mountain Chardonnay, Okanagan Falls
International: Champagne de Venoge Cordon Bleu, Champagne, France

THE JERUSALEM ARTICHOKE, also called a sunchoke or topinambur, is a flowering plant native to North America grown throughout the world for its tuber, which is used as a root vegetable. Despite its name, the Jerusalem artichoke has no relation to Jerusalem, and little to do with artichokes. The name Jerusalem is due to folk etymology; when the Jerusalem artichoke was first discovered it was called Girasole, the Italian word for sunflower. The Jerusalem artichoke is a type of sunflower. Over time the name Girasole transformed into Jerusalem. When cooked the Jerusalem artichoke tastes like a cross between a radish and an artichoke, but with a pronounced silky texture.

ROASTED TOMATO SOUP

Serves 6

FOR THE SOUP

12 large (about 4 lb/2 kg) tomatoes, washed, stemmed, and quartered

½ cup (125 mL) extra virgin olive oil

¼ cup (60 mL) good-quality balsamic vinegar

12 large garlic cloves, peeled

1 Tbsp (15 mL) fresh thyme leaves or summer savory

1 tsp (5 mL) fine sea salt

½ tsp (2 mL) freshly ground pepper

1 cup (250 mL) yellow onions, finely chopped

1 bay leaf

pinch of salt

2 cups (500 mL) lightly packed fresh basil leaves, plus few leaves torn for garnish

2 cups (500 mL) rich chicken stock (or vegetable stock for a vegetarian soup), warm

juice and zest of 1 lemon

FOR THE GARNISH

chopped chives

cubes of melting cheese, like fontina or friulano

I start making roasted tomato soup in the second week of September when there is still an overabundance of tomatoes in our gardens and I just can't eat yet another luscious tomato and basil salad. Roasted tomato soup has a great depth of flavor that heralds the cool nights of early fall. I have also made this soup with smoked tomatoes that we put in our stone smoker for about an hour. It was delicious.

Preheat the oven to 425°F (220°C). Line a baking sheet with parchment paper.

In a large bowl, mix the tomatoes, ¼ cup (60 mL) of the oil, the vinegar, garlic, thyme, salt, and pepper. Spread the tomatoes out on the prepared baking sheet. Roast the tomatoes in the oven until very dark in spots, about 35–40 minutes. Remove and allow to cool slightly.

In a large pot over medium heat, combine the remaining oil, the onions, bay leaf, and salt. Cook until the onions are very soft, 8–10 minutes, stirring occasionally. Add the 2 cups (500 mL) of basil leaves and sauté with the onions for about 1 minute.

Add the roasted tomatoes and stock to the saucepan. Bring the mixture to a simmer and cook for 10 minutes, uncovered. Season to taste with salt and pepper and then transfer the tomato mixture to a blender. Start the motor at a slow speed and increase speed gradually until the mixture is very smooth. Strain the blended soup through a fine mesh sieve back into the pot. Adjust the soup for seasoning and add the lemon juice and zest.

When ready to serve, bring the soup to a simmer over medium heat. Garnish with chopped chives.

CHEF'S TIP

As a variation, garnish with cubes of a melting cheese, like fontina or friulano, as for the Chickpea Soup with Fontina (see page 142).

SUGGESTED WINE PAIRING

BC: Wild Goose Rosé, Okanagan Falls

International: Château Silex "Elogé" Rosé, A.O.C. Costières de Nîmes

ROASTED SQUASH AND PEAR SOUP

Serves 10

FOR THE SOUP

2 large butternut squash or Kuri squash, peeled, de-seeded, and cubed in 2-inch (5-cm) pieces

4 Bartlett or Anjou pears (firm, but not too ripe), cut into 2-inch (5-cm) pieces

1 Tbsp (15 mL) vegetable oil

salt

freshly ground pepper

1 onion, diced

1 celery stalk, diced

1 carrot, peeled and diced

1 bay leaf

1 Tbsp (15 mL) unsalted butter

4 cups (1 L) chicken stock

4 cups (1 L) unfiltered apple juice or fresh cider

1 tsp (5 mL) salt

1 tsp (5 mL) freshly ground pepper

2 Tbsp (30 mL) cold unsalted butter, cut into small pieces

1 Tbsp (15 mL) rice wine vinegar

juice and zest of 1 lemon

FOR THE GARNISH

stale white bread, cut into ½-inch (1-cm) cubes

2 Tbsp (30 mL) salted butter, melted

chopped parsley

This soup is a favorite in early fall in mid-September, when the weather begins to change and you crave comforting warm soup. I have added ripe pears (which are always in abundance in our orchard at the same time that the squash begin to ripen in the garden), as well as apple juice for a bit of sweetness.

Preheat oven to 375°F (190°C).

Begin the soup by roasting the squash and pears. Toss the squash and pear pieces in the vegetable oil and season with salt and pepper. Place in a large enough roasting pan to accommodate all the pieces without overcrowding (to prevent steaming) and roast for 45 minutes, until all the pear and squash pieces are slightly caramelized. Turn the pieces only once while roasting.

While the squash is roasting, prepare a mirepoix (see page 133). Sweat the onion, celery, carrot, and bay leaf in the butter until soft. Add the roasted squash and pear pieces. Pour the chicken stock and apple juice overtop the vegetables. Bring to a boil and reduce heat to a simmer. Season to taste with salt and pepper. Simmer the soup, uncovered, for half an hour to amalgamate the flavors.

While the soup is simmering, prepare the garnish. Sauté the bread cubes in the melted butter until light golden brown. Finish toasting them in the oven at 200°F (95°C) for 10 minutes to ensure that they are dried out, but will not brown further.

Transfer the soup to a blender and purée until smooth. Strain the blended soup through a fine mesh sieve into a clean pot to give the soup a very silky texture. Add more hot stock or water if the purée is too thick — it should be pourable, not stodgy.

Right before serving, put the hot soup back into the blender. While the blender is running, add the cold butter chunks, one at a time. This will give the soup a wonderful sheen and silky consistency. Check the seasoning of the soup and adjust to taste with salt and pepper. Add the rice wine vinegar and lemon juice and zest.

Serve the soup in warm soup bowls. Garnish with a few croutons and some chopped parsley.

SUGGESTED WINE PAIRING

BC: Elephant Island Dry Pear Wine, Naramata

International: Montresor Pinot Grigio, Veneto, Italy

WILD RICE AND MUSHROOM SOUP

Serves 6

7 oz (200 g) oyster mushrooms or
   chanterelles, cleaned, stems discarded
3½ oz (100 g) cremini mushrooms
   (brown button), cleaned
2 tsp (30 mL) dried porcini mushrooms,
   soaked in ½ cup (125 mL) water to
   rehydrate (reserve the soaking water)
12 dried morels, soaked in ½ cup
   (125 mL) water to rehydrate (reserve
   the soaking water)
1 Tbsp (15 mL) vegetable oil
2 Tbsp (30 mL) unsalted butter
1 small shallot, finely chopped

1 small clove garlic, finely chopped
salt
freshly ground pepper
cayenne to season
½ cup (125 mL) brandy
3 cups (750 mL) light chicken stock
1½ cups (375 mL) whipping (35%)
   cream
1 cup (250 mL) cooked wild rice
juice of 1 lemon

FOR GARNISH
chervil leaves or finely chopped chives

DEGLAZING is using a small amount of liquid (about enough to cover the bottom of the pan by no more than ¼ inch/0.5 cm), usually stock, wine, broth, or water, to loosen bits of caramelized, flavorful food particles from the bottom of a pan after cooking. A spatula, whisk, or wooden spoon is used to scrape up the little attached bits. The heat should be on high to reduce the amount of liquid and further intensify the flavors. I sometimes also deglaze with vinegar if what I'm cooking is particularly fatty (like duck) and will benefit from the counterpoint of some acid in the final sauce.

I have a soft spot for wild mushroom soup, and I have fond memories of a delicious version my friend Ian Philip made for me at a dinner party years ago. I was reminded of his soup recently at the Vancouver Fairmont Airport Hotel on a layover on my way to Toronto. That quick soup and salad lunch was the best pre-flight lunch I have ever had. I returned from my trip inspired to make a soup that would live up to the ones I had previously enjoyed. I love the textures of the chewy wild rice and mushrooms together with brandy and cream.

Finely slice the oyster and cremini mushrooms. Leave the porcini mushrooms as they are and slice half of the morels into fine rounds and slice the other half lengthwise.

Heat the oil in a cast-iron frying pan over medium-high heat. Add the mushrooms and sweat for about 5 minutes. When the mushrooms begin to release their juices, add the butter, shallot, and garlic. Season to taste with salt, pepper, and cayenne, and continue to cook for 5 minutes. Deglaze the pan, with the mushrooms still in it, with the brandy. Add the chicken stock, reserved mushroom soaking liquid, and bring to a boil. Cook for 10 minutes, and then add the cream and return to a boil. Using a slotted spoon, remove half of the mushroom pieces and reserve in a bowl. Pour the soup into a blender and blend until smooth. Return the blended soup to the pot and add the cooked wild rice and the reserved mushroom pieces for texture. Bring the soup back up to a slow simmer on medium heat, check the seasoning, and add the lemon juice and a tiny pinch of cayenne to taste. Keep warm until ready to serve.

To serve, ladle the hot soup into warm soup bowls. Scatter some of the chervil leaves or chopped chives over the soup and serve.

SUGGESTED WINE PAIRING
BC: Kettle Valley "Adra Station" Reserve Chardonnay, Naramata
International: Faiveley Mercurey Blanc, Burgundy, France

STOCKS

A good soup is only as good as its stock, and no store-bought version can compare with the real thing made in your own kitchen.

COURT BOUILLON

Makes 12 cups (3 L)

2 carrots, peeled and chopped
4 stalks celery, chopped
1 leek, both white and green parts, washed and chopped
1 onion, peeled and chopped
1 head garlic, halved and skin on
1 bouquet garni, containing parsley, thyme, and bay leaf
4 black peppercorns
1 lemon, halved
1 tomato, quartered
1 bottle (750 mL) white wine
8 cups (2 L) water
½ tsp (2 mL) salt

Combine the carrots, celery, leek, onion, garlic, bouquet garni, peppercorns, lemon, tomato, wine, water, and salt in a large pot. Bring to a boil over medium heat. Reduce heat to low and simmer, uncovered, for 30 minutes. Strain immediately, pressing solids gently to release as much liquid as possible.

VEGETABLE STOCK

Makes 4 cups (1 L)

1 medium onion, thinly sliced
1 leek, green part only, thinly sliced
1 tomato, blanched, seeded, and chopped
1 fennel bulb, thinly sliced
2 stalks celery, roughly chopped
2 carrots, roughly chopped
3 cloves garlic
6 mushrooms (or saved pieces and stalks)
4 black peppercorns
2 sprigs thyme
5 cups (1¼ L) cold filtered water

Combine the onion, leek, tomato, fennel, celery, carrots, garlic, mushrooms, peppercorns, thyme, and water in a large pot. Bring to a boil over medium heat. Reduce heat to low and simmer, uncovered, for 45 minutes. Strain immediately through a fine mesh sieve, pressing the solids gently to release as much liquid as possible.

Vegetable stock can be used immediately, refrigerated for up to 1 week, or frozen for up to 2 months in an airtight container.

CHICKEN STOCK

Makes about 12 cups (3 L)

1 Tbsp (15 mL) vegetable oil
2 lb (1 kg) chicken backs, necks, and
  a few wings
2 sprigs thyme
2 bay leaves
1 medium carrot, coarsely chopped
1 medium onion, coarsely chopped
1 leek, both white and green parts, finely
  sliced
2 cloves garlic, halved
1 stalk celery, coarsely chopped
2 peppercorns

Preheat oven to 450°F (230°C).

In a large roasting pan, heat the oil over high heat, add the chicken pieces, and bake in the oven for 45 minutes. The chicken bones will stick to the pan and give the stock its dark color. You can also roast the chicken bones in a cast-iron pan on the stovetop until the bones are a deep golden color. If you want a light chicken broth, omit the roasting process.

Remove the roasted bones from the pan and put them in a large stockpot. Add the thyme and bay leaves, cover with cold water, and bring to a boil. Lower the temperature as soon as the liquid reaches a boil, and as the stock begins to simmer, skim the froth and fat off the top of the pot.

After the first skimming, add the carrot, onion, leek, garlic, celery, and peppercorns and let the stock simmer, uncovered, very gently for 6–8 hours or overnight. This gentle simmering will yield a flavorful, clear broth. Skim the stock throughout its cooking process.

Strain the stock carefully through a fine mesh sieve. It can be used as is, but for a more intense flavor, reduce by half over low heat.

The stock can be refrigerated for up to 1 week or frozen in an airtight container for up to 2 months.

LAMB, BEEF, AND VEAL STOCKS

Makes 8–12 cups (2–3 L)

2 lb (1 kg) lamb, beef, or veal bones
3 medium carrots, cut in chunks
2 medium onions, cut in chunks
4 stalks celery, cut in chunks
1 head garlic, cut in half with skin on
2 Tbsp (30 mL) tomato paste
5 sprigs thyme
1 bay leaf
5 peppercorns

Preheat oven to 450°F (230°C). Lightly grease 2 roasting pans with vegetable oil.

Roast the bones in a single layer in one pan for about 40 minutes, turning occasionally, until dark brown. In the other pan, roast the carrots, onions, celery, garlic, and tomato paste until caramelized.

Remove the fat from the bone pan. Deglaze both pans with a little water or wine. Transfer the contents of both pans to a stockpot along with the thyme, bay leaf, and peppercorns. Add enough cold water to cover. Over medium heat, simmer, uncovered, for 4–6 hours, skimming off impurities periodically. The stock ingredients should always be at least three-quarters covered by water. If the level falls below that level, add more cold water.

Remove from the heat and allow to cool slightly. Strain through a fine mesh sieve into a clean container, discarding all the solids. For a more concentrated flavor, you can reduce the stock by half at this point. Cool to room temperature and refrigerate until needed. Remove the congealed fats before using.

Lamb, beef, and veal stock will keep in the refrigerator for up to 1 week or can be frozen in an airtight container for up to 3 months.

FIRST COURSES &
COMPOSED SALADS

COMPOSED SALAD OF DU PUY LENTILS WITH ROASTED BEETS, WALNUTS, AND CHÈVRE WITH ORANGE-TARRAGON DRESSING

Serves 8

FOR THE LENTILS
1 shallot, finely diced
1 carrot, finely diced
1 celery rib, finely diced
2 Tbsp (30 mL) olive oil
1 cup (250 mL) du Puy lentils (small French lentils)
½ cup (125 mL) white or rosé wine
1 bay leaf
1 sprig thyme
1 clove garlic, peeled and left whole
4 cups (1 L) hot water (about)

FOR THE BEETS
2 lb (1 kg) beets
2 Tbsp (10 mL) vegetable oil
salt
freshly ground pepper

FOR THE ORANGE-TARRAGON DRESSING
1 small shallot, minced
¼ cup (60 mL) red wine vinegar
¼ cup (60 mL) extra virgin olive oil
1 Tbsp (15 mL) grainy mustard
1 Tbsp (15 mL) honey
1 tsp (5 mL) salt
1 tsp (5 mL) freshly ground black pepper
juice and zest of 1 lemon
juice and zest of 2 oranges
½ cup (125 mL) fresh tarragon leaves, pulled off their stems and finely chopped, plus more chopped leaves for garnish

fresh goat cheese or hard crottin, to crumble
1 cup (250 mL) walnuts, toasted and roughly chopped

I often serve this cold bistro-style salad in the summertime. The combination of earthy lentils, toasted walnuts, and beets are balanced by the tangy chèvre and orange zest in the dressing. This salad can be served as a composed salad on individual plates or family-style as a large salad.

To prepare the lentils, sauté the diced shallot, carrot, and celery in the olive oil in a large heavy-bottomed casserole. Add the lentils and lightly toast them until you can hear them start to crackle a little bit (about 2 minutes). This gives them a nutty flavor. Deglaze (see page 150) the pan with the wine. Add the bay leaf, thyme, and garlic to the pot.

Do not add salt to legumes when they are cooking as it will toughen their skins.

Add enough hot water to the pot to generously cover the lentils. Bring the water and lentils to a boil and then turn the heat down to a bare simmer. Cook the lentils gently and cover with the lid left slightly ajar, until they're cooked though and tender, but still firm. Add more water to the pot if necessary, but be sure not to cook the lentils into mush! They need to have some firmness when they're cooked as they'll be tossed with dressing to make a cold salad. When the lentils are cooked through and all the water has been absorbed, turn the lentils out onto a baking sheet to cool to room temperature.

Preheat oven to 400°F (200°C).

While the lentils are cooking, prepare the beets. If the beets are young and tender, just leave their skins on and cut them in half. If they're old, they should be peeled and cut into quarters. Toss the beets in the vegetable oil and salt and pepper and place on a baking sheet to roast. Roast the beets for about 1 hour until fork-tender (this may vary depending on how fresh the beets are), being sure that they do not burn toward the end of the cooking time. Lower the heat to 350°F (180°C) if the beets do start to burn. Remove from the oven and cool to room temperature. Reserve a few of the beets for garnish (the rest will be mixed in with the lentils).

To prepare the dressing, place the minced shallot in the red wine vinegar. Let sit for 10 minutes so that it absorbs the vinegar. Combine the oil, mustard, honey, salt, pepper, lemon juice and zest, orange juice and zest, and tarragon with a whisk in a small bowl. Combine the acidulated shallots with this mixture right before tossing the salad.

To serve the salad, toss the slightly cooled lentils and roasted beets with half of the dressing in a large bowl. Because the lentils will still be slightly warm, they will absorb the dressing, making them very flavorful. If you're serving the salad family-style, place the lentils in a serving bowl or long dish and top with the roasted beets. Crumble the fresh goat cheese on top of the beets and sprinkle with the toasted walnuts. Drizzle the remaining orange and tarragon dressing overtop the salad and garnish with chopped fresh tarragon. If you're serving the salad individually, place a large spoonful (about ¼ cup/60 mL) of dressed lentils in the center of a small plate and arrange the roasted beet slices off-center over the lentils. Crumble the chèvre and walnuts over the salad and drizzle with a little extra dressing and chopped tarragon.

SUGGESTED WINE PAIRING
BC: Joie Pinot Noir Rosé, Naramata
International: Domaine L'Hortus Rosé Pic St. Loup, Coteaux du Languedoc, France

GATHERED GREENS TOPPED WITH FRESH HONEYCOMB, BLUE CHEESE, AND TOASTED HAZELNUTS

Serves 4

FOR THE DRESSING

1 small shallot, minced
2 Tbsp (30 mL) red wine vinegar
¼ cup (60 mL) extra virgin olive oil
1 Tbsp (15 mL) grainy mustard
1 Tbsp (15 mL) honey
1 tsp (5 mL) salt
1 tsp (5 mL) freshly ground black pepper
juice and zest of 1 lemon

FOR THE GARNISH

⅔ lb (300 g) fresh honeycomb, cut into
    pieces about 3 × ⅛-inch (7.5 ×
    0.3-cm) thick, 1 piece per plate
⅔ lb (300 g) Roquefort-style blue
    cheese (cow or goat's milk), sliced
    into pieces about 3 × ⅛-inch (7.5 ×
    0.3-cm) thick, 2 pieces per plate
½ cup (125 mL) hazelnuts, toasted,
    skinned, and slightly crushed
honey for drizzling the finished plates
fleur de sel for garnish

FOR THE SALAD

A MIX OF ANY WASHED AND TORN
GATHERED GREENS SUCH AS:

½ head red leaf lettuce
1 small bunch baby spinach
½ bunch young arugula leaves
snipped beet tops
1 cup (250 mL) mâche or lamb's lettuce
1 bunch watercress
1 bunch curly endive or frisée

FINE HERBS, PICKED INTO SPRIGS AND
GENTLY WASHED, SUCH AS:

flat-leaf parsley
chervil
tarragon
basil
chives
edible flower petals (like pansies, chive
    blossoms, nasturtiums, or calendula)

I started serving this composed salad to showcase some of the best local products of our area: fresh honeycomb from the Similkameen Apiary in Cawston, blue cheese from Poplar Grove or Carmelis Goat Cheese Artisan in Kelowna, and fresh hazelnuts from the Naramata Bench. This salad is a wonderful balance of flavors, combining the bitter mixed greens with the sweet honeycomb, toasty nuts, and salty, creamy cheese. It was a hit every weekend as most people had never tried fresh honeycomb before.

For the dressing, place the minced shallot in the red wine vinegar and let sit for 10 minutes. Combine the olive oil, mustard, honey, salt, pepper, and lemon juice and zest in a small bowl and whisk together. Add the acidulated shallot right before tossing the salad.

Prepare the salad greens and herbs by gently washing them and drying them with a salad spinner; reserve between damp towels. Pick herbs into sprigs, and reserve in water until ready to serve.

Place the honeycomb pieces onto a piece of waxed paper. Place the blue cheese pieces onto a separate piece of waxed paper. Keep both the honeycomb and cheese in a cool place until needed.

Gently toss together the herbs and greens with your hands in a large stainless-steel bowl. Add the dressing, and toss gently. Add the dressing to the greens right before serving or the salad will wilt from the vinegar!

Place the honeycomb on the bottom of a rimmed bowl. Place 2 pieces of blue cheese beside the honeycomb. Place a handful of dressed greens gently on top and sprinkle with the toasted hazelnuts as garnish. Finish the salad with a spoonful of extra dressing and a thin drizzle of honey (the honey will sit on the salad leaves like spun sugar), as well as a little fleur de sel for a textural garnish. Serve immediately.

SUGGESTED WINE PAIRING
BC: La Frenz "Alexandria," Naramata
International: Ernst Loosen "Dr L" Riesling, Mosel, Germany

SALT is edible in basically 2 types: table salt and sea salt. They are chemically identical, containing mainly sodium chloride. Table salt is mined from deposits left by dried-up or receded sea; sea salt is extracted from evaporated seawater. From these 2 types of salt several varieties are produced, differing somewhat in composition (presence of additional minerals), form (size and shape of the crystal), color, taste, and intended use.

>> Table salt is often mixed with iodine (and called iodized salt) and often contains anti-caking agents. It has a very fine crystal and is intensely salty.

>> Pickling salt is a fine-grained salt used for pickling and canning. Like kosher salt, it contains no additives, such as anti-caking agents, which would cloud the brine.

>> Sel gris or gray sea salt is unprocessed, retaining various minerals. Produced near the town of Guérande in Brittany, France, it is said to smell of the sea. It's generally used to season already cooked dishes to take advantage of its delicate flavor.

>> Fleur de sel is a very expensive kind of sel gris, and is not actually gray but creamy-white in color. It's harvested from the thin white film that forms on the surface of the salt marshes in Brittany and is therefore quite costly! I like to use it to finish dishes to add a nice textural crunch.

>> Hawaiian alaea salt takes its name and reddish color from the red clay (alaea) found along the shores in Hawaii. It's also generally used for seasoning already cooked dishes.

>> Rock salt is grayish in color. It's an unrefined salt, containing many minerals and impurities. Inedible, it's used in ice cream machines and for melting ice and snow on the roads. It should not be confused with coarse pickling salt.

>> Kosher salt is so named because it's used for koshering purposes, i.e., drawing blood from meat. It's a coarse salt that generally contains no additives. Because of the large size of the crystals, about twice as much kosher salt is required to achieve the same taste intensity as would be needed using regular table salt. Also, because the salt is flaked, it tends to dissolve quickly, making it a favorite cooking salt for chefs.

PAIN D'ÉPICE CROUTONS WITH GOAT CHEESE AND RADISHES

Serves 4

FOR THE PAIN D'ÉPICE

1 cup, plus 2 Tbsp (280 mL) sugar
¾ cup (175 mL) honey
2½ tsp (12 mL) baking soda
¼ tsp (1 mL) salt
1¼ cup (310 mL) boiling water
3 Tbsp (45 mL) rum
1 tsp (5 mL) powdered anise
2 tsp (10 mL) ground cinnamon
4 cups (1 L) all-purpose flour, sifted

FOR THE GOAT CHEESE

6 oz (175 mL) fresh goat cheese
1 Tbsp (15 mL) whole (3.5%) milk
salt
freshly ground pepper
1 tsp (5 mL) lemon zest
1 Tbsp (15 mL) finely minced chives
12 French breakfast radishes (long pink
    and white ones), washed and leaves
    left on

This recipe was given to me by John Taboada of Portland's Navarre Restaurant. This is a lovely spring dish to make as an appetizer or amuse buche. The root of the dish is to capture the spirit and historicism of the "kingly" Loire Valley in France, which is also the market garden of France, famous for root vegetables like Nantes carrots and long pink and white radishes. John describes the dish as a combination of crispy textures: the crisp croutons and crunchy radishes are complemented by the aromatic pain d'épice and the spicy character of the radishes. Since the pain d'épice is better a day or 2 old, make it ahead of time. It's also important to slice the loaf very thinly and toast it to get the full effect of this bread's fabulous aromatics. John describes the bread's history as "medieval."

Preheat the oven to 350°F (180°C). Grease and line a 9 × 5 × 3-inch (2-L) loaf pan with parchment paper.

To prepare the pain d'épice, combine the sugar, honey, baking soda, and salt in a bowl. Pour the boiling water overtop, and let the sugar dissolve. Stir in the rum, anise, and cinnamon and then fold in the flour. Pour the batter into the prepared pan and bake for one hour. When ready to serve, slice the bread very thinly and toast into croutons. Note that this loaf recipes yields more bread than necessary to make enough croutons for the dish. The loaf freezes well, so make as many croutons as desired and freeze the rest of the bread.

For the goat cheese, cream the goat cheese with the milk, salt and pepper to taste, and the lemon zest.

Fold in the chives and shape the cheese into a quenelle or oval.

To plate the dish, place 3 radishes per person on a small plate. Place 2 croutons next to the radishes and put a small quenelle of goat cheese on top of each crouton. This is a simple, fresh, aromatic appetizer.

SUGGESTED WINE PAIRING

BC: Stag's Hollow Sauvignon Blanc, Okanagan Falls
International: Chateau Gaudrelle Vouvray "Sec Tendre,"
Loire Valley, France

HARICOT VERT VINAIGRETTE
SERVED À L'ALSACIENNE

Serves 8 as a small starter or 4 as a meal

2 lb (1 kg) French green beans (or
    asparagus, in season)

FOR THE GARNISH

3 large eggs hard boiled (or 1 egg
    poached per serving)
6½ oz (200 g) smoked bacon, cut into
    fine strips or lardons
6 salt-packed anchovies, filleted and
    rinsed
2 ripe tomatoes cut into a concassé
    (see page 141)
3 Tbsp (45 mL) chopped parsley

FOR THE VINAIGRETTE

2 Tbsp (30 mL) finely chopped shallot
2 Tbsp (30 mL) red wine vinegar
¼ cup (60 mL) extra virgin olive oil
salt
freshly ground pepper

This is as classic a bistro dish as they come. It's a fabulous way to begin a summer meal when green beans are at their peak. If you want to make this salad into a full meal, you can poach a fresh egg and top the salad with it, instead of just crumbling a bit of hard-boiled egg on it.

Prepare a large bowl of ice water.

Prepare the beans or asparagus by snapping off the less-tender bits of the asparagus stalks or bean ends. Leave the tails on the ends of the beans. In a large pot of boiling, salted water, blanch the beans for 1 minute until they turn bright green and are slightly tender, but still crisp (al dente). Refresh the beans in the ice water to stop them from cooking and to shock in their vibrant green color. When cool, discard the water and pat the vegetables dry.

While the beans are cooling, prepare the eggs and lardons. Separate the yolks and whites of the boiled eggs, finely chop or grate them, and set aside until needed. Heat a cast-iron pan on medium heat and slowly render the bacon until crispy. Remove with a slotted spoon onto a paper towel and reserve. Check the saltiness of the anchovies and soak, if necessary, in several changes of cold water to remove excess salt. Drain and squeeze the anchovies so that they're quite dry and slice them into small strips, being careful to remove any large bones.

Prepare the vinaigrette by combining the shallot, vinegar, olive oil, and salt and pepper in a bowl and whisking until the oil is emulsified.

To serve the salad, toss the beans gently with the vinaigrette in a large bowl. Arrange the beans on individual plates or large platter in a single layer. To serve on individual plates, wrap the strips of anchovy around the bottom of the beans, top the bean bundles with a scattering of the chopped egg, crispy lardons, and tomato concassé, and drizzle some of the remaining vinaigrette over the beans. If serving with a poached egg, omit the chopped egg and top the beans with the egg at the very last second. Sprinkle with the chopped parsley and serve immediately.

SUGGESTED WINE PAIRING

BC: Pentâge Rosé, Penticton
International: Druet Bourgueil Rosé, Loire Valley, France

CHEF'S TIP

If neither asparagus or beans are in season try substituting fresh blanched and shelled fava beans for the green beans. Toss them with some curly endive.

SHAVED FENNEL SALAD

Serves 6–8

FOR THE SALAD
2 fennel bulbs
7 oz (200 g) hard, salty goat or sheep
    cheese like Manchego or locally,
    Carmelis Lior

FOR THE DRESSING
2 Tbsp (15 mL) lemon juice
2 Tbsp (15 mL) extra virgin olive oil
zest of 1 lemon
1 tsp (5 mL) salt
1 tsp (5 mL) freshly ground pepper

fennel fronds for garnish
lemon juice and zest for garnish

This salad is delicious on its own or as an accompaniment to any ceviche, fritters, or fried fish appetizer for a cold composed plate. The fresh juiciness of the fennel is a nice contrast to something fried. I love buying fennel from the farmer's market in the early spring when Zaparango Farm in Cawston sells perfect, beautiful baby fennel bulbs.

Prepare the salad by removing the ribs from the fennel bulbs with a vegetable peeler. Being very careful, use a mandoline (and the guard!) to slice the fennel bulb into extremely thin, feather-like pieces. Go slowly and take your time. If you don't have a mandoline, thinly slice the fennel bulb with a sharp knife. Plunge the fennel shavings into a bowl with ice and water and a bit of lemon juice or vinegar. The cold acidulated water will keep the fennel from turning brown and make it curl up, like peacock feathers.

While the fennel shavings are chilling, make the dressing by combining the lemon juice, olive oil, lemon zest, salt, and pepper in a bowl and whisking until the olive oil is emulsified.

To plate the salad, drain the water from the fennel and pat the shavings dry. If you're serving the salad family-style, lay the thin pieces of fennel on a large platter and shave the cheese into thin, long strips (thin enough to almost see through) overtop the fennel. Drizzle the dressing over the platter. If you're serving the salad as an accompaniment to a fried food, place a mound of the dressed salad in the middle of a small plate and top with your fried food. If serving ceviche, lay the ceviche on a small plate first and then top the ceviche with a small amount of the salad.

Finish off with an extra squeeze of lemon juice and the zest, and a few chopped fennel fronds.

SUGGESTED WINE PAIRING
BC: Herder Pinot Gris, Cawston
International: Somamariva Prosecco di Conegliano, Veneto, Italy

CHEF'S TIP
Ceviche is a wonderfully fresh way to serve delicate or tender seafood. That's because a ceviche "cooks" the fish without actually adding heat. Instead, a high-acid marinade "denatures" the protein and cooks the seafood quickly. To make a spot prawn or scallop ceviche, thinly slice 6 scallops into 4–6 pieces or butterfly 6 spot prawns. To make the marinade, combine 2 Tbsp (30 mL) fresh lime juice, 1 tsp (5 mL) lime zest, half a finely diced serrano or jalapeño pepper, 1 Tbsp (15 mL) mirin, 1 Tbsp (15 mL) rice wine vinegar, and 1 Tbsp (15 mL) finely chopped red onion. Toss the sliced shellfish in the marinade for about 1 minute and then let sit for 30 minutes. Drain before serving.

CHEF'S TIP
Try adding blood orange or grapefruit segments to this salad when winter citrus is in season.

KITCHEN MANDOLINES are hand-operated kitchen tools with adjustable blades often mounted in a frame with movable legs. They can slice food, especially firmer vegetables like potatoes, carrots, squash, and cucumbers, much thinner than can be achieved by using a knife, no matter what a person's skill level may be. The extremely sharp, razor-like blade is mounted between two flat, rectangular surfaces, which can be adjusted to separate from each other in a downward motion. The legs of a kitchen mandoline are set up at a downward angle, with the blade facing away from the user. If you are using a Japanese slicer ("Benriner"), hold the slicer at a 20-degree angle to the cutting board. An adjusting screw or handle, underneath the flat surfaces, opens and closes the gap between the two surfaces, determining the size and shape of the pieces of food to be sliced. The word "safety" cannot be stressed enough when it comes to safely using a kitchen mandoline. Do not be afraid of the mandoline—use the guard for safety and use firm pressure when slicing.

PISSALADIÈRE

Makes two 12-inch (30-cm) rounds or one long rectangular tart

Serves 6–8 people as a first course with salad

2 Tbsp (30 mL) extra virgin olive oil

8 large onions, cut in half and thinly sliced into half-moons

2 Tbsp (30 mL) fresh thyme leaves, stripped from their stalks

3 cloves garlic, cut into thin slices

½ tsp (2 mL) ground sea salt

1 tsp (5 mL) freshly ground pepper

1 recipe quick puff pastry (see page 286) or store-bought puff pastry, kept cold

16 anchovy fillets, packed in oil (drained and de-boned)

1 cup (250 mL) sun-dried olives or kalamata olives, pitted

¼ cup (60 mL) salt-packed capers, well rinsed and patted dry

Pissaladière can be found in the window of any boulangerie or seaside café in the South of France. It's rather like a cheeseless pizza, garnished with the salty, earthy combination of caramelized onions, olives, and anchovies. Its name comes from the Provençal word "pissalat," an anchovy purée. It can be eaten hot or cold and makes a tremendous lunch on its own, served with a salad, or cut into smaller pieces to be served as a snack.

In a large cast-iron or heavy-bottomed frying pan, gently heat the oil on medium heat and add the sliced onions and thyme. Stir the onions with a wooden spoon into they are evenly coated with oil. When the onions have turned translucent, add the garlic slices. Add the salt and pepper, stirring the onions occasionally, and rubbing the caramelized bits off the bottom of the pan. Lower the heat to medium-low and cook down the onions and garlic until very soft and fully caramelized, continuing to stir every 5 minutes or so. The onions will have turned a golden brown color, but should not become crispy. This should take about 20 minutes.

While the onions are cooking, preheat the oven to 400°F (200°C). Roll out the cold puff pastry into a long rectangle between 2 pieces of parchment paper. Raise the edges of the dough to form a crust around the entire edge of the tart. Work quickly to keep the dough cold. Once rolled out, put the dough back into the freezer while you wait for the onions to finish caramelizing.

To prepare the pissaladière, spread the caramelized onions evenly over the puff pastry. Cover the onions with the anchovy fillets in a cross-hatch pattern. Place the pitted olives between the diamond shapes of the anchovies to garnish. Sprinkle the capers over the tart.

Bake until the rim of the puff pastry has turned golden brown, about 30–40 minutes. It is important that the puff pastry is full cooked in the middle of the pie and not just around the edges. Resist the urge to take it out of the oven too early. When the pie is cooked, take it out of the oven and cool on a wire rack. Pissaladère is traditionally served at room temperature in Provence.

SUGGESTED WINE PAIRING
BC: Joie Pinot Noir Rosé, Naramata
International: Domaine Houchart Cote de Provence Rosé, Provence, France

RED ONION AND THYME TARTE TATIN

Serves 8–12

FOR THE SAVORY PÂTE BRISÉE

1⅔ cups (400 mL) all-purpose flour

½ tsp (2 mL) salt

6 Tbsp (90 mL) cold unsalted butter,
  cut into pieces

1 egg yolk

3 Tbsp (45 mL) cold water

FOR THE TARTE TATIN

½ cup (125 mL) sugar

2 Tbsp (30 mL) unsalted butter

2 Tbsp (30 mL) cider vinegar

1 tsp (5 mL) salt

2 lb (1 kg) red onions, peeled and halved

2 Tbsp (30 mL) fresh thyme leaves,
  pulled off their stems and chopped

This dish is a savory version of the classic apple tarte Tatin. It makes a wonderful lunch dish when served with a simple green salad. I first made this when I was an apprentice at the Agora Restaurant at the Art Gallery of Ontario in Toronto with chef Anne Yarymowich.

For the pâte brisée, combine the flour and salt in a food processor fitted with a steel blade. Add the butter pieces and then pulse the machine until the dough resembles coarse cornmeal. Add the egg yolk and water and pulse until the dough just comes together. Do not overwork the dough. Turn the dough out onto a clean work surface and bring it together into a ball. Press the ball into a disk, wrap in plastic wrap, and let rest in the refrigerator for at least 1 hour before rolling out.

When rested, roll out the dough into a disk slightly larger than the circumference of the frying pan you will be using to make the tarte Tatin. Let rest in the refrigerator again until ready to use.

Meanwhile, begin preparing the onion Tatin. Heat a cast-iron pan over medium heat and sprinkle the sugar into the bottom of the pan. Do not stir this melting sugar or it will crystallize and not melt properly. Once the sugar has melted and caramelized slightly, add the butter chunks. You can now stir the sugar and butter to combine them. Add the vinegar and salt to acidulate the caramel and make it savory. Arrange the onion halves, cut side up, in concentric circles on top of the caramel. They should fill the pan completely and be tightly packed. Sprinkle the onions with chopped thyme leaves. Cook the onions on top of the stove over medium heat until a deep golden caramel forms and the onions are slightly softened. The onions will produce juice that must evaporate slightly before the onions themselves will caramelize. Remove from the heat and let the onions cool slightly. Drain off any excessive juice, or the pastry will be soggy. Leave only enough juice to coat the bottom of the pan.

Preheat the oven to 425°F (220°C).

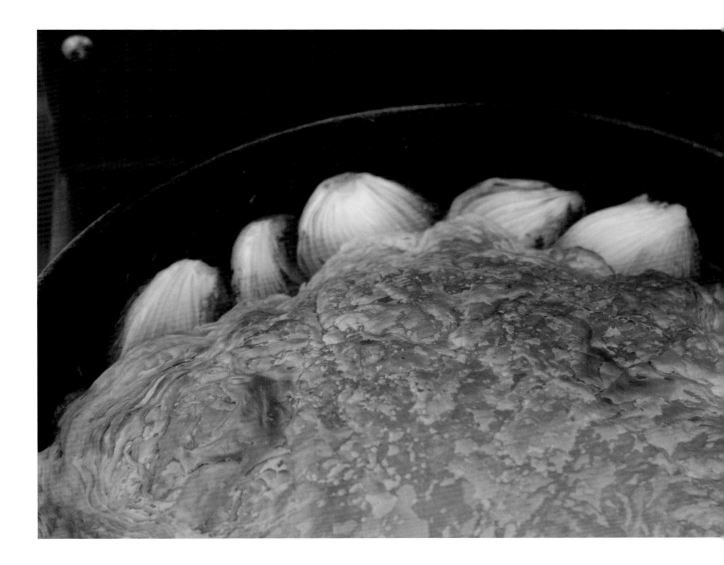

Take the rolled pastry from the refrigerator. Set the pastry on top of the onions so that they are completely covered, tucking the pastry in at the edges. Work fast so that the dough does not soften from the heat of the onions.

Bake until the pastry is crisp and golden brown, about 25–30 minutes. Let the tart cool in the pan for 5–10 minutes before unmolding onto a large tray or plate. It is very important to do this with great care, covering your arms with towels so that excess caramel does not splash on them. If any onions stick to the bottom of the pan, transfer them to the top of the tart with a spatula. Serve the tart warm, with crème fraîche or a side of goat cheese.

SUGGESTED WINE PAIRING

BC: La Frenz "Alexandria," Naramata
International: Gaston Huet "Le Mont" Vouvray Demi-sec, Loire Valley, France

ALSATIAN ONION TART

Serves 8 as an appetizer course

FOR THE PASTRY

2 cups (500 mL) all-purpose flour

¾ cup (180 mL) cold unsalted butter, cut into ½-inch (1-cm) cubes

½ tsp (2 mL) salt

4–5 Tbsp (60–75 mL) ice water

FOR THE FILLING

4 bacon slices (¼ lb/125 g), cut crosswise into lardons (⅛–1/16-inch/0.03–0.01-cm wide strips)

3 Tbsp (45 mL) unsalted butter

2 lb (1 kg) onions, halved lengthwise and very thinly sliced crosswise (about 10 cups/2.5 L)

1¼ tsp (7 mL) salt

1 tsp (5 mL) freshly ground white pepper

1 cup (250 mL) crème fraîche or sour cream

4 large eggs

½ tsp (2 mL) freshly grated nutmeg

½ tsp (2 mL) ground coriander

This is a classic Alsatian appetizer and a perfect pairing for an aromatic wine like a "gentil" blend of Riesling, Gewürtz, Pinot Blanc, and Muscat. It's delicious served with a small salad for a starter course or sliced as a small canapé.

To make the pastry, blend together the flour, butter, and salt in a bowl with your fingertips or a pastry blender (or pulse in a food processor) until most of the mixture resembles coarse meal with some small (roughly pea-sized) butter lumps. Drizzle evenly with 4 Tbsp (60 mL) ice water and gently stir with a fork (or pulse in a food processor) until incorporated. Squeeze a small handful of the dough. If it doesn't hold together, add more ice water, ½ Tbsp (7.5 mL) at a time, stirring (or pulsing) until just incorporated, then test again. Do not overwork the mixture, or the pastry will be tough. Turn out the mixture onto a cold work surface and gather the dough together with a pastry scraper. Press into a ball, and then flatten into a disk. Wrap the dough in plastic wrap and chill in the refrigerator until firm, at least 1 hour.

Roll out the dough onto a floured surface with a floured rolling pin (or between 2 pieces of parchment paper) into a 14-inch (35-cm) round and fit it into an 11-inch (28-cm), removable bottom tart pan that is at least 1¼ inches (3 cm) deep. Trim away any excess dough, leaving a ½-inch (1-cm) overhang, then fold the overhang over the pastry and press against the side to reinforce the edge. Lightly prick the bottom of the pastry with a fork and chill until firm, about ½ hour. Preheat oven to 400°F (200°C).

Line the chilled shell with foil and fill with pie weights or beans. Blind-bake (see page 270) until the pastry is set and pale golden along the rim, about 15–20 minutes. Carefully remove the foil and weights and bake the shell until golden all over, about 10–15 minutes more. Transfer the shell to a rack.

While the shell is baking, prepare the onion filling. Render the bacon in a frying pan over medium heat, stirring occasionally, until crisp, about 6–8 minutes. Transfer the bacon with a slotted spoon onto paper towels to drain and pour off the excess bacon fat. Add the butter to the pan in which the bacon was rendered and cook the onions, seasoned with salt and white pepper, over medium heat, stirring, until softened, about 2 minutes. Cover the surface of the onions with a round of parchment paper or cover the frying pan with a tight-fitting lid and continue to cook, lifting the parchment paper or lid to stir frequently, until the onions are very soft and pale golden, about 20 minutes. Stir in the bacon, then remove from the heat and cool for 10 minutes. While the onions are cooling, whisk together the crème fraîche, eggs, nutmeg, coriander, and more salt and white pepper in a large bowl, then stir in the onions. Pour the filling into the tart shell, spreading over the onions evenly, and bake until the filling is set and the top is a dark golden color, about 25–35 minutes. Serve warm or at room temperature.

SUGGESTED WINE PAIRING

BC: Joie "A Noble Blend", Naramata

International: Pfaffenheim Pinot Gris, Alsace, France

ASPARAGUS WITH TRUFFLED GOAT CHEESE SABAYON

Serves 8

3 lb (1.5 kg) asparagus (or golden beets or green beans)
6 large egg yolks
½ cup (125 mL) white wine
6 oz (175 g) goat cheese, at room temperature
1 Tbsp (15 mL) whole (3.5%) milk

1 Tbsp (15 mL) freshly squeezed lemon juice
½ cup (125 mL) whipping (35%) cream
salt
2 Tbsp (30 mL) minced chives
drizzle of truffle oil (optional), or use the truffle goat cheese from Salt Spring Island

Asparagus and creamy goat cheese are a natural combination. I've also used this recipe with sliced, roasted golden beets or steamed green beans instead of asparagus. This sauce is also delicious with salmon or smoked trout.

This recipe as been adapted from a recipe that Karen Barnaby gave to Mara Jernigan at Fairburn Farm in the Cowichan Valley. Mara made this incredible creation right in front of me as I was perched on a stool in her teaching kitchen. I had to have the recipe and now make it often at Joie when the first wild asparagus appears in the orchard!

Bring a pot of salted water to a rolling boil and prepare an ice-water bath. If you're using green beans instead of asparagus, tip and tail them. Plunge the asparagus or beans into the boiling water and cook for 1–2 minutes (depending on the thickness of the asparagus or beans). Plunge them into the ice-water bath to shock in their bright green color and stop the cooking process. Leave in the ice-water bath until cool.

Whisk the egg yolks and wine together in a metal bowl. Place the bowl over a double boiler and continue whisking until the mixture thickens and triples in volume.

In a separate bowl, beat the goat cheese until smooth. Gradually beat the milk and lemon juice into the goat cheese. Fold the egg yolk and wine mixture into the cheese.

Beat the whipping cream until soft peaks form and then fold into the yolk and cheese mixture. Stir in half of the chives. Season with salt to taste. Cover and refrigerate, if necessary, before using. The sabayon should be used immediately for best results. I would suggest making it right before you plan on serving it to take advantage of all the fluffy air that you just worked so hard to put into the sabayon.

To serve, arrange the asparagus or beans on a small plate, or on a large platter if you are serving the dish family-style. Top with the sabayon and sprinkle with the remaining chives. Drizzle over the truffle oil or goat cheese if using. Serve immediately.

SUGGESTED WINE PAIRING
BC: Lake Breeze Semillon, Naramata
International: Fouassier Sancerre, Loire Valley, France

CRISPY SWEETBREADS WITH SAGE BROWN BUTTER EMULSION

Serves 6

FOR THE CRISPY SWEETBREADS
1¾ lb (800 g) sweetbreads
8 cups (2 L) court bouillon (see page 152)
1 tsp (5 mL) salt
pinch of freshly ground white pepper
all-purpose flour to dredge
2–3 Tbsp (10–15 mL) clarified butter
   or neutral vegetable oil

FOR THE SAGE BROWN BUTTER
EMULSION
½ lb (250 g) unsalted butter
1 cup (250 mL) fresh sage leaves, stalks
   removed
1 egg yolk
zest and juice of 1 lemon
salt

FOR THE GARNISH
fried capers

CLARIFIED BUTTER is butter that has been rendered to separate the milk solids and water from the butter fat. Typically it is produced by melting butter and allowing the different components to separate by density. Some solids float to the surface and are skimmed off; the water and the remainder of the milk solids sink to the bottom and are left behind when the butter fat is poured off. The non-butter fat components are discarded. Clarified butter has a higher smoke point than regular butter, and is therefore preferred in some cooking applications, such as sautéing.

I love sweetbreads. Visiting chef Jason Schubert made these delicious textural delights one week for our first course. He served them with an aioli-like sauce, made with leftover sage brown butter we had in the refrigerator. It was a delicious experiment. The salty garnish of the fried sage leaves and fried capers is a nice contrast to the richness of the sweetbread itself.

Soak the sweetbreads in water for 6 hours in the refrigerator, changing the water 2 or 3 times. Prepare an ice-water bath. Blanch the sweetbreads in the court bouillon, brought up to a simmer (or water infused with 1 bay leaf, 1 lemon, 1 carrot, and 1 onion), for 20 minutes. Plunge into the ice water. When the sweetbreads are cool, peel off the membrane and trim any tough parts. Portion into 2-oz (50-g) pieces, and flatten slightly with your hand.

Line a flat baking tray with clean kitchen towels. Move the sweetbreads to the tray, cover with clean kitchen towels, and top with a second baking tray. Weigh the trays down with 8 lb (3.5 kg) of weights, evenly distributed. Refrigerate overnight or for at least 8 hours.

To make the sage brown butter emulsion, slowly melt the butter in a heavy-bottomed saucepan. Keep the butter at a bare simmer until it turns a golden brown color (all the milk solids will caramelize slowly), about 30–40 minutes. Add a handful of fresh sage leaves and let simmer for about 10 minutes. Right before serving, increase the heat to crisp the sage leaves, being careful not to burn the butter. Using a slotted spoon, remove the crispy sage leaves from the butter and drain on a paper towel. Reserve for garnish.

To make the emulsion, very slowly start to drizzle the warm (but not hot) sage brown butter into the egg yolk to temper it, and then whisk like crazy until the sauce begins to thicken. Continue to whisk, adding the brown butter in a slow stream to emulsify the sauce. When the sauce becomes too thick to drizzle, add the lemon juice with the zest to achieve the correct consistency and season to taste with salt. Reserve until ready to serve, keeping the sauce barely warm.

To serve the sweetbreads, remove from the refrigerator, season with salt and pepper, dredge in flour, and pan-fry in clarified butter over medium heat until brown and crispy, 3–4 minutes per side.

Once the sweetbreads are done, transfer them to warm plates. Drizzle the sage brown butter emulsion overtop and garnish with crispy sage leaves and fried capers.

SUGGESTED WINE PAIRING

BC: Sumac Ridge "Stellar's Jay" Brut, Summerland
International: Monmousseau Brut, Loire Valley, France

CHEF'S TIP

To fry capers, heat 2 Tbsp (30 mL) pure olive oil in a frying pan over medium-high heat. Rinse 3 Tbsp (45 mL) salt-packed capers and pat dry between 2 pieces of paper towel. Fry the capers for about 1–1½ minutes until golden and the caper begins to unfurl a bit (capers are the pickled buds of a Mediterranean flower). Remove the capers from the pan with a slotted spoon, drain on another paper towel, and let cool before using as a garnish.

DUCK RILLETTES SERVED WITH DRIED PEAR COMPOTE

Makes 8 small ramekins of rillette

FOR THE RILLETTES

4 confited duck legs (any other confited meat could be substituted here, like rabbit, pork, or boar)
¼ cup (60 mL) minced shallots
2 roasted or confited garlic cloves
1 Tbsp (15 mL) cognac
4 Tbsp (60 mL) unsalted butter
½ tsp (2 mL) freshly ground white pepper
¼ tsp (1 mL) ground nutmeg
¼ tsp (1 mL) ground allspice
¼ tsp (1 mL) salt
2 Tbsp (30 mL) fat, reserved from the confit

FOR THE DRIED PEAR COMPOTE

1 Tbsp (15 mL) vegetable oil
1 onion, finely chopped
½ cup (125 mL) sugar
¼ cup (60 mL) balsamic vinegar
2 cups (500 mL) soft, dried pears, roughly chopped (other dried fruit can be substituted, such as apricots, prunes, or figs)
1 cup (250 mL) unfiltered apple juice

"Rillette" is just a fancy word for potted meat that is shredded and served in its own fat. I like to serve rillette with a mix of good mustard, cornichons, and dried fruit chutney or compote and a small side salad of herbs for a first course. Try this recipe that my chef friend Jason Schubert created using the dried pears and apple juice from our orchard. Serve this delicious condiment with any charcuterie, cold roasted meats, or cheese plate.

For the rillette, combine the duck legs, shallots, garlic, cognac, butter, pepper, nutmeg, allspice, and salt in the bowl of an electric mixer fitted with a dough hook. Beat at medium speed for about 1 minute, or until everything is well mixed. Alternatively, use a food processor, taking care not to purée the mixture or let it turn into a paste. The texture should have the consistency of finely chopped meat. Use immediately or place in an airtight container, drizzle some of the reserved fat over the top, and refrigerate for up to 1 week.

To make the compote, heat the vegetable oil in a large saucepan and sauté the onion until soft. Sprin-

kle the sugar over the softened onion and continue to cook until a light caramel forms. Once the caramel is golden, deglaze (see page 150) the pan with the balsamic vinegar. Cook the onions down until they are glazed.

Add the chopped pears to the glazed onion and deglaze with the apple juice. Cook the pears down until they are soft and mushy. Add more juice if necessary to completely soften the dried pears. Cool the compote before serving.

To serve, press the rillette into small ¼ cup (60 mL) ramekins, or shape the mixture into a quenelle or oval and serve with warmed croutons, fresh crusty bread, or brioche (see page 175) and a large quenelle of the compote on each plate.

SUGGESTED WINE PAIRING
BC: Wild Goose "Autumn Gold," Okanagan Falls
International: Philippe Delesvaux Coteaux du Layon-Anjou, Loire Valley, France

BRIOCHE

Makes 2 nice loaves

FOR THE STARTER

1¼ cups (310 mL) hard flour (see
    page 309)
1 tsp (5 mL) granulated sugar
¾ tsp (4 mL) fresh yeast or 1¼ tsp
    (6 mL) active dry yeast
½ cup (125 mL) whole (3.25%) milk

FOR THE MAIN DOUGH

8 whole eggs
¼ cup (60 mL) granulated sugar
3 Tbsp (45 mL) active dry yeast
1 Tbsp (15 mL) salt
2¼ cups (560 mL) all-purpose flour
1½ cups (375 mL) unsalted butter

1 whole egg for egg wash
1 tsp (5 mL) water

My friend chef Dana Ewart learned this recipe for perfect brioche from chef James MacGuire at Montreal's Boulangerie Le Passe-Partout.

For the starter, mix together the flour, sugar, fresh yeast, and milk by hand, kneading gently until smooth. Place in a bowl and cover with a damp towel. Allow to ferment for 3 hours, or up to overnight.

Flour a baking tray.

In the bowl of a standing mixer, combine the starter with the eggs, sugar, yeast, and salt. Mix in the flour a little at a time. When the flour is entirely combined, increase the speed and beat with a dough hook for 10 minutes.

While the dough is mixing, plasticize the butter. This is done by placing it between 2 sheets of parchment paper and beating it with a rolling pin until it's the same consistency as the dough. When the dough is mixed thoroughly, begin adding small amounts of the plasticized butter. Each addition must be completely mixed in before adding the next. This is to ensure a proper emulsification of the butter. When all the butter

is mixed in, beat for 2–3 minutes more and pour onto the floured baking tray. Wrap well with plastic wrap. Allow the dough to ferment in the refrigerator for 4 hours, or up to overnight.

Remove the dough from the refrigerator, punch out the air, and rotate the dough once. Cut it into the desired amounts. The dough can now be frozen for up to 1 month, or baked.

To bake the brioche, punch it to wake up the yeast, shape it into a buttered loaf pan or a fluted cylinder mold, and proof it until it doubles in bulk (about 30 minutes).

Preheat the oven to 425°F (220°C). Combine the whole egg with the water to make an egg glaze. Brush over the dough and bake until golden and the loaf sounds hollow when tapped. For large and tall brioches, bake at 425°F (220°C) for 15 minutes, then lower the heat to 375°F (190°C) and continue baking 20–30 minutes longer. For small brioches, bake at 425°F (220°C) for 15–25 minutes.

TONNATO TONNATO

Serves 8

FOR THE TUNA LOIN

1 whole tuna albacore loin
   (about 1 lb/500 g)
½ cup (125 mL) salt
½ cup (125 mL) brown sugar
1 Tbsp (15 mL) fennel seeds
¼ tsp (1 mL) chili flakes
1 Tbsp (15 mL) coriander seeds
1 whole star anise

or 1 package of pre-sliced smoked tuna

FOR THE CAPER, ANCHOVY, AND TUNA MAYONNAISE

1 (5-oz/160-g) can Italian tuna packed in
   olive oil
1 whole large egg
¼ cup (60 mL) capers packed in salt,
   well rinsed
4 anchovy fillets packed in oil, de-boned
1 clove garlic, minced
juice and zest of 1 lemon
½ tsp (2 mL) salt
freshly ground pepper
½ cup (125 mL) olive oil

This dish is a play on a traditional Italian dish called vitello tonnato that is usually made with sliced, cold roasted veal shin with a tuna, anchovy, and caper mayonnaise. This is my summer BC version of this dish, using local tuna loin that I smoke here on the farm.

Make a rub for the tuna by putting the salt, sugar, fennel seeds, chili flakes, coriander seeds, and star anise into a spice mill, blender, or mortar and pestle to grind into a fine powder. Rub the tuna loin with the spice mixture until coated and put it on a rack in the refrigerator on a baking sheet, uncovered, to cure overnight. The salt and sugar in the curing mixture will "cook" or denature the outside of the tuna, leaving the center of the tuna raw. Rinse the loin well with water and pat dry before slicing it. If you're going to smoke the loin, pat it dry after rinsing it and return it to the refrigerator to form a sticky layer that the smoke will adhere to. Smoke the tuna in a home smoker or on your barbecue (see page 182). Note that you do not want to cook the tuna, only gently smoke it, keeping the temperature of the smoker at around 200°F (95°C) for 1 hour. You can also make this dish with store-bought smoked tuna or simply use tuna that has been cured already.

To make the mayonnaise, put the tuna and its oil, along with the egg, capers, anchovy fillets, garlic, lemon juice and zest, and salt and pepper into the bowl of a food processor to blend. While the motor is running, add the olive oil in a slow stream until it becomes emulsified and the mayonnaise is creamy. Check the consistency and add more olive oil and a bit of warm water, if necessary. You should be able to drizzle the mayonnaise. Check the seasoning of the mayonnaise for salt and lemon juice. If the flavor is "flat," add more lemon juice and a pinch of salt.

To assemble the dish, cut the tuna loin very thinly and arrange on a chilled plate in a layer of concentric circles, just enough to cover the entire plate in one layer. Drizzle the smoked tuna with the caper, anchovy, and tuna mayonnaise.

Serve with crusty bread, olive oil–soaked crostini, or Onion and Poppy Seed Crackers (see page 184). This dish is also delicious garnished with deep-fried capers.

SUGGESTED WINE PAIRING
BC: Blue Mountain Brut, Okanagan Falls
International: Regaleali Rosé, Sicily, Italy

VENISON CARPACCIO WITH PICKLED BEET AND PARSLEY AND ONION SALAD

Serves 4

1¼ lb (550g) loin of venison, cut into
⅛inch (0.3-cm) slices

FOR THE PICKLED BEETS

5 lb (2.2 kg) red beets — smaller beets are
    better for canning
1 cup (250 mL) brown sugar
3 cups (750 mL) cider vinegar
4 cloves
2 bay leaves
1 cinnamon stick or 2 Tbsp (30 mL)
    cassia bark, broken up
1 tsp (5 mL) salt

FOR THE PARSLEY AND ONION SALAD

1 large Walla Walla or sweet onion, cut
    into very thin slices
1 large bunch flat-leaf parsley, roughly
    chopped
juice and zest of 1 lemon

¼ cup (60 mL) extra virgin olive oil
    (the best you have)
splash of sherry vinegar
2 tsp (10 mL) fleur de sel

A carpaccio is meat or fish sliced very thin and not cooked but marinated. You can eat beef, venison, and many types of fish like this. For this dish, it's absolutely essential that the meat be trimmed clean of any trace of sinew or fat. My friend Jason Schubert made this dish and served it at one of our Orchard Dinners in 2005. I have included a preparation for pickled beets in this recipe (the recipe is my mom's—she makes tremendous pickled beets!) but if you don't want to make the beets yourself, a jar of quality pickled beets can be substituted.

Put the venison slices between 2 large pieces of plastic wrap. Bang them with a rolling pin (not too hard) and then roll them out, still between the sheets of plastic, until they become very thin. Transfer the slices onto plates. This is tricky as the slices are delicate, so peel off one piece of film and then invert the meat onto a cold plate and peel off the top layer. Allow to stand for about 1 hour at room temperature.

Scrub the beets clean, removing the stalks and leaves and stringy tail. Place them in a large pot with their skins on, cover with water, and bring to a simmer. When fork-tender, remove the beets from the pot and drain. Let the beets cool slightly before peeling them by rubbing the skins. The skins should come off quite easily. Cut the beets in half or into quarters (depending on their size) and transfer to a bowl or to hot, sanitized canning jars.

Make a brine by combining the sugar, vinegar, cloves, bay leaves, cinnamon stick, and salt. Bring the brine to a boil and pour over the beets. Let the heat of the brine seal the canning jars. Leave the beets to sit overnight in a covered bowl if using them right away.

To prepare the salad, soak the sliced onions in ice-cold water for 10 minutes, rinsing often. This will take the acidic sting out of the onions as well as making them crisp. Chop the parsley with a sharp knife once in both directions so it still has some life to it (making sure not to "mulch" it!). Rinse and pat dry the onion slices. Drain the beet pieces, which should now be pickled from their brine. Combine the beet pieces with the onion, parsley, and lemon juice and zest.

To serve the carpaccio, take the plate with the thin venison slices and place a small handful of the salad on top of the carpaccio in the middle of the plate. Drizzle over the good olive oil and a splash of sherry vinegar. Top the carpaccio with a pinch of fleur de sel for texture.

SUGGESTED WINE PAIRING
BC: Blue Mountain Pinot Noir, Okanagan Falls
International: Fattoria di Basciano Chianti Rufina, Tuscany, Italy

BUCKWHEAT BLINIS
WITH CURED SOCKEYE SALMON

Serves 8

FOR THE CURED SALMON

1 side of sockeye or spring salmon
   (about 1–2 lb/500 g–1 kg)
½ cup (125 mL) salt
½ cup (125 mL) brown sugar
1 Tbsp (15 mL) fennel seeds
1 Tbsp (15 mL) coriander seeds
1 Tbsp (15 mL) dried dill
6 juniper berries
1 tsp (5 mL) white pepper
pinch of chili flakes
zest of 1 lemon

FOR THE BLINIS

2 lb (1 kg) yellow-fleshed potatoes, like
   Yukon gold or Sieglinde, skins on
4 Tbsp (60 mL) buckwheat flour
2 Tbsp (30 mL) crème fraîche or sour
   cream
6 large eggs
2 tsp (10 mL) salt
½ tsp (2 mL) freshly ground white
   pepper

FOR THE GARNISH

¼ cup (60 mL) crème fraîche
1 Tbsp (15 mL) finely chopped chives

I love classic blinis. This recipe uses some of the great heirloom potatoes that I can buy from the farmer's market and incorporates the traditional use of buckwheat flour. We smoke as much fish as possible in the smoker at Joie. If you don't have access to a home smoker, simply cure the salmon and weigh it down gravlax-style, before slicing it.

Begin the cured salmon by making the rub. Put the salt, sugar, fennel seeds, coriander seeds, dill, juniper berries, pepper, and chili flakes into a mortar and pestle. Grind everything into a fine powder. Add the lemon zest to the powder after it has been ground. Rub the salmon fillet with the spice mixture until coated, put in the refrigerator on a rack on a baking sheet, and cover with a piece of parchment paper to cure overnight. Weigh down the fillet with another baking sheet placed over the parchment paper, held down with full bottles of wine or something similar in weight. The salt and sugar in the curing mixture will "cook" or denature the outside of the fish, leaving the center of the fish somewhat raw.

Once cured, rinse the fillet well with water and pat dry. If you want, you can now eat the salmon in this cured state or proceed to smoke it. If you're smoking the fish, leave it to dry in the refrigerator for several hours until a sticky film develops. This will allow the smoke to adhere to the salmon. Smoke the salmon in a home smoker or in your barbecue (see pg 182). Note: you do not want to cook the fish, only gently smoke it.

The fish will smoke for a short time, about 1 hour.

To begin the blinis, place the potatoes in salted water, bring to a boil, and simmer, covered, until thoroughly cooked. Drain and, while the potatoes are still warm, peel them and press them through a fine mesh sieve or ricer. This will keep the potatoes fluffy and not produce a gluey mass when processed. Quickly work in the buckwheat flour with a fork or spoon and mix in the crème fraîche. Add 1 egg and mix in until the batter is smooth. Add the remaining eggs one at a time, mixing well after each addition. Season with salt and freshly ground white pepper. The batter should have the texture of pancake batter. If necessary, add a bit more sour cream or milk to reach the right consistency.

Preheat a nonstick pan over medium heat until very hot. Spoon about 1 teaspoon (5 mL) of the batter into the pan. Cook until the bottom is golden brown, 2–3 minutes, turn, and cook the other side for a further minute. Place the cooked blinis on a small baking sheet and keep warm.

When ready to serve the blinis, place a thin slice of salmon on each blini and top with some crème fraîche and finely chopped chives for garnish.

SUGGESTED WINE PAIRING

BC: Blue Mountain Brut Rosé, Okanagan Falls
International: Champagne Gosset Grande Rosé,
Champagne, France

APPLEWOOD SMOKED SALMON AND MIZUNA WITH WARM ROASTED FINGERLING POTATOES AND HORSERADISH CRÈME FRAÎCHE

Serves 6

FOR THE POTATOES

2 Tbsp (30 mL) vegetable oil
2 Tbsp (30 mL) olive oil
1 tsp (5 mL) coarse sea salt
freshly ground pepper
1 Tbsp (15 mL) fresh rosemary, roughly
    chopped
1 tsp (5 mL) paprika
2 lb (1 kg) fingerling or nugget potatoes,
    scrubbed and dried

FOR THE HORSERADISH CRÈME FRAÎCHE
DRESSING

1 cup (250 mL) crème fraîche
3 Tbsp (45 mL) prepared horseradish
½ tsp (2 mL) salt
½ tsp (2 mL) freshly ground pepper
juice and zest of 1 lemon
freshly chopped chives

1¼ lb (600 g) smoked salmon or trout
    (see page 179 for house-cured salmon)
2 cups (500 mL) baby mizuna leaves,
    washed and spun for garnish

These potatoes are a delicious creamy accompaniment to a cold smoked-fish plate or as a salad on their own as part of a picnic. This dish can also be made with roasted beets and drizzled with the horseradish crème fraiche instead of tossed in it.

Preheat oven to 400°F (200°C).

For the potatoes, mix the oils with the salt, pepper, rosemary, and paprika. Cut the potatoes in half, toss in the oil and spice mixture, and spread out on a baking sheet. Do not crowd the potatoes or they will steam and not get crispy. Use 2 pans if necessary.

Roast the potatoes for 15 minutes, and then reduce the oven temperature to 350°F (180°C) until the potatoes are golden and crisp on the outside and tender in the middle, about half an hour. Turn the potatoes only once during cooking to ensure crispiness.

Meanwhile, prepare the dressing. Mix together the crème fraîche, horseradish, salt, pepper, and lemon zest and juice in a large bowl. Reserve a small amount of dressing (about ¼ cup/60 mL) for drizzling over the individual plates. Add a little more lemon juice if necessary to help it drizzle better.

While the potatoes are still warm, toss to coat in the dressing.

To serve, place a small mound of the dressed potatoes on a small plate with a small piece (4-oz/100-g portion) of smoked salmon or trout beside it. Top the potatoes and the smoked fish with a small handful of the mizuna. Drizzle over a spoonful of the reserved dressing.

SUGGESTED WINE PAIRING

BC: Lake Breeze Blanc de Noirs, Naramata
International: Boony Doon Vin Gris de Cigare, Santa Cruz
California, USA

CHEF'S TIP

The dressed potatoes can be served on their own as part of a picnic, or the salad can be plated individually on small plates with some smoked salmon or trout. Try roasted beets instead of the potatoes.

Crème fraîche (pronounced 'krem-fresh') is a thick and smooth soured cream with a rich and velvety texture. This matured cream has a nutty, slightly sour taste produced by culturing pasteurized cream with natural bacteria. Crème fraîche can be bought but it is very simple to make your own by gently heating whipping cream (35% fat) and then stirring in some buttermilk at a 2:1 ratio. This mixture is left to sit, slightly covered, in a warm place for about 24 hours. It is ready when it is thick, with the consistency of thick cream. The benign live bacteria in the buttermilk will multiply and protect the cream from any harmful bacteria. Once the crème fraîche has thickened sufficiently, cover and place in the refrigerator. It will continue to thicken and take on a more tangy flavor as it ages. Crème fraîche will keep in the refrigerator for about 7–10 days. It is used in both savory and sweet dishes and makes a wonderful accompaniment for tarts. It can also be whipped, along with a little sugar, and used in place of whipped cream.

HOUSE-CURED WILD SPRING SALMON
SERVED À L'ALSACIENNE

Serves 6

FOR THE CURED SALMON
½ cup (125 mL) salt
½ cup (125 mL) sugar
1 Tbsp (15 mL) fennel seeds
1 Tbsp (15 mL) coriander seeds
1 Tbsp (15 mL) dried dill
6 juniper berries
1 tsp (5 mL) white pepper
pinch of chili flakes
zest of 1 lemon
1 side of sockeye or spring salmon

FOR THE CHOUCROUTE
1 Tbsp (15 mL) duck fat
½ cup (125 mL) smoked bacon, cut into
    thin strips or lardons
2 cups (500 mL) peeled and thinly sliced
    onions
1 medium onion, left whole
4 whole cloves
1 tsp (5 mL) mustard seeds
1 tsp (5 mL) coriander seeds
½ tsp (2 mL) freshly ground white
    pepper
2 juniper berries, crushed
1 Tbsp (15 mL) cassia bark or broken-up
    cinnamon stick
2 cups (500 mL) Riesling or other
    aromatic white wine
1 cup (250 mL) sauerkraut, rinsed and
    drained
1 bay leaf

SMOKING on your barbecue requires that you use the "indirect heat method" to keep the heat and smoke source, i.e., charcoal and wood chips, off to the sides of the barbecue grill so the heat does not directly cook your food. Instead you use low heat to slowly cook your food. A loose rule of thumb might be one hour slow cooking per pound of meat.

Any dish served with sauerkraut in French cooking is referred to as being prepared "à l'Alsacienne." This is an interesting dish as there are textural and temperature differences within the piece of seared salmon. The spice in the choucroute is echoed in the cure for the fish and the smoky bacon is complementary to the smoked, cured salmon.

Put the salt, sugar, fennel seeds, coriander seeds, dill, juniper berries, white pepper, and chili flakes into a spice mill, blender, or mortar and pestle. Grind them into a fine powder to make a rub for the salmon. Add the lemon zest to the powder after it has been ground. Rub the salmon with the spice mixture until well coated and put in the refrigerator on a rack on a baking sheet, covered with a piece of parchment paper, to cure overnight. Weigh down the salmon with another baking sheet placed over the parchment paper, held down with full bottles of wine or something similar in weight that is heavy enough to hold down the sheet. The salt and sugar in the curing mixture will "cook" or denature the outside of the fish, leaving the center of the fish somewhat raw. Once cured, rinse the salmon well with water and pat dry. If you want, you can now eat the salmon in its cured state or proceed to smoke it.

If you are smoking the salmon, leave it to dry in the refrigerator for several hours until a sticky film develops on the fish. This will allow the smoke to adhere to the salmon. Smoke the salmon in a home smoker or in your barbecue. Note that you do not want to cook the fish, only gently smoke it. The heat of the smoker should not exceed 200°F (95°C). The fish will only smoke for a short time, about 1 hour.

To prepare the choucroute, melt the duck fat in a large saucepan on medium heat. Sauté the bacon un-til almost crispy and then add the sliced onions. Cook for about 10 minutes until the onions are transparent. Stud the whole onion with the cloves and put the mustard seeds, coriander seeds, pepper, juniper berries, and cassia bark into a spice grinder and grind into a fine powder.

Add the wine, sauerkraut, ground spices, bay leaf, and studded whole onion to the saucepan and continue to cook until all the liquid is absorbed. Discard the bay leaf and season to taste with salt and freshly ground white pepper. Keep warm until needed.

To serve the dish, cut 2-oz (50-g) portions of the cured salmon and sear 1 side only (skin side down) in a hot pan coated with oil. Serve over a small amount of warm choucroute for an appetizer course.

SUGGESTED WINE PAIRING

BC: Golden Mile Riesling, Oliver
International: Trimbach "Clos St Hune" Riesling, Alsace, France

To start your barbecue smoker, mound the charcoal off to one side, let it burn, and when it gets ashen or the charcoal turns white, then spread out the coals and add your wood for smoke. The heat and smoke will rise up one side of your barbecue, cool slightly, and come down the other side where your food is — a simple sort of convection oven. It is important that you put a pan of water in the bottom of your barbecue grill and put the coals and wood chips off to one side or around the water pan. A water pan will help keep the temperature constant and keep your foods from completely drying out. Position the food over the water pan, not the charcoal. It's important to keep the barbecue grill temperature under 220°F (100°C), otherwise you'll cook your food, rather than smoke or slow cook it.

ONION AND POPPY SEED CRACKERS

Makes 36 crackers

1 medium onion	1 tsp (5 mL) baking powder
1 large egg	2 Tbsp (30 mL) poppy seeds
1/3 cup (75 mL) vegetable oil	1 Tbsp (15 mL) granulated sugar
2 tsp (10 mL) salt	1/4 tsp (1 mL) freshly ground pepper
2 cups (500 mL) all-purpose flour	

My friend Dana Ewart shared this recipe with our students during her artisanal baking workshop. These crackers are an excellent garnish to cheese and charcuterie boards as well as an accompaniment for salmon or tomato tartar (see page 186).

In the bowl of a food processor fitted with the blade attachment, purée the onion. One medium onion will yield approximately 1 cup (250 mL) purée. Measure 1 cup (250 mL) liquid onion and return to the bowl of the mixer or place in a stainless steel bowl. Add the egg, oil, and salt and whisk to combine. Reserve.

Sift the flour together with the baking powder in a bowl or on a board. Sprinkle on the poppy seeds, sugar, and pepper. Toss lightly to combine. Make a well in the center of the dry ingredients and pour in the wet ingredients. Mix in one direction until the dough is fully combined. Lightly knead the dough, flouring as needed, for 2 minutes. Wrap tightly in plastic wrap and rest in the refrigerator for 1 hour.

Preheat oven to 325°F (160°C).

This dough is best rolled between 2 pieces of parchment paper that have been well floured. Roll as thinly as possible without tearing the dough. Cut the dough with a pizza roller, or a knife, into any desired shape.

Bake the crackers until evenly golden, about 5 minutes. Remove from the oven and cool the crackers on a wire rack. Or place the baked crackers on a mold while still warm if you want to make them into quirky shapes!

CHEF'S TIP

Try replacing the poppy seeds with cumin, black pepper, or anise seeds for a different flavor.

WILD SOCKEYE SALMON TARTAR

Serves 6

1 lb (500 g) fresh salmon fillet, all skin
   and bones removed
2 shallots, finely diced
1 bunch chives, finely diced (about 2
   Tbsp/30 mL)

juice and fine zest of 1 lemon
2 Tbsp (30 mL) olive oil
salt
freshly ground pepper

I love making this tartar with sockeye salmon because of its deep color. In combination with the green chives, the little morsels of salmon coated in shiny olive oil look like little jewels. This dish is beautiful served on its own with a tiny herb salad, on a crouton, or as a garnish in a chilled soup.

Chill the cutting board, bowl, and knife you will be using to make the tartar. When preparing raw ingredients, it is important to keep all equipment cold.

Prepare an ice-water bath.

Cut the salmon very evenly and finely into ½-inch (1-cm) dice. To make this step easier, first make 3- × ½-inch (7.5- × 1-cm) wide strips of salmon (or "batons") and then cut these strips into tiny cubes. Do not use a food processor to do this or the salmon will become mush. The texture of the final tartar depends on the uniformity of the salmon dice. Keep the chopped salmon in a cold bowl in an ice-water bath while you continue your preparation.

Add the shallots, chives, and lemon juice and zest to the salmon pieces. Add the olive oil gradually to bind the tartar. Season the tartar with salt and pepper to taste. Keep chilled and cover until ready to use.

To serve the tartar, place about 1 Tbsp (15 mL) on a crouton or cracker (see Onion Poppy Seed Crack-

ers on page 184) or in the bottom of a soup bowl to garnish a soup like Asparagus and Sorrel Soup (see page 138) or Chilled Yellow Tomato Soup (see page 134).

SUGGESTED WINE PAIRING
BC: Joie Pinot Noir Rosé, Naramata
International: Artazuri Rosado, Navarra, Spain

TOMATO CONFIT TARTAR

Serves 8

FOR THE CONFIT

3 lb (1.5 kg) tomatoes (preferably
   heirloom varieties)
5 cloves garlic, peeled and left whole
1 Tbsp (15 mL) coarse sea salt
5 whole peppercorns
5 sprigs thyme
4 cups (1 L) extra virgin olive oil
   (enough to roughly submerge the
   tomatoes)

FOR THE TARTAR

2 shallots, finely diced
2 Tbsp (30 mL) chives, finely diced
juice and zest of 1 lemon
salt
freshly ground pepper
1 Tbsp (15 mL) oil from the confit

Tomato confit is delicious on its own, but when made into a tartar it's divine, especially when spread onto croutons. It's an excellent dish to make when the garden is full of heirloom tomatoes or when you just couldn't say no at the market.

For the confit, peel the tomatoes (see page 187) and discard the skins. Keep the tomatoes whole.

Preheat oven to 175°F (90°C).

Place the tomatoes in a large casserole dish or braising pot. Sprinkle over the garlic cloves, salt, pepper, and thyme. Cover with enough olive oil to submerge the tomatoes. Place in the oven for at least 4–6

hours—overnight is good—until the tomatoes have poached and absorbed lots of flavor. Remove the tomatoes from the cooking liquid and reserve the oil to use in pasta or in other sauces and dressings. Keep the liquid in an airtight jar in the refrigerator.

For the tartar, cut the whole, confited tomatoes in quarters and de-seed them. Chop the tomato quarters very evenly and finely into ½-inch (1-cm) dice. Add the shallots, chives, lemon juice and zest, and salt and pepper. Add some of the confit olive oil to bind the tartar.

Serve the tartar as a spread or shape it into a quenelle or oval on croutons rubbed with a clove of garlic and sea salt and drizzled with olive oil and a little herbed salad.

SUGGESTED WINE PAIRING

BC: Township 7 Rosé, Naramata
International: Bellevue La Foret Rosé, Cotes du Frontonnais, France

PEELING TOMATOES is easy to do. Bring a large pot of water to the boil. While waiting for the pot to boil, score the bottom of the tomatoes with a X. Plunge the tomatoes into the boiling water for 30 seconds, to just loosen their skins, not to cook them. Plunge the blanched tomatoes into an ice-water bath to loosen the skins further. The skin should peel off easily and can be discarded.

COUNTRY LAMB AND OLIVE TERRINE WITH CELERIAC REMOULADE

Serves 12, generously

FOR THE TERRINE

½ lb (225 g) barding fat (sliced back fat),
    bacon, or caul fat
1 Tbsp (15 mL) butter
1 medium onion, chopped
1 lb (500 g) ground lamb leg (half
    fat–half lean) or cheek meat
½ lb (225 g) ground pork
½ lb (225 g) ground lamb liver or
    chicken livers
2 cloves garlic, finely chopped
¼ tsp (1 mL) allspice
pinch of ground cloves
pinch of freshly ground nutmeg
2 eggs, beaten
¼ cup (60 mL) brandy or cognac
1 Tbsp (15 mL) salt
1 Tbsp (15 mL) white pepper
½ lb (225 g) thick-sliced cooked pickled
    tongue or ham, cut into strips
½ cup (125 mL) kalamata olives, pitted
½ cup (125 mL) pistachios, shelled and
    lightly toasted

FOR THE GARNISH

1 bay leaf
sprig of thyme

FOR THE MAYONNAISE

2 egg yolks
2 tsp (10 mL) white wine vinegar
1 tsp (5 mL) Dijon mustard
salt
freshly ground black pepper
1 cup (250 mL) vegetable oil

FOR THE REMOULADE

½ celeriac, peeled and grated
    juice of 1 lemon
1 Tbsp (15 mL) Dijon mustard
handful fresh flat-leaf parsley, chopped
salt

My chef friend Jason Schubert and I made this recipe with lamb livers we had been given from a whole local lamb. The lamb meat and livers can be substituted with veal or pork cheeks if you like. We served the terrine with celeriac remoulade (shredded raw celery root coated in a rich and tangy mayonnaise) and a pear compote. Celeriac remoulade is a classic accompaniment to any charcuterie.

Line a 9- × 5-inch (2-L) terrine mold or loaf pan with the barding fat, bacon, or caul fat, reserving some for the top (overhanging the sides, to be folded up after). Keep the lined mold cool while preparing the stuffing.

Preheat oven to 350°F (175°C).

If grinding the meat at home, make sure your meat grinder parts and blades are cold, and ensure all meat and fat is cold as well. This will keep the fats

from emulsifying while being ground. To prepare the meat mixture, melt the butter in a small pan and fry the onion slowly until soft but not brown. Remove the pan from the heat and cool slightly. In a bowl, mix together the ground lamb, pork, livers, onions, garlic, spices, eggs, brandy, and salt and pepper. Beat with a wooden spoon to blend in the seasonings. Beat the mixture for 2–3 minutes, until it holds together. To test the seasoning or salt level, fry a small piece of the mixture and taste. Remember that the terrine will be served cold and therefore the perception of salt will be dulled.

To assemble the terrine, spread one-third of the meat mixture in the bottom of the lined terrine, add a layer of half the ham or tongue strips and olives, and top with another layer of stuffing and then with pis-

tachios. Repeat until you have 3 layers of filling and 2 layers of ham or tongue, finishing with the stuffing layer. Fill the mold to the brim, as the terrine will shrink as it cooks. Cover the top of the terrine with the barding fat, bacon, or caul fat overhanging the sides of the terrine mold. Set a bay leaf and thyme sprig in the center of the finished terrine for garnish. Cover the terrine mold with a tight-fitting lid or aluminum foil.

Bake the terrine in a water bath in the oven for 1¼–1½ hours until cooked. Check the internal temperature of the terrine for doneness with a meat thermometer—it should be at least 140°F (60°C) to be cooked through. Do not cook the terrine above 160°F (70°C) or its color will be gray instead of pink. Once cooked, remove the terrine from the water bath and cool. Once cool, put the terrine in the refrigerator and

(continued next page)

(continued from previous page)

press weight it down with a full wine bottle or another heavy pot overnight.

To make the mayonnaise, place the egg yolks, vinegar, mustard, and salt and pepper to taste into a food processor and blend until pale and creamy. With the motor running, pour in enough oil, in a steady stream, until the mayonnaise is thick.

For the remoulade, peel the celeriac and then slice it as thinly as possible using a mandolin if you have one (see page 165). Stack the slices 3 or 4 at a time on top of each other and cut into long, thin julienne strips or matchsticks. Place the celeriac, lemon juice, mustard, seasoning, and parsley in a large bowl. Mix together well and stir in the home-made mayonnaise. Season to taste. Mix to combine and serve.

Let the terrine's flavors mellow in the refrigerator for several days before eating. Serve the terrine in the mold or in slices with celeriac remoulade or with pear compote (see page 174), a small herb salad, and toasted slices of brioche (see page 175).

SUGGESTED WINE PAIRING
BC: Nichol Syrah, Naramata
International: Château Pesquie "Les Terrasses" Côte du Ventoux, Rhone Valley, France

GOAT CHEESE PANNACOTTA

Makes 12 small ramekins

1 cup (250 mL) goat milk
1 cup (250 mL) whipping (35%) cream
1 tsp (5 mL) salt
1 cup (250 mL) fresh goat cheese,
    softened, or goat yogurt

6 sheets gelatin, soaked in cold water,
    or 2 packets powdered gelatin
juice and zest of 1 lemon

This recipe is delicious served with beets. Tangy goat cheese and earthy beets are a marriage made in heaven. "Panna" is Italian for cream and pannacotta is literally cooked cream set with gelatin. This recipe was passed on to me by my chef friend Jason Schubert. He substituted the usual full cream for goat milk and fresh goat cheese and the result is a silky first course that's not too rich and overwhelming. Try to use Carmelis lebane or goat yogurt, which is my preferred cheese, if you can get your hands on some.

Grease 12 small ramekins well with butter and set them on a baking sheet. Combine the milk, cream, and salt in a pot and stir over medium heat until warm. Add the goat cheese to the warm cream, whisking to avoid lumps. Add the gelatin to the pot and stir until the gelatin is dissolved and all the ingredients are well combined. Add the lemon juice and zest. Stir well. Pour the pannacotta liquid into the greased ramekins, cover with plastic wrap, and refrigerate until set, about 2 hours. The longer the better, however.

To serve the pannacotta, use a blow torch to warm the outside of the ramekins to unmold them easily. If you don't have a blow torch, dunk the ramekins into a warm water bath, being careful not to get water inside them. Run a paring knife along the rim of the ramekin when warm. Unmold the pannacotta onto a small plate by flipping the warmed ramekin upside down, and then holding on to the inverted ramekin and plate as one,

give the whole works a shake. The pannacotta should release itself from the ramekin when lifted a little.

Serve with roasted beets sliced into a carpaccio, or Venison Carpaccio with Pickled Beet and Parsley and Onion Salad (see page 178).

SUGGESTED WINE PAIRING
BC: Pentâge Semillon, Penticton
International: Henri Bourgeois "Petit Bourgeois" Sauvignon Blanc, Loire Valley, France

TORTILLA DE PATAS

Serves 4–6

¾ cup (175 mL) extra virgin olive oil
2 onions, finely sliced into half-moons
2 lb (1 kg) yellow-fleshed potatoes (like
   Yukon Gold), peeled and diced

6 fresh large eggs, lightly beaten in
   a large bowl
½ tsp (2 mL) salt
freshly ground black pepper

This first course is a traditional Spanish tapas, but can be served as a first course celebration of our farm-fresh eggs! Essentially a tortilla is a Spanish omelet (not unlike an Italian frittata) but with a different technique. The tucking motion of the edges while the torta cooks is key to the dish. We had a torta battle between two of our students and visiting chef John Taboada over the proper way the potatoes and onions should be prepared for this particular dish. The girls, armed with the knowledge of their Spanish grandmother, won the battle with their perfectly round torta.

Heat the oil in a large frying pan and cook the onions until soft. Add the potatoes and cook over medium heat until almost done but before they begin to brown, about 10 minutes. Break the potatoes up a bit with a spatula, and then transfer to the bowl with the eggs. Stir the potatoes around to cover well with the egg, and season with salt and pepper.

Remove most of the oil from the skillet, leaving only about 1 Tbsp (15 mL). Add the egg mixture, reduce the heat to low, and cook the omelet slowly until golden and firm enough to flip. Keep tucking the edges under with a spatula as the tortilla cooks. Carefully flip the tortilla, slipping it onto another plate if necessary, and cook until done. It should still be soft inside, and about 1 inch (2.5 cm) thick.

Cut the tortilla into wedges and serve immediately, or let cool to room temperature and serve on individual plates.

SUGGESTED WINE PAIRING

BC: La Frenz Alexandria Muscat, Naramata
International: Cameron Winery "Vino Pinko,"
Oregon, USA

SARDINE ESCABECHE

Serves 6

12 whole sardines
1 cup (250 mL) all-purpose flour,
    seasoned with salt, pepper, and
    paprika
½ cup (125 mL) olive oil
½ cup (125 mL) red wine vinegar
1 medium onion, sliced thinly
2-inch (5-cm) strip orange zest

1 sprig fresh thyme
1 sprig fresh rosemary
1 fresh bay leaf
4 garlic cloves, crushed
2 dried red chilies
1 tsp (5 mL) salt
1 small bunch fresh flat-leaf parsley,
    roughly chopped

Escabeche is a traditional Spanish tapas preparation that is essentially hot brine poured over small pan-fried oily fish. This recipe is delicious made with sardines or mackerel. Serve an escabeche as a cold fish course to begin a summer meal.

    Gut, scale, and remove the heads from the sardines and then dust them in the seasoned flour. Fry them in half of the olive oil for 1 minute on each side and then transfer to a shallow dish.

    Add the vinegar, onion, orange zest, thyme, rosemary, bay leaf, garlic, chilies, and salt to a pot, bring the mixture bring to the boil, and simmer for about 15 minutes. Add the parsley and the remaining olive oil. Pour the hot marinade over the sardines and leave until cold.

    To serve, remove the sardines from the marinade. Serve 2 sardines on a small plate with some of the pickled onions from the brine as a first course or put out on a platter with toothpicks for tapas.

SUGGESTED WINE PAIRING
BC: Elephant Island Little King Brut, Naramata
International: Lustau Amontillado Dry Solera Reserva Los Arcos, Jerez Spain

SALT COD FRITTERS

Serves 6

1 lb (500 g) dried salt cod

2 cups (500 mL) whole (3.25%) milk

1 garlic clove, peeled and left whole

1 bay leaf

4 medium white-fleshed potatoes, like
  Russets, skins on

1 Tbsp (15 mL) salt

2 large eggs, beaten slightly

1 medium Spanish onion, finely minced

2 garlic cloves, minced

1 handful fresh flat-leaf parsley,
  finely chopped

salt

freshly ground pepper

8 cups (2 L) vegetable or peanut oil, for
  frying

lemon wedges for garnish

Salt cod fritters are traditional Spanish tapas. They make an excellent first course when served with a small green salad or icy-cold shaved fennel. Note that you need to begin to prepare this dish the day before you plan to eat it.

Starting a day ahead, soak the dried cod in cold water in the refrigerator for 12–24 hours, changing the water several times to remove most of the salt. Drain and rinse the cod, and put it in a large pot. Add the milk and enough water to cover the cod by 1 inch (2.5 cm). Cooking cod in milk keeps it really moist. Add the peeled garlic clove and bay leaf. Simmer gently over medium-low heat for 20–25 minutes, until the cod is tender and pliable. Drain and rinse well, then flake the cod into a bowl with your hands, removing any little bits of skin and bone.

While the cod is simmering in the milk, cover the potatoes with cold water and 1 Tbsp (15 mL) salt and bring to a boil. Simmer the potatoes, covered, until fork-tender. Drain and cool the potatoes slightly under cold running water. While the potatoes are still warm, peel them and press them through a fine mesh sieve or ricer. This will keep them fluffy, and they will not become a gluey mass when processed. Combine the po-

tato, flaked salt cod, beaten eggs, onion, garlic, parsley, and salt and pepper by gently folding together. Do not beat the mixture or it will be gluey. The batter must be stiff enough to form oval shapes with 2 wet spoons. If the batter is too loose, add a little flour.

When ready to serve the salt cod fritters, heat the vegetable oil to 375°F (190°C) in a large heavy pot. Fry a few fritters at a time by spooning an oval of batter into the oil until it floats and turns golden brown. Do not crowd the pot or the temperature of the oil will drop and the fritters will soak up oil. When the fritters are golden, remove them from the oil with a slotted spoon and place onto a paper towel or newspaper and season them with salt. Eat immediately.

Serve 1 salt cod fritter with a small green salad or Shaved Fennel Salad (see page 164) as an appetizer course or serve a few with a larger salad for a nice summer lunch.

SUGGESTED WINE PAIRING

BC: Hawthorne Mountain See Ya Later Brut, Okanagan Falls

International: Masia Vallformosa Cava Brut, Penedes Spain

SALT COD was once one of the most valuable commodities in the world. It was the sustainable protein for most of Europe for about 500 years. Before refrigeration, most of Europe survived on salted, air-dried cod fillets. When used in cooking, salt cod is first soaked to remove much of the salt. It's reconstituted in simmering milk enhanced with garlic and then used a million different ways: as a means of adding salt to food (similar to the way anchovies are used), folded into stews, or mixed with creamy, soft, cooked potatoes.

MARINATED OLIVES

Makes 2 cups (500 mL)

1 tsp (5 mL) chili flakes
1 tsp (5 mL) coriander seeds
1 tsp (5 mL) fennel seeds
½ tsp (2 mL) whole black peppercorns
1 bay leaf, crumbled
1 Tbsp (15 mL) dried oregano

3 cloves garlic, thinly sliced
zest of 1 orange
zest of 1 lemon
½ cup (125 mL) olive oil
2 cups (500 mL) mixed olives

Salty, garlicky marinated olives are the best antipasti or tapa that I can think of to accompany a glass of rosé wine. Make a double batch of these olives and keep them in your fridge at all times. They just get better the longer they sit.

In a mortar and pestle, roughly crush the chili flakes, coriander and fennel seeds, and peppercorns. Put these crushed spices into a large mixing bowl and then add the bay leaf, oregano, garlic, and the orange and lemon zests. Pour over the olive oil and toss with the mixed olives. Refrigerate in an airtight jar for up to 3 months.

FRIED ALMONDS

Makes 1 cup (250 mL) or tapas for 4

1 Tbsp (15 mL) olive oil
1 cup (250 mL) peeled almonds

2 tsp (10 mL) tamari
coarse sea salt

Fried almonds are a savory snack that begs for another aperitif before dinner. The addition of tamari makes these almonds even more mouthwatering.

Heat the olive oil in a frying pan. Add the almonds and move them around the pan constantly for about 1 minute. Be careful not to burn the almonds. They turn golden brown very quickly once the oil is hot and it can be a matter of seconds before they start to burn. When the almonds have browned, sprinkle over the tamari. Let the heat of the almonds and the pan glaze the nuts. Remove the almonds from the frying pan and place on a plate covered with paper towel. Sprinkle with coarse sea salt and leave to cool before eating.

MAIN COURSES

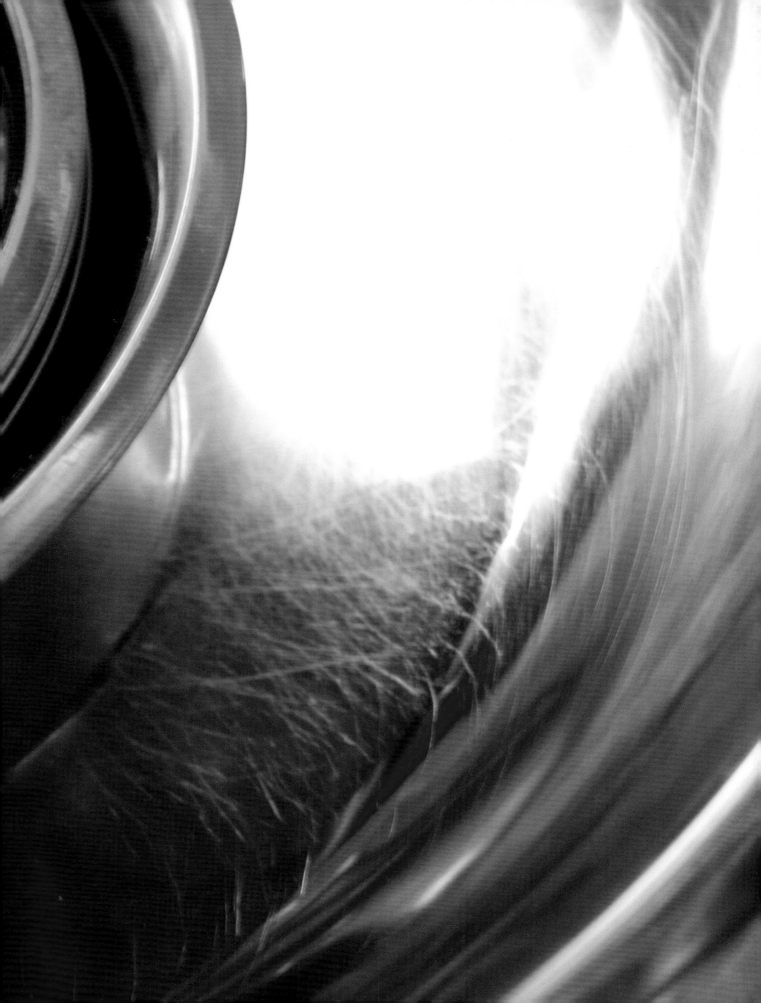

NARAMATA BENCH SYRAH BRAISED OXTAILS

Serves 6

4 Tbsp (60 mL) olive oil
2 cloves garlic, finely chopped
¾ cup (175 mL) onion, cut into ¼-inch
  (0.5-cm) dice
¾ cup (175 mL) carrot, cut into ¼-inch
  (0.5-cm) dice
1½ cups (375 mL) celery, cut into ¼-inch
  (0.5-cm) dice
2½ lb (1.25 kg) oxtail, cut at the natural
  joints

1½ cups (375 mL) full-bodied red
  wine like Merlot or Syrah
1 (14-oz/398-mL) can Italian tomatoes,
  seeded, drained, and coarsely chopped
2 cups (500 mL) beef stock, warm
2 bay leaves
2 sprigs rosemary, tied together
salt
freshly ground pepper
1 bunch parsley, roughly chopped

I love braised oxtails with their sticky braising liquid resulting from the natural cartilage in the tail. I recently had the pleasure of having a (giant) "braised oxtail sandwich" at Seattle's Salumi. I enjoyed it so much that I cooked up a batch of oxtails when I arrived home. It's so much tastier than your average beef stew. Eat the oxtails on the bone with wide herbed egg noodles in their own juice or as a ragù in a sandwich that would make any meatball envious!

Preheat oven to 300°F (150°C).

Heat 2 Tbsp (30 mL) of the olive oil in a large heavy-bottomed ovenproof pot. Add the garlic, onion, carrot, and celery. Sauté over medium heat, stirring frequently, until the vegetables are lightly caramelized.

In a separate pan, heat the remaining olive oil over medium-high heat. Add some of the oxtail pieces and season. Brown the oxtails on all sides for about 8 minutes. The oxtails will have to be sealed in several batches since overcrowding causes the meat to steam rather than seal. Be careful not to burn the bottom of the pans as they will be deglazed after sealing the oxtails. As the pieces of oxtail are browned, put them in the large pot, uncovered, on top of the sautéed vegetables. Deglaze the sauté pans with the red wine to remove any caramelized bits. Pour the wine from the pans into the pot with the oxtails and vegetables. Add

the tomatoes, warm beef stock, bay leaves, and rosemary sprigs and season with salt and pepper. Over medium heat, bring the pot to a simmer. Cover and place in the oven. Cook for 2½–3 hours, turning the oxtails once during cooking. When done, the meat should be very tender and fall easily off the bone.

Transfer the oxtails and vegetables to another pot and cover to keep warm. Return the braising liquid left in the pan to the heat. With a ladle, skim off any excess fat and reduce over medium heat to concentrate the flavors. When you have reached the desired consistency for the sauce, season to taste with salt and pepper. Add the chopped parsley and serve.

To serve, ladle the reduced braising liquid over the oxtails and serve with wide egg noodles with butter and herbs. You can also take the oxtail meat off the bones and shred it. Place the shredded oxtail meat in the reduced braising liquid and you now have a delicious ragù to eat with garlic toast or in a long baguette sandwich in place of meatballs.

SUGGESTED WINE PAIRING
BC: La Frenz Shiraz "Reserve," Naramata
Internatational: Paolo Scavino "Bric del Fiasc"
Barolo, Piedmont, Italy

BOEUF BONNE FEMME

Serves 4

4 Tbsp (60 mL) unsalted butter
¼ lb (125 g) smoked bacon, cut into
   strips or lardons
16 pearl onions, peeled
1 lb (500 g) brown mushrooms
1 cup (250 mL) carrots, cut into 2-inch
   (5-cm) pieces
2 small garlic cloves, peeled and crushed
1 lb (500 g) beef shank, shin, or shoulder,
   cut into 1-inch (2.5-cm) cubes

salt
freshly ground pepper
2 cups (250 mL) red wine
2 cups (250 mL) brown veal stock
2 Tbsp (30 mL) all-purpose flour
1 tsp (5 mL) tomato paste
1 bouquet garni (bay leaves, thyme, leek,
   black peppercorn, and 3 cloves
   wrapped in a leek leaf)

This is a classic French bistro stew that I like to make when the weather begins to turn cold. "Bonne Femme" is a term that refers to comforting home cooking that your grandma or "good wife" would make. Does anyone know where I can find myself a French wife? She sure would be handy around the farm and during harvest to feed us. Résumés at Joie are always welcome . . . I remember teaching this recipe to one of my all-time favorite students, Lanny Mann. I wonder if I could tempt Lanny out of retirement to come cook for us. I sure hope he's cooking this recipe for his "good wife" Kathy.

Melt the butter in a large heavy-bottomed pot over medium heat. Add the bacon and cook it over medium heat until it begins to turn golden. Add the onions, mushrooms, and carrots and cook for 3 minutes until the onions begin to soften and the mushroom begin to brown. Now add the garlic.

Transfer the bacon, onions, mushrooms, carrots, and garlic to a clean pot and cover to keep warm. Increase the heat to high, season the cubes of beef, and then add them to the original pot to brown on all sides. You may have to do this in several batches as overcrowding will cause the meat to steam rather than seal. Transfer the meat to the pot containing the bacon and vegetables, leaving as much fat as possible in the bottom of the pot. Keep the meat and vegetables warm.

Combine the wine and stock and gently warm through. Over medium heat, stir the flour into the pot that the meat was browned in and cook until it begins to turn a light brown. If there's not enough fat to make a roux, add some more butter. Stir in the tomato paste. Add the warmed wine and stock mixture, little by little, whisking constantly.

Bring to a boil, stirring if necessary. Strain this mixture through a fine mesh sieve over the meat and vegetables and add the bouquet garni. Bring to a boil, cover, and simmer for about 1½–2 hours. When done, the meat will be very tender.

Remove the meat, bacon, and onions from the pot and keep warm in the oven, tenting the pot with aluminum foil. The meat will stay moist if it's covered with a little of the cooking liquid. Strain the cooking liquid through a fine mesh sieve into a clean saucepan. If necessary, reduce the cooking liquid until it's well flavored and slightly thickened. Return the meat, bacon, and onions to the liquid and gently warm through. Check the seasoning and adjust to taste.

To serve, place a portion of the stew on a warm plate or in a shallow bowl and serve with some crusty bread and good butter.

SUGGESTED WINE PAIRING
BC: Laughing Stock "Portfolio" Meritage, Naramata
International: Benziger "Tribute" Meritage, Sonoma, California

VENISON TENDERLOIN STUFFED WITH CHANTERELLE MUSHROOMS WITH A CASSIS JUS

Serves 4

FOR THE VENISON

2 large (1.5-lb/750-g) venison tenderloins
7 oz (200 g) (about 12 slices) thinly sliced prosciutto
6 leaves Swiss chard, stems removed, leaves blanched and refreshed
2 Tbsp (30 mL) vegetable oil

FOR THE MUSHROOMS

1 Tbsp (15 mL) butter
2 large shallots, finely diced
1 lb (500 g) fresh chanterelle mushrooms (or a mixture of other fresh wild mushrooms)
¼ cup (60 mL) white wine
1 Tbsp (15 mL) tamari or soy sauce
¼ cup (60 mL) finely sliced fresh chives
juice and zest of 1 lemon

FOR THE CASSIS JUS

1 tsp (5 mL) unsalted butter
1 shallot, finely minced
1 carrot
1 bay leaf
1 tsp (5 mL) tomato paste
1 cup (250 mL) Elephant Island cassis
3 cups (750 mL) dark reduced veal stock
1 clove garlic
1 sprig thyme

I made this dish the summer that my chef friends Cam and Dana Ewart arrived from the coast with a giant box of chanterelle mushrooms they'd picked. Being obsessed with the ballottine and stuffing things into boned-out meat, I of course butterflied some delicious venison tenderloins that Richard Ynetma sent me from his fallow deer farm in Enderby. I finished the dish with a reduction of cassis from our neighbors at Elephant Island Orchard Winery. Butterflying tenderloin is an excellent way to make a cherished, expensive piece of meat go a long way.

Prepare the venison tenderloins by taking a whole loin and butterflying it into a flat piece. Do this by making an incision along the length of the loin halfway through its thickness. Once the initial cut has been made, make pockets on either side of the incision that open up the meat toward the cutting board. Keep making these "pocket cuts" until the tenderloin lies flat. Line a piece of plastic wrap with the thin prosciutto slices and place the flattened tenderloins on top. Season well with salt and pepper.

A BALLOTTINE is a rolled piece of lean meat that is usually stuffed with something fatty and then barded or wrapped with something else fatty to keep a lean bird, like pheasant, moist. Ballottines are meant to be sliced to display the stuffing inside.

Prepare the Swiss chard by blanching it in a pot of boiling water and refreshing it in an ice-water bath or under cold running water. Pat dry and lay out in large pieces on a kitchen towel to dry. When the leaves are dry, place them over the tenderloins to cover the meat.

For the mushrooms, heat the butter in a frying pan over medium heat. Sauté the shallots until softened and then add the mushrooms. Cook down the mushrooms until they begin to caramelize slightly and then deglaze the pan with the wine and the tamari. Simmer the mushrooms until the wine mixture glazes the mushrooms. Cool this mixture slightly by spreading it out on an unlined baking sheet.

Once the mushroom mixture is cool, place half the mixture (in the first one-third of the loin, closest to you) on each of the chard-lined tenderloins. Begin to roll the tenderloin into a large log, being careful to keep the mushroom mixture in the log. Keep the log tight by cinching it with the plastic wrap. Think of rolling a giant maki roll, if you've ever hand-rolled sushi. Peel the plastic wrap away from the log and tie the prosciutto-wrapped venison loin with butcher's twine to keep it intact while cooking.

Prepare the jus by heating a saucepan over medium heat and adding the butter, shallot, carrot, and bay leaf. Sauté the vegetables until slightly caramelized and then add the tomato paste to coat. Deglaze the pot with the cassis. Reduce the cassis with the vegetables to a syrup. Once reduced, add the veal stock, bring to a boil, lower the temperature to a slow simmer, and reduce again by half. Let the veal stock reduce while the venison is cooking. To serve the sauce, strain through a fine mesh sieve into a clean saucepan and adjust the seasoning if necessary.

Preheat oven or barbecue to 400°F (200°C).

Heat a cast-iron frying pan with the vegetable oil and sear the venison log on each side until slightly golden and firm. Finish cooking the tied loin on the upper rack of the barbecue or in the oven on a rack for about 15 minutes. To judge the doneness of the log, give it a poke. It should be fairly firm to the touch, not soft. Let the log rest, uncovered, for 5 minutes in a warm place before you slice into it.

To serve, I slice the log into beautiful medallions, crispy on the outside and full of chanterelles on the inside. Cut the log into 2-inch (5-cm) thick slices with a sharp knife. The slices can be laid out on a plate and finished with a ladle of jus overtop. Serve the venison with du Puy lentils for an earthy dish with the mushrooms or with a creamy potato gratin.

SUGGESTED WINE PAIRING
BC: Le Vieux Pin "Apogée" Merlot, Oliver
International: Bava "Stradivario" Barbera d'Asti, Piedmont, Italy

ROASTED LEG OF LAMB STUFFED WITH ORANGE ZEST, BLACK OLIVES, AND BASIL WITH ANCHOVY AIOLI

Serves 6

FOR THE LAMB

1 4–6-lb (2.5-kg) leg of lamb, bone-out and butterflied

1 tsp (5 mL) black peppercorns

2 Tbsp (30 mL) fresh rosemary, taken off its stocks

1 large bunch of basil

zest of 2 oranges

zest of 1 lemon

4 cloves garlic, peeled

1 cup (250 mL) kalamata olives or sun-cured black olives, pitted and roughly chopped

1 anchovy fillet, de-boned

1 Tbsp (15 mL) olive oil

1 Tbsp (15 mL) coarse sea salt or kosher salt

freshly ground pepper

FOR THE AIOLI

juice of 2 lemons

1 large egg yolk

1 cup (250 mL) olive oil

1 cup (250 mL) grapeseed oil

½ clove garlic, minced

1 tsp (5 mL) anchovy paste

3 Tbsp (45 mL) water (for lengthening out the aioli)

salt

freshly ground pepper

I like to serve this dish with panisse (fried chickpea fritters). They're fantastic for dipping into the aioli. The earthy flavor of the anchovy is a perfect complement to the savory lamb. I even enjoy serving this dish as cold sliced lamb with crusty bread to make sandwiches with the aioli.

Preheat oven to 425°F (220°C).

Wash the lamb and pat it dry; a dry skin will ensure crispiness. Score the fat slightly. Run a boning or paring knife along and around the shank bone to make a deep pocket in which to stuff the aromatics. Run your finger into the pocket to make it deeper.

Grind together the peppercorns, rosemary, basil, orange and lemon zests, garlic, olives, anchovy, and oil into a rough paste in a mortar and pestle. Stuff the paste into the cavity you made along the bone or stuff the butterflied leg, roll it back up, and tie the roast with butcher's twine. The stuffing will flavor the meat from the inside out.

Rub the outside of the lamb leg generously with coarse sea salt and freshly ground pepper.

Place the leg in the oven, preferably right on to one of the racks to ensure that the heat will circulate

all the way around the roast, cooking it evenly and forming a crust on the outside. Place a roasting pan under the roast to catch all the fat and cooking juices. If you're not comfortable with this method, place the lamb on a rack or a trivet for an admittedly less messy approach! You can also use a rotisserie on the barbecue or oven for terrific results.

Cook the meat for about 15 minutes to seal, and then lower the heat to 350°F (180°C) for the remainder of the cooking time, about 1 hour for medium-rare lamb. Note: lamb is cooked best at this degree of doneness.

Meanwhile, prepare the aioli. Add a few drops of lemon juice to the egg yolk. Add the oil very slowly, drop by drop, to start the emulsification process between the oil and the yolk, whisking constantly. As the yolk and oil start to come together and thicken slightly as you whisk, add the minced garlic and anchovy paste, as well as a pinch of salt and some pepper (it's important to season as you go along). Continue to add the oil

in a slow stream, whisking constantly. Begin to alternate adding the lemon juice, oil, and water to lengthen out the aioli. The finished product should be more like a thick sauce than a mayonnaise. Check the seasoning of the finished aioli and add more salt or lemon juice and zest if necessary. Keep the aioli in the refrigerator until the lamb is ready to be served.

When the lamb has reached an internal temperature of 135°F (57°C) at its thickest part, take it out of the oven and rest for 15 minutes in a warm place so its internal juices can recirculate and will not run out when the roast is carved). Serve the lamb slices with a side of panisse (see page 264) and a generous dollop of aioli for dipping.

SUGGESTED WINE PAIRING
BC: Pentâge "Pentâge," Penticton
International: Le Vieux Donjon Chateauneuf du Pape, Rhone Valley, France

AUTUMN ROASTED LEG OF LAMB STUFFED WITH CHESTNUTS, CURRANTS, AND CHANTERELLES WITH PAN JUS

Serves 6

FOR THE STUFFING

1 lb (500 g) fresh chestnuts, shelled and peeled, chopped coarse, or ¾ lb (375 g) vacuum-packed whole chestnuts or rehydrated dried chestnuts, chopped coarse (about 2 cups/500 mL)

2 large shallots, finely diced

4 Tbsp (60 mL) olive oil

2 cloves garlic, finely chopped

1 Tbsp (15 mL) fresh thyme, finely chopped

¼ lb (125 g) fresh chanterelles, cut in quarters if they are large, left whole if they're tiny

½ cup (125 mL) white or rosé wine

zest of 1 lemon

½ cup (125 mL) currants, plumped in 2 cups (500 mL) hot water

FOR THE LAMB

1 leg of lamb (about 4 lb/2 kg), de-boned and fat side scored

salt

freshly ground black pepper

2 carrots, cut into large chunks

1 onion, halved

2 celery ribs, cut into large chunks

1 bulb garlic, skin on

1 bay leaf

olive oil for the roasting pan

1 cup (250 mL) lamb stock

sherry vinegar

This gorgeous leg of lamb combines my favorite fall flavors. When sliced, the boneless leg of lamb reveals its marbled chestnut, chanterelle, and currant stuffing. Serve this dish with a potato gratin (page 254) or Boulanger potatoes (see page 257).

Prepare the chestnuts by cutting an X on the round side of each chestnut. Spread them in 1 layer on a baking pan, add ¼ cup (60 mL) water, and bake for 10 minutes, or until the shells open. Remove the chestnuts, a handful at a time, and shell and peel them while they are still hot.

Sauté the shallots in the oil in a large frying pan and add the garlic, thyme, and mushrooms. Sauté until the mushrooms are slightly golden and have released all their juices. Deglaze the pan with the wine and simmer until the wine and mushroom juices have glazed the mushrooms. Add the lemon zest, coarsely chopped chestnuts, and plumped currants. Let the stuffing cool slightly.

Preheat oven to 450°F (230°C).

Take the lamb and place it fat side down on a cutting board, making sure the inside is well seasoned with salt and pepper. Put the stuffing in the middle of the leg along its whole length. Start rolling the lamb from 1 side to the other. Tie with 6 separate pieces of string along the length of the rolled-up leg.

Roughly chop the carrots, onion, and celery and break up the bulb of garlic. Put all the vegetables and bay leaf into the center of the roasting pan and drizzle some oil overtop. Drizzle the lamb roll with more olive oil. Season again with salt and pepper and place on top of the vegetables in the roasting dish. Place the roasting pan in the oven. Cook for half an hour, lower the temperature to 350°F (180°C), and cook for a further half hour. Baste the lamb as it roasts to make it golden. Add the stock into the bottom of the roasting pan and cook another 15 minutes.

Take the roast out of the oven and let rest, uncovered, in a warm place for 15 minutes and then remove the string. While the roast is resting, take the roasting pan with its pan juices and strain into a pot through a fine mesh sieve, making sure to push the roasted garlic through the sieve. Bring the pan jus to a boil and let it reduce slightly. Adjust the seasoning of the jus if necessary with salt and pepper and a bit of sherry vinegar.

Slice the roast into medallions to show off the beautiful stuffing inside and serve with the natural gravy from the roasting dish.

SUGGESTED WINE PAIRING
BC: Herder "Josephine" Meritage, Cawston
International: Quinta do Vale Donna Maria, Douro, Portugal

BRAISED ENDERBY LAMB SHANKS

Serves 6–8

FOR THE BRAISE

2 Tbsp (30 mL) vegetable oil

1 cup (250 mL) onion, cut into ¼-inch (0.5-cm) dice

¾ cup (175 mL) carrot, cut into ¼-inch (0.5-cm) dice

½ cup (125 mL) celery, cut into ¼-inch (0.5-cm) dice

2 Tbsp (30 mL) unsalted butter

3 cloves garlic, finely chopped

2 strips lemon peel

1 strip orange peel

8 lamb shanks, 1¼-inch (3-cm) thick, tied round with string

salt

freshly ground pepper

1 cup (250 mL) dry red wine

1½ cups (375 mL) dark lamb (or veal) stock

1½ cups (375 mL) canned Italian tomatoes, coarsely chopped, with their juice

6 dried porcini mushrooms, rehydrated in 2 cups (500 mL) boiling water

2 sprigs thyme

1 sprig rosemary

2 bay leaves

½ cup (125 mL) sherry vinegar

¼ cinnamon stick (optional)

FOR THE GREMOLATA

½ bunch flat-leaf parsley, roughly chopped

1 bunch basil, roughly chopped

1 bunch mint, roughly chopped

zest of 1 lemon

½ tsp (2 mL) sea salt

1 tsp (5 mL) coarsely cracked black pepper

GREMOLATA is a traditional accompaniment to the Italian dish osso buco (veal shanks). Typically, it contains garlic, parsley, and grated lemon peel. It may also be eaten as an accompaniment to buttered noodles and green vegetables like beans. Some recipes add mint leaves to the typical gremolata, which makes it a better accompaniment for lamb. I find a gremolata mixture is a fresh way to finish a heavy, braised dish.

I love eating braised lamb shanks in the winter. It's a dish that just gets better all week long. You can serve the braised lamb shanks on the bone or you can shred the meat and eat it as a ragù. This recipe also works well with veal shanks if you want to make osso bucco.

Preheat oven to 300°F (150°C).

Heat 1 Tbsp (15 mL) of the vegetable oil over medium heat in the large pot that will be used for braising. Add the diced onion, carrot, and celery and cook until the vegetables are lightly browned. Add the chopped garlic and lemon and orange peel and continue to sauté for 1 more minute. Once the vegetables are lightly browned, remove the pot from the heat.

Season the shanks with salt and pepper on both sides. Heat the remaining oil in a cast-iron frying pan over medium-high heat. When the oil is hot, but not smoking, brown the lamb on all sides. It may be necessary to brown the shanks in batches, as overcrowding the pan will cause the meat to steam, rather than seal. Stand the shanks side by side on top of the vegetables in the braising dish.

Remove the fat from the sauté pans and set the pans over high heat. Deglaze the pans with the wine and boil briskly for about 3 minutes. With a whisk, loosen any caramelized bits from the bottom of the pans. Strain this liquid through a fine mesh sieve over the lamb shanks in the pot. In the same pan, bring the stock to a simmer and add the canned tomatoes with their juice, the porcini mushrooms and rehydrating liquid, thyme, rosemary, and bay leaves, and return to a simmer. Season to taste with salt and pepper. Pour into the braising dish containing the lamb and vegetables. Bring the entire contents of the braise to a simmer on the stovetop over medium-high heat. Cover tightly with aluminum foil and cook in the oven for 3–4 hours, basting and flipping the shanks only once during cooking. If the shanks are handled too much the meat may fall away from the bone. When done, the shanks should be very tender when pierced with a fork.

For the gremolata, combine the parsley, basil, mint, lemon zest, salt, and pepper together in a bowl.

Remove the shanks from the pot, remove the string, and then place the shanks in a dish and cover to keep warm. Remove the flavoring vegetables from the pot and add them to the dish with the lamb shanks, making sure to discard the bay leaf and herbs. Reduce the braising liquid by half to thicken the sauce. Add the sherry vinegar to the reduced sauce to balance its flavors. Season to taste with salt and pepper.

When ready to serve, return the lamb shanks and the flavoring vegetables to the pot with the reduced braising liquid in it, back to the heat. Skim any excess fat from the top. Adjust seasoning to taste. Place a lamb shank on a warm place or in a shallow bowl. Ladle some of the braising liquid over the shank. Sprinkle the gremolata overtop each portion.

SUGGESTED WINE PAIRING
BC: Osoyoos Larose Meritage, Osoyoos
International: Aldo Conterno "Il Favot" Langhe, Piedmont, Italy

NAVARIN PRINTANIER

Serves 8

FOR THE NAVARIN

2 Tbsp (30 mL) unsalted butter

2 Tbsp (30 mL) vegetable oil

2.5 lb (1.25 kg) boneless lamb leg or
    shoulder, cut into 1-inch (2-cm) cubes

salt

freshly ground pepper

2 carrots, peeled and quartered

2 onions, peeled and quartered

2 tsp (10 mL) sugar

1 cup (250 mL) white wine

4 cups (1 L) lamb stock, warm

4 garlic cloves, peeled and left whole

1 bouquet garni with bay leaf, thyme,
    rosemary, and black peppercorns tied
    in a leek green

1 28-oz (796-mL) can plum tomatoes
    with juice, roughly chopped

FOR THE SPRING VEGETABLE GARNISH

16 pearl onions or baby garlic cloves,
    peeled

1 lb (500 g) small new potatoes, skin on
    and cut into 1-inch (2-cm) pieces

1 lb (500 g) baby turnips, cut into 1-inch
    (2-cm) pieces

1 lb (500 g) baby carrots, cut into 1-inch
    (2-cm) pieces

balsamic vinegar or lemon juice to finish

½ lb (250 g) green beans, cut into 1-inch
    (2-cm) pieces

1 cup (250 g) fresh shelled peas or fava
    beans

FOR GARNISH

finely chopped chervil and chives

fresh mint leaves

Navarin is a classic fresh bistro stew and "printanier" means spring, hence the use of first lamb and baby spring vegetables and herbs of the year in this dish.

Melt the butter and oil in the bottom of a heavy-bottomed pot set over medium heat. Season the lamb with salt and pepper and seal the lamb in the pan. It may be necessary to do this in several batches as overcrowding will cause the meat to steam rather than seal. Remove the lamb from the pan and reserve in a warm place.

Add the peeled and quartered carrots and onions and cook until they begin to color. Remove the vegetables and return the lamb to the pot. Sprinkle with the sugar and allow it to caramelize. The caramelized sugar will give the finished sauce a glossier finish and a slight sweetness. Once the sugar has caramelized, return the vegetables and deglaze the pan (see page 150) with the white wine.

Slowly add the warm stock to the pan and bring to a simmer. Add the garlic, bouquet garni, and tomatoes. Simmer the stew for 45 minutes–1 hour (longer if using lamb shoulder), until the meat is tender.

Remove the lamb from the pot with a slotted spoon and place into a clean pot. Reduce the sauce and the flavoring vegetables left in the pot until it thickens slightly. This is an excellent way to thicken a stew without using flour. It is healthier and will result in a cleaner- and fresher-flavored stew. When the sauce has reduced by half, strain it through a fine mesh sieve into the pot with the lamb pieces, discarding any flavoring vegetables left in the sieve. Add the spring vegetable garnish of onions or baby garlic, potatoes, turnips, and carrots and cook until the vegetables are tender.

To finish the navarin, ensure that the sauce is well flavored. Add a little vinegar or lemon juice and some salt to season. Just before serving, add the beans and peas and cook until they are tender and bright green.

To serve, place some stew in warm, shallow bowls, evenly distributing the vegetables and meat. Garnish with the chervil, chives, and mint.

SUGGESTED WINE PAIRING

BC: Twisted Tree Syrah, Osoyoos
International: Chateau St. Cosme Cotes du Rhone, Rhone Valley, France

SPANISH ROAST PORK LOIN
IN FENNEL SAUCE

Serves 8

FOR THE PORK

2 Tbsp (30 mL) chopped fresh rosemary
4 garlic cloves, chopped
1 tsp (5 mL) freshly ground black pepper
1 tsp (5 mL) fennel seeds
salt
1 3-lb (1.5-kg) loin of pork, chined
   (backbone removed) and then cut
   between the backbone and ribs,
   creating a pocket)
1 Tbsp (15 mL) unsalted butter
2 Tbsp (30 mL) extra virgin olive oil

FOR THE FENNEL SAUCE

¼ cup (60 mL) unsalted butter
1 fennel bulb, sliced
salt
½ cup (125 mL) whole (3.5%) milk
1 cup (250 mL) white wine

This recipe is yet another classic combination of pork and fennel. The sauce, however, is a distinctly Spanish preparation as it uses milk in the emulsification of the sauce. This delicious recipe was taught at Joie by chef John Taboada of Navarre Restaurant in Portland. We paired it with my recipe for Moorish Rice Pilaf (see page 251) for a dish that John said his Spanish grandmother would be proud of.

Prepare the pork by mixing together the rosemary, garlic, pepper, fennel seeds, and salt to taste. Stuff this mixture into the pocket you made between the backbone and ribs. Tie the meat and bone together with butcher's twine.

Preheat oven to 350°F (180°C).

In a roasting pan, melt the butter with the olive oil over low heat. Add the meat, seal the loin, and transfer to the oven. Roast for about 1½ hours, basting occasionally. Alternatively, roast the loin on a rotisserie and it will baste itself as it cooks.

Meanwhile, prepare the fennel sauce. In a small pot melt 1 tsp (5 mL) of the butter. Add the sliced fennel, salt to taste, and a little water, enough to just cover the bottom of the pan. Cover and cook over low heat until the fennel is tender, about 10 minutes. Pour the contents of the pot into a blender with the rest of the butter and the milk. Process until very smooth.

Rest the meat for about 15 minutes in a warm place. Carve the loin by cutting in between the ribs and arrange the slices on a warm platter. Keep warm. Pour off the fat from the roasting pan. Deglaze the cooking juices, with the white wine over medium heat, scraping the pan well (see page 150). Bring to a boil and cook for a couple of minutes. Do not stir. Add the fennel sauce and stir well. Pour the sauce through a fine mesh sieve over the meat and serve piping hot.

SUGGESTED WINE PAIRING

BC: Mount Boucherie "Summit" Syrah, Westbank
International: Teofilo Reyes Tinto Crianza, Ribera del Duero, Spain

BRAISED BOAR CHEEKS WITH
APEX MOUNTAIN BOLETUS MUSHROOMS

Serves 6–8

3 Tbsp (45 mL) pure olive oil
1 cup (250 mL) onion, cut into ¼-inch
  (0.5-cm) dice
¾ cup (175 mL) carrot, cut into ¼-inch
  (0.5-cm) dice
½ cup (125 mL) celery, cut into ¼-inch
  (0.5-cm) dice
6 cloves garlic, finely chopped
8 large cheeks of boar, veal, or lamb,
  your preference
salt

freshly ground pepper
1 cup (250 mL) dry red wine
½ lb (250 g) dried porcini mushrooms,
  rehydrated in 2 cups (500 mL) boiling
  water
1½ cups (375 mL) pork or veal
  stock (chicken is fine, too)
1 cup (250 mL) unfiltered apple juice
2 sprigs thyme
2 bay leaves
½ cup (250 mL) sherry vinegar

I love any kind of cheek meat: boar cheeks, lamb cheeks, veal cheeks, halibut cheeks . . . Cheeks come from, as you would imagine, the jowl of an animal. They're all collagen and melt down when braised into tender pieces of meat surrounded by a sticky, jammy sauce. In winter I serve the cheek meat with a creamy potato gratin, and in summer, I omit the starch and serve the boar cheek as a ragù on top of a sauté of oyster mushrooms and green beans with bacon, finished with some grainy mustard for a lighter summer dish.

Preheat oven to 300°F (150°C).

Heat 1 Tbsp (15 mL) of the olive oil over medium-high heat in the pot you will be using to braise the meat. Add the diced onion, carrot, and celery and cook until the vegetables are lightly browned. Add the chopped garlic and continue to sauté for 1 more minute. Once the vegetables are lightly browned, remove the pot from the heat.

While the vegetables are browning, heat the vegetable oil in a cast-iron frying pan over medium-high heat to seal the cheek meat. It may be necessary to brown the cheeks in batches, as overcrowding the pan will cause the meat to steam, rather than seal. When the cheeks are browned, transfer them to the pot containing the now caramelized vegetables. Remove the fat from the sauté pans used to sear the cheeks and place the pans over high heat. Deglaze the pans with the wine (see page 150) and boil briskly for about 3 minutes. Use a whisk to loosen any caramelized bits from the bottom of the pans. Add the porcini mushrooms plus their hydrating liquid, stock, apple juice,

thyme, and bay leaves. Bring the whole mixture to a boil. Strain this liquid through a fine meshed sieve over the cheeks in the pot. Season to taste with salt and pepper. Bring the entire contents of the braise to a simmer on the stovetop. Cover tightly with aluminum foil and cook for 3–4 hours, basting and flipping the cheeks only once during cooking. When done, the cheek meat should feel very tender when pierced with a fork.

To serve, remove the cheeks from the pot and spread out on a baking sheet to cool. When cooled enough to shred, but still warm, break apart the cheek meat with your hands. Reserve the meat and keep warm. Remove the flavoring vegetables from the pot, especially the porcini mushrooms, and reserve. Discard the bay leaf and thyme. Reduce the braising liquid by half to thicken the sauce. Add the sherry vinegar to balance the flavors of the reduced sauce and season to taste with salt and pepper.

When ready to serve, transfer the cheek meat and the flavoring vegetables to the pot with the reduced braising liquid in it, and heat through. Skim off any excess fat from the top. Adjust seasoning to taste. Serve the cheek meat, bound together by the sauce, with a sauté of green beans, mushrooms, and bacon or a creamy potato pavé.

SUGGESTED WINE PAIRING
BC: Golden Mile Pinot Noir, Oliver
International: Castello di Quercetto Chianti Classico,
Tuscany, Italy

CHOUCROUTE GARNI

Serves 6

FOR THE CHOUCROUTE

1 Tbsp (15 mL) rendered duck or goose fat

½ cup (125 mL) smoked bacon, cut into thin lardons or strips

2 cups (500 mL) peeled and thinly sliced onions

1 medium onion, left whole

4 whole cloves

1 tsp (5 mL) mustard seeds

1 tsp (5 mL) coriander seeds

½ tsp (2 mL) white pepper

2 juniper berries, crushed

1 Tbsp (15 mL) cassia bark or broken up cinnamon stick

4 cups (1 L) Riesling or other aromatic white wine

2 cups (500 mL) drained sauerkraut

1 bay leaf

TO FINISH

A selection of fine German or Alsatian charcuterie:

1 lb (500 g) smoked pork loin

3 knackwurst

3 fresh weisswurst

½ lb (250 g) Polish kielbasa

1 smoked pork hock

½ lb (250 g) slab bacon

4 legs of duck confit (or crisped goose breasts if you have roasted a goose for the fat)

1 lb (500 g) goose liver sausage or liverwurst

1 lb (500 g) new potatoes, skin left on

I've been known to roast a goose before making choucroute just so I could have the goose fat for braising the sauerkraut. I use the remaining roasted goose breasts to top the choucroute platter along with the sausages and smoked porky treats. Roasting a whole goose is not necessary, however, as using rendered duck fat will do. You can buy this at any good charcuterie or German deli. I like visiting Oyama Meats at Granville Island in Vancouver as they not only sell duck fat but also have a dreamy selection of sausages and pork "garni." Having choucroute garni is an event—invite your friends! Tell them to bring a bottle of great Alsatian Riesling and their appetites!

Preheat oven to 350°F (180°C).

Melt the duck fat in a large pot over medium heat. Sauté the bacon and onions for about 10 minutes, or until the bacon is cooked and the onions are transparent. Stud the whole onion with the cloves and put the mustard seeds, coriander seeds, white pepper, juniper berries, and cassia bark into a spice grinder and grind into a fine powder. Add the wine, sauerkraut, bay leaf, studded whole onion, and ground spices to the pot and bring it to a simmer over medium heat. Cover and bake in the oven for 1 hour or until all the liquid is absorbed. Discard the bay leaf and

then season to taste with salt and more freshly ground white pepper.

Remove the pot from the oven and add the piece of pork loin, sausages, and slab bacon. Cover the meats with the now Riesling-braised choucroute. Cook for another half an hour, or until the pork loin is cooked and the sausages are heated through. Finish the breasts and the goose liver sausage in a frying pan and add to the other charcuterie on top of the sauerkraut.

While the meats are in the final stage of cooking, boil the new potatoes and keep them warm until needed.

Drain the sauerkraut, removing the herbs and spices, and mound it in the center of a large, warm platter. Slice the sausages, pork loin, and bacon and place around the sauerkraut. Add the crisped goose breasts or crisped duck confit and the soft pâté–like sausage. Arrange the boiled new potatoes around the sauerkraut. Serve a variety of mustards with the choucroute. Allow each person to serve themselves a portion.

SUGGESTED WINE PAIRING

BC: Joie "A Noble Blend," Naramata
International: Domaine Marcel Deiss Engelgarten Bergheim, Alsace, France

CRISPY PORK BELLY BRAISED IN JOIE'S ORCHARD APPLE JUICE

Serves 8

FOR THE BELLY
5 lb (2.2 kg) pork belly
1 Tbsp (15 mL) coriander seed
1 Tbsp (15 mL) fennel seed
1 tsp (5 mL) chili flakes
1 whole star anise
¼ cup (60 mL) sugar
¼ cup (60 mL) salt

FOR THE BRAISE
1 Tbsp (15 mL) vegetable oil
6 garlic cloves, peeled and left whole
salt
freshly ground pepper
1 medium onion, finely chopped
2 celery ribs, chopped
2 carrots, peeled and chopped
1 cup (250 mL) white wine
1 cup (250 mL) pork or chicken stock, warm
2 cups (500 mL) unfiltered apple juice or fresh cider, warm
4 sprigs fresh thyme, tied together

¼ cup (60 mL) sherry or apple cider vinegar

This delicious dish is irresistible with its melting, crispy skin and fork-tender belly meat. It's wonderful served on top of braised purple cabbage or melted Savoy cabbage with a tangy sauce made from a reduction of its braising juices. I make this dish to celebrate the wonderful bellies that arrive from the two pigs I buy from Crannòg Brewery every year. They eat nothing but spent beer mash from the brewery. Pork bellies are easily found at Asian grocery stores or Chinatown butcher shops.

Begin your preparations the day before you're going to serve the pork belly. Trim the fat cap from the belly, leaving only ½ inch (1 cm) of fat. Score this remaining fat. Lightly toast the coriander seeds, fennel seeds, chili flakes, and star anise in a dry pan and then coarsely grind them with the sugar and salt in a spice grinder or in a mortar and pestle. Rub this spice mixture into the pork, both front and back. Put the belly onto a wire rack and leave uncovered in the refrigerator overnight.

The following day, scrape the spices off the fat side of pork and rinse the whole belly with cold water. Pat the belly dry and season well with salt and pepper.

To prepare the braise, heat a large, heavy frying pan over medium heat and add the vegetable oil and the belly to the hot pan, fat side down. When the fat is nicely browned, transfer the pork to a casserole or roasting pan, fat side up.

Preheat oven to 300°F (150°C).

Pour off most of the fat from the frying pan in which the belly was seared. Add the garlic, onion, celery, and carrots. Sauté until just tender and then add salt and pepper to taste. Add the wine to deglaze the pan (see page 150) and cook until the pan is almost dry, glazing the vegetables. Pour this vegetable mixture over the pork in the roasting pan. Add the warm chicken stock and apple juice, thyme, and salt to taste. Put the lid on the braising pot or cover the roasting pan with foil. Cook in the oven for 2½–3 hours, or until the pork

is fork-tender. Let the belly cool in the braising liquid.

To serve, remove the pork from its braising liquid, divide into 6 pieces and set aside. Skim the fat from the braising liquid and strain through a fine mesh sieve into a clean pot. Bring the braising liquid to a boil, add the sherry vinegar, and reduce by two-thirds until sauce has almost a glaze-like consistency and is sticky. Meanwhile, heat a cast-iron frying pan over medium-high heat and render the fat side of the pork over medium-high heat. When nicely browned, lower the heat to medium and brown the remaining sides.

Serve the crispy braised pork belly fat side up on top of braised purple cabbage and spoon the reduced sauce overtop the pork.

SUGGESTED WINE PAIRING
BC: Joie Riesling, Naramata
International: Bischofliche Ayler Kupp Riesling Spatlese, Mosel, Germany

FENNEL-MARINATED PORK LOIN STUFFED WITH ITALIAN SAUSAGE

Serves 6

FOR THE RUB
2 Tbsp (30 mL) fennel seeds
5 dried bay leaves
2 Tbsp (30 mL) sea salt
1 tsp (5 mL) chili flakes

FOR THE PORK LOIN
4 lb (2 kg) pork loin, bone-out and butterflied

FOR THE STUFFING
3 sprigs fresh rosemary
3 garlic cloves
1 tsp (5 mL) coarse sea salt
2 Tbsp (30 mL) olive oil
1 Tbsp (15 mL) balsamic vinegar
1 tsp (5 mL) freshly ground pepper
6 hot Italian or fennel sausages, casing removed

This dish is a delicious way to remind yourself of Tuscany. Pork loin (not to be confused with pork tenderloin) is very affordable and goes a long way. Make this dish for dinner and then use the cold leftover pork slices for sandwiches or panini the next day.

To make the rub, grind the fennel seeds, bay leaves, sea salt, and chili flakes in a spice grinder. Score

the pork roast on the fat side and rub the spice mixture into the roast. Let marinate overnight.

Preheat oven or barbecue to 425°F (220°C).

Put the rosemary, garlic, and salt in a mortar and pestle and grind into a paste. Add the oil and balsamic vinegar. Rub this paste into the inside of the butterflied pork loin. Stuff the sausage meat inside the loin, roll up the loin, and tie securely with butcher's twine for roasting.

Roast the meat for 15 minutes to seal in its juices and then lower the oven temperature to 325°F (160°C). Roast until the internal temperature of the pork reaches 140°F (60°C), about 1 hour. Baste the roast every 15 minutes to ensure a golden crust and a juicy interior. If you are using a barbecue, seal the pork at a high temperature with the lid up and then cook the pork on the upper rack for about 1½ hours with the lid down (the internal temperature of the barbecue should remain around 250°F/120°C). If you have a barbecue rotisserie, this is the time to use it! The delicious pork loin will baste itself on the rotisserie.

Let the roast rest, tented by aluminum foil, for at least 15 minutes before slicing. Serve with lentils or soft polenta drizzled with sage brown butter (see page 240).

SUGGESTED WINE PAIRING
BC: Alderlea Pinot Noir, Cobble Hill, Vancouver Island
International: Coltibuono Chianti Classico, Tuscany, Italy

ESCALOPE OF CRANNÒG PORK WITH MUSHROOMS IN A GRAINY MUSTARD CREAM SAUCE

Serves 6–8

FOR THE PORK

3 pork tenderloins (about 3 lb/1.5 kg)
salt
freshly ground pepper
1 Tbsp (15 mL) vegetable oil

FOR THE GRAINY MUSTARD CREAM SAUCE

3 Tbsp (45 mL) butter
2 shallots, finely minced
1 lb (500 g) oyster mushrooms (or chanterelles or shaggy manes if they are in season), torn into pieces

¼ cup (60 mL) grainy Dijon mustard
¼ cup (60 mL) brandy
2 cups (500 mL) whipping (35%) cream
zest of 1 lemon
3 Tbsp (45 mL) finely chopped parsley, plus more for garnish
1 bunch basil, cut into a chiffonade (see page 250)

FOR THE GARNISH

12 cherry tomatoes, de-seeded and cut into cubes

This delicious dish is made with the cherished loin of the pigs I buy every year from the Crannòg Brewery in Sorrento. It is a fresh and light dish, despite the creamy sauce. If you don't use oyster mushrooms, make sure you use mushrooms with gills, as they soak up the tangy cream sauce. I like to serve this dish with roasted potatoes, rösti, or egg noodles.

Cut each pork tenderloin width-wise into 3 or 4 portions. Take each portion, 1 at a time, cover with plastic wrap, and pound with a meat tenderizer or rolling pin. Be sure to pound the meat across its grain. Pound each portion into an escalope about 1 inch (2 cm) thick. Season both sides with salt and pepper.

Heat a large frying pan over medium-high heat until hot. Coat the hot pan with the vegetable oil and sear the escalopes, 2 at a time, very quickly on both sides. Do not crowd the pan or the escalopes will steam, instead of sear. Reserve the cooked escalopes on a covered platter until ready to eat. You can also hold them in a 200°F (95°C) oven while you make the sauce. Leave the fat in the pan.

To make the sauce, melt the butter with the fat from searing the pork and then add the shallots. When the shallots are translucent, add the oyster mushrooms, season with more salt and pepper, and sauté until tender. Remove the mushrooms and reserve. Add the mus-

tard to the shallots and cook for 1 minute. With the shallots still in the pan, deglaze the pan (see page 150) with the brandy. Simmer to let the alcohol burn off. Add the cream a little at a time, whisking the mixture constantly, ensuring that the cream does not split because of the acidity of the mustard. After all the cream has been added, bring the sauce to a gentle simmer and let the cream reduce by half. Season the sauce after it has reduced. Do not let the cream boil or the sauce will separate.

To assemble the dish, increase the oven temperature to 350°F (180°C) and warm through the pork escalopes. To finish the sauce (do this right before plating the dish), add the lemon zest, chopped parsley, basil, and the reserved oyster mushrooms. Adjust the seasoning to taste. Plate the pork with some roasted potatoes or egg noodles. Ladle the sauce over the escalopes, making sure that every plate gets some mushrooms. Finish each plate with chopped parsley, cherry tomatoes, and freshly ground black pepper.

SUGGESTED WINE PAIRING

BC: Golden Mile Pinot Noir, Osoyoos
International: Domaine Marcel Deiss "Burlenberg" Pinot Noir, Alsace, France

RABBIT MARBELLA

Serves 4

FOR THE RABBIT

1 Tbsp (15 mL) olive oil

1 large (3–4-lb/2-kg) rabbit or organic, free-range chicken, cut into 8 pieces

1 tsp (5 mL) salt

freshly ground pepper

1 onion, cut into 1-inch (2.5-cm) pieces

1 large carrot, cut into 1-inch (2.5-cm) pieces

1 rib celery, cut into 1-inch (2.5-cm) pieces

6 cloves garlic, peeled and left whole

1 cup (250 mL) white wine

4 cups (1 L) chicken stock, warm

2 bay leaves

1 large sprig fresh thyme

FOR THE GARNISH

1 cup (250 mL) dried prunes or other dried fruit (I used dried pears from our orchard), cut into small dice

1 cup (250 mL) warm sherry vinegar

1 cup (250 mL) green Spanish green olives, pitted and halved

½ cup (125 mL) capers, well rinsed and roughly chopped

juice and zest of 1 lemon

chopped parsley

This dish is my version of the classic chicken "Marbella," which is an Andalusian dish that uses the salty/ sweet combination of green olives, capers, and dried fruit (classically prunes). I like to braise my rabbit or chicken pieces first and make a reduction sauce out of the braising liquid, finishing the dish with the green olives, capers, and dried fruit. I enjoy using rabbit for this dish because I have access to delicious, local rabbits, but it works equally well with good-quality free-range chicken.

Preheat oven to 300°F (150°C).

Heat the olive oil in a cast-iron frying pan over medium heat. Season the meat well with salt and pepper and brown in the oil until golden on both sides. Reserve the meat, keeping it warm in a bowl tented with aluminum foil. In the same pan, brown the onion, carrot, celery, and garlic in the fat from the meat. Cook until slightly caramelized. Once caramelized, deglaze the frying pan with the wine (see page 150) and simmer while scraping the bottom of the pan with a whisk. Place the vegetables in a large roasting pan or heavy flameproof casserole, and add the meat overtop. Pour the wine and warm chicken stock over the meat and vegetables. Add the bay leaves and thyme and bring everything to a simmer on the stove top. Once the braising pot is hot, place in the preheated oven and braise for about 2½–3 hours until the meat falls away from the bones.

Meanwhile, prepare the garnish by plumping the dried fruit in a pot with the sherry vinegar and simmering until the fruit is rehydrated. Pit the olives, chop the capers, and reserve in a separate bowl.

To finish the dish, remove the braised rabbit from the pot and pull the meat away from the bones. Reserve the meat in a bowl in a warm place. Strain the braising liquid through a fine mesh sieve over a high-lipped frying pan (with a large surface area for speedy reduction) and bring the strained liquid to a boil. Turn down the heat to medium and reduce the braising liquid by two-thirds. Add the chopped garnish to the pan (including any leftover vinegar) and the shredded braised meat. This should form a ragù-like stew, with the meat and garnish surrounded by flavorful sauce. Adjust the seasoning of the sauce by adding more sherry vinegar or salt if necessary. Right before serving, add the juice and zest of 1 lemon to the dish for freshness.

Serve the braised rabbit on its own as a stew or on top of soft polenta (see page 260) or with rice in true Spanish spirit. Top the dish with a handful of chopped parsley.

SUGGESTED WINE PAIRING

BC: Nichol Syrah, Naramata

International: La Rioja Alta Gran Reserva 904, Rioja, Spain

BRAISED RABBIT WITH CRÈME FRAÎCHE, DIJON, AND THYME

Serves 4

1 whole rabbit (a whole chicken can be substituted if rabbit is unavailable)

FOR THE SHORT STOCK
2 Tbsp (30 mL) vegetable oil
1 onion, cut into quarters, skin on
2 ribs celery or lovage, roughly chopped
1 large carrot, peeled and roughly chopped
2 cloves garlic, left whole
2 bay leaves
1 large sprig rosemary
2 sprigs thyme

FOR THE BRAISE
salt
freshly ground pepper
2 Tbsp (30 mL) vegetable oil
2 cups (500 mL) white wine (un-oaked Chardonnay or Pinot Blanc) or try using rosé

2 thyme branches
1 bay leaf
6 whole cloves garlic

FOR THE SAUCE
½ cup (125 mL) crème fraîche or sour cream
2 Tbsp (30 mL) grainy Dijon mustard
zest of 1 lemon
1 Tbsp (15 mL) thyme leaves, finely chopped
salt
freshly ground pepper

FOR THE LOINS
4 oz (125 g) pancetta, thinly sliced onto waxed paper
1 Tbsp (15 mL) vegetable oil
1 Tbsp (15 mL) chopped thyme

This delicious recipe makes me think of southern Burgundy. Bring on the traditional two-hour wine country lunch! When we make this recipe in our Saturday morning market cooking classes, it would never fail to freak everyone out. Most were convinced that they would not enjoy their rabbit lunch. Lo and behold, by the time class finished and the smell of rabbit braising in wine had whetted everyone's appetites, plates were licked clean and the crispy loin bits were the first to disappear.

Cut the rabbit into 4 parts (2 front legs and 2 rear legs), reserving the carcass and neck for the short stock. If using a rabbit, also remove its 2 loins, carefully preserving some of the belly flap for rolling later. If you're not comfortable doing this, have your butcher do it for you. Reserve the meat pieces in a bowl.

Begin the short stock by cutting the carcass into

4 smaller pieces with a cleaver. In a hot cast-iron frying pan, cover the bottom of the pan with the vegetable oil and sear the meat on each side until caramelized and golden. Add the onion, celery, carrot, garlic, and the bay leaves, rosemary, and thyme. Cover with clean, cold water and bring to a boil. Lower the heat to a gentle simmer. Do not stir the stock, as stirring will cause the liquid to become turbid and cloudy. The goal is to produce a clear, golden broth. Gently simmer the stock, uncovered, for about half an hour.

While the short stock is simmering, begin the braise. Season the rabbit pieces with salt and pepper. Heat another heavy-bottomed frying pan and cover the bottom with the vegetable oil. Sear the rabbit pieces until golden on each side, add the thyme, bay leaf, and garlic cloves. Add enough wine to just barely cover the rabbit (about half a bottle, depending on how large

your pan is). Bring to a boil and then lower the heat to a bare simmer. Lightly cover the pan with aluminum foil to make a loose lid and let the pieces braise until tender, about 2 hours. Remove the pieces of rabbit when it's done cooking, tent with aluminum foil, and reserve in a warm place. Reserve the braising liquid in the same frying pan.

To make the sauce, strain the short stock through a fine mesh sieve into the pan with the reserved braising liquid. Skim off any fat or impurities that have floated to the surface of the combined liquids. Take this combination of flavorful liquids and reduce by half over medium heat. Add the crème fraîche and Dijon mustard and reduce by half again. Just before serving, add the lemon zest and chopped thyme and adjust the seasoning with salt and pepper. Keep the sauce warm. Caution: do not boil the sauce once the crème fraîche

has been added; simmer only or the cream will split.

While the sauce is reducing, begin preparing the loins. Season loins with salt, pepper, and chopped thyme. Roll the belly flap around the loin meat, tucking in the short end, to ensure that the loin is of even thickness for even cooking. Wrap this log with the pancetta by rolling the loin like sushi while pulling back the waxed paper. Sear the pancetta-covered loin in the oil in a hot cast-iron pan. Cook the loins for about 10 minutes after they are seared on each side, either in the oven at 400°F (200°C) or on the stovetop over medium heat, to ensure that they are cooked through.

To serve, reheat the rabbit pieces in a bit of sauce or on the grill briefly, to warm through. Place your starch (crispy polenta, fresh egg noodles, or roasted potatoes) in the bottom of a rimmed bowl. Cut the loin pieces into small 1-inch (2.5-cm) medallions and cut

(continued next page)

(continued from previous page)

the leg in half, separating the leg and the thigh meat. Each portion should have a piece of each kind of meat placed on top of the starch, topped with a medallion of loin meat. Spoon the finished sauce over the meat and drizzle a bit around the bottom of the bowl. Serve immediately.

SUGGESTED WINE PAIRING
BC: Blue Mountain Gamay Noir, Okanagan Falls
International: Louis Jadot Rose de Marsannay, Burgundy, France

PANCETTA is an Italian form of bacon. It's pork belly that has been salt cured and spiced, and dried for about three months (but usually not smoked).

PHEASANT CACCIATORE

Serves 4–6

3 Tbsp (45 mL) vegetable oil
1 3-lb (1.5-kg) pheasant, cut into 8 pieces
½ cup (125 mL) pancetta (about
    3½ oz/100 g), cut into thin strips
1 medium onion, finely chopped
8 garlic cloves, roughly chopped
4 anchovy fillets
½ lb (250 g) dried porcini mushrooms,
    re-hydrated and juice reserved
3 sprigs rosemary
6 bay leaves
4 crushed juniper berries

1 red bell pepper, chopped
2 Tbsp (30 mL) Marsala
1 28-oz (796-mL) can plum tomatoes,
    chopped and juice strained of its seeds
4 cups (1 L) dark chicken stock, warm
½ cup (125 mL) red wine (robust Chianti
    or Nebbiolo)
1 tsp (5 mL) salt
½ tsp (2 mL) dried chili flakes or half
    a peperoncino
1 Tbsp (15 mL) chopped parsley

Cacciatore is the Italian version of the French chasseur, a rustic and robust hunter's stew. This recipe uses a game bird that is braised, rather than sautéed. I have also used pancetta instead of bacon and Marsala instead of red wine. I have tried to replicate the delicious version that our guest chef Jason Schubert cooked up for our guests and served with potato and Parmigiano Reggiano ravioli during the summer of 2005.

Heat the oil in a heavy-bottomed pot over medium heat. Season the pheasant and add it to the hot pan to seal in the juices. Do this in batches, so that the meat will caramelize and not steam. Reserve the pheasant pieces in a bowl.

Add the pancetta and chopped onion to the pot and sauté until the pancetta is golden and the onions are translucent. Add the garlic, anchovies, porcini mushrooms, rosemary, bay leaves, juniper berries, and red pepper. Deglaze the pan (see page 150) with the Marsala, scraping the caramelized bits off the bottom of the pan. Put the pheasant pieces overtop the vegetables, add the chopped tomatoes and their juice, and cover with the warm chicken stock and red wine. The meat should be surrounded by liquid, but not submerged. Add more liquid if necessary. Cover the pot with a lid or with aluminum foil with holes poked in it to let some steam escape, and braise the pheasant for 2–3 hours in a slow oven at 300°F (150°C). Alternatively, cook on the stovetop, simmering the pheasant, covered, until the meat is almost falling off the bone, about 1 hour.

Remove the rosemary and bay leaves before serving. Take out the pheasant pieces and keep warm. Reduce the braising liquid if necessary to thicken the sauce. Serve the cacciatore with soft or crispy polenta, white beans and rosemary, or fresh pasta.

SUGGESTED WINE PAIRING
BC: Quail's Gate "Family Reserve" Pinot Noir, Westbank
International: Isole e Olena Chianti Classico,
Tuscany, Italy

CRISPY SKINNED PHEASANT WITH LEMON AND BLACK PEPPER JUS

Serves 4

FOR THE PHEASANT
1 whole pheasant (about 3–4 lb/2 kg)
4 oz (125 g) (about 6 slices) prosciutto,
    cut into 3-inch (7.5-cm) pieces
16 fresh sage leaves
salt
freshly ground pepper
1 Tbsp (15 mL) vegetable oil

FOR THE LEMON AND BLACK PEPPER JUS
1 tsp (5 mL) unsalted butter
1 shallot, finely minced
1 clove garlic, roughly chopped
1 carrot
1 sprig thyme
1 bay leaf
1 tsp (5 mL) tomato paste
1 Tbsp (15 mL) sherry vinegar
1½ cup (375 mL) dark reduced chicken
    or other poultry stock
juice and zest of 1 lemon
freshly ground pepper
lemon wedges for garnish

This recipe is inspired by the classic Tuscan preparation of a weighted, pressed chicken. I've chosen to use local pheasant to prepare this dish. Pheasant has a deeper, slightly gamier flavor than regular chicken and marries well with the earthy, salty flavors of the sage and prosciutto. The best part of this recipe is the juicy meat with the ultra crispy skin that turns translucent, revealing the pretty sage leaves tucked under the skin.

You will also need a brick, a second cast-iron pan, or a dinner plate with a heavy bowl of water to place on top of the pheasant pieces while they are cooking to weigh them down.

Preheat oven to 400°F (200°C).

Cut the pheasant into 8 parts, with the bones out. Begin by removing the wing tips (leaving the wings attached to the breast). Remove both legs from the pheasant and cut each into 2 pieces, separating the legs and thighs (this should give you 4 pieces in total). Tunnel-bone out the legs and thighs if you're feeling confident; if not, leave the bones in. Note: the bone-in leg pieces will take longer to cook than the boneless legs. Remove the breasts from the breast bone, with the wings still attached (this cut is called a "supreme") and cut each breast into 2 pieces, giving you 4 pieces of breast meat in total. Be careful not to rip the skin while de-boning the pheasant as we need the skin intact to make it crispy.

Slide your pinky finger under the skin of all of the pheasant pieces to loosen it from the meat. This will make a pocket for the sage leaves and prosciutto. Stuff the prosciutto pieces under the skin of the pieces. Follow the prosciutto with 2 sage leaves each per piece of pheasant, placing them on top of the prosciutto. Flatten out the pheasant skin on top of the stuffing and season the pheasant pieces front and back with salt and pepper.

For the jus, heat a pot over medium heat and then add the butter, shallot, garlic, carrot, thyme, and bay leaf. Sauté the vegetables and then add the tomato paste to coat. Deglaze the pot with the vinegar and add the chicken stock. Bring the stock to a boil and then lower the temperature to a slow simmer. Let the sauce reduce by half while the pheasant is cooking. To serve the sauce, strain through a fine mesh sieve into a clean saucepan and finish the sauce with the lemon juice, zest, and freshly ground black pepper.

To cook the pheasant, heat a cast-iron frying pan and drizzle over the vegetable oil until the bottom of the pan is barely coated with oil. When the oil is very hot, but not smoking, place the pheasant skin side down in the pan and place the weight on top. Be sure not to crowd the pan with the pheasant pieces or the pheasant will steam and not get crispy. Cook the pheasant in 2 batches if you don't have 2 cast-iron pans. Cook for about 4 minutes on the skin side until very golden and then remove the weight and flip over to sear the other side. Place the weight down again and cook the meat through for another 4–5 minutes for the boneless pieces. If you've left the bone in the leg meat, you may have to finish these pieces in a hot oven for another 7–10 minutes. The pheasant is done when both sides are crispy and flattened. When pricked, the juices should run clear. Be sure to rest the finished pieces, uncovered, for a few minutes in a warm place before serving them.

Serve the pheasant with the lemon and black pepper jus. Extra lemon wedges add a fresh juicy hit of citrus to balance all that saltiness.

SUGGESTED WINE PAIRING
BC: Pentâge Pinot Noir, Penticton
International: Fattoria di Selvapiana "Bucherciale" Chianti Rufina Riserva, Tuscany, Italy

PHEASANT BALLOTTINES STUFFED WITH MORELS, PISTACHIOS, AND SOUR CHERRIES

Serves 4

FOR THE PHEASANT BALLOTTINES

1 3-lb (1.5-kg) free-range or wild
    pheasant, cut into 4 pieces and
    de-boned (or use 4 pheasant breasts
    with the wing left on) – reserve the
    bones for short stock
salt
freshly ground pepper
3½ oz (100 g) (about 8 slices)
    prosciutto, thinly sliced onto waxed
    paper
2 Tbsp (30 mL) vegetable oil

FOR THE STUFFING

3 thyme sprigs, woody stems removed
1 rosemary sprig, woody stem removed
2 shallots, minced
10 dried morel mushrooms, re-hydrated
    and chopped
2 Tbsp (30 mL) pistachios or pine nuts,
    toasted

¼ cup (60 mL) sour cherries, chopped
    (or substitute plumped currants)
1 tsp (5 mL) salt
½ tsp (2 mL) white pepper
7 oz (200 g) foie gras terrine, fondant,
    or torchon

FOR THE SHORT STOCK

2 Tbsp (30 mL) vegetable oil
1 onion, quartered, skin on
2 ribs celery, roughly chopped
1 large carrot, peeled and roughly
    chopped
2 garlic cloves, left whole
2 bay leaves
1 large sprig sage
2 sprigs thyme
4 cups (2 L) water, poultry, or veal stock
    to cover the bones

This was the first Joie dish that I created specifically from the ingredients from our area. It combined the delicious pheasant I was getting from North Okanagan Game Meat with the jewel-like sour cherries from Claybank Farms and the morels from the 2003 Okanagan Mountain Park fire. It became an instant hit and was served up many times at the orchard table during the summer of 2004.

Butterfly the pheasant breasts to make pockets for the stuffing. Season the boneless legs and breasts with salt and pepper.

For the stuffing, combine the thyme, rosemary, shallots, re-hydrated morels, pistachios, sour cherries, and salt and pepper in a stainless-steel bowl or in the bowl of a heavy mortar and pestle. Pound well to form a paste. Adjust seasoning to taste.

Place a small round of the foie gras in the pocket of the butterflied pheasant breast and in the boneless legs. Press down slightly. Over the foie gras, fill each of the legs and breasts with about 2 Tbsp (30 mL) of the stuffing. Roll the pheasant tightly and wrap the rolled flesh in prosciutto (2 strips per piece); tie the bundle with kitchen string or butcher's twine. Sear the outside of the rolls in the 2 Tbsp (30 mL) vegetable oil until golden. Refrigerate until needed or continue the cooking process.

For the short stock, cut the pheasant carcass into 4 smaller pieces with a cleaver. In a hot cast-iron frying pan, cover the bottom of the pan with the 2 Tbsp (30 mL) vegetable oil and sear the carcass pieces and leg bones on each side until caramelized and golden. Add the onion, celery, carrot, garlic, bay leaves, sage, and thyme. Cover with cold water or stock and bring to a boil. Once the short stock has reached a boil, turn down the heat and simmer gently, uncovered, about 30 minutes. Do not stir the stock, as stirring will cause the

liquid to become turbid and cloudy. The goal is to produce a clear, golden broth.

To make the sauce, strain the short stock through a fine mesh sieve into a clean pot. Skim off any fat or impurities that float to the surface and reduce the sauce by half over medium heat.

Preheat oven or barbecue to 350°F (180°C).

Finish cooking the ballottines in the oven or on the grill for about 15 minutes, until the center is cooked through. Test the internal temperature with a meat thermometer (it should register 170°F/75°C), or prick the meat to see that the juices run clear.

To serve the ballottines, take the pheasant from the oven and let rest for 5 minutes to let the juices recir-culate. Slice the ballottines in half on the bias and serve both pieces on warm plates so that the inside can be seen. Serve with du Puy lentils napped with sage brown butter (see page 263) and the sauce.

SUGGESTED WINE PAIRING

BC: Pentâge Gamay, Penticton
International: Marcel Lapierre Morgon, Beaujolais, France

COQ AU VIN

Serves 4

FOR THE CHICKEN

1 4-lb (2-kg) free-range chicken

4 Tbsp (60 mL) unsalted butter

1 Tbsp (15 mL) vegetable oil

½ lb (250 g) slab bacon, cut into thin strips or lardons

24 pearl onions, blanched and peeled

2 cups (500 mL) quartered button mushrooms

3 Tbsp (45 mL) all-purpose flour

3 cups (750 mL) dry white wine (Chardonnay or something not too aromatic)

1 cup (250 mL) chicken stock, warm

1 clove garlic, crushed

salt

freshly ground pepper

FOR THE GARNISH

2 Tbsp (30 mL) chopped parsley

Coq au vin is classic wine country food—especially in the Burgundy region of eastern France. Be aware that it will only be as good as the chicken that you use, so buy the best free-range, local chicken that you can find.

Cut the chicken into 8 pieces, leaving the bones in. Heat 1 Tbsp (15 mL) of the butter and the vegetable oil in a sauté pan over medium-high heat. Add the bacon and cook until almost browned. Add the pearl onions and continue to cook until both the onions and bacon are lightly browned. Add the mushrooms to the pan with the onions and bacon and cook over medium heat until the mushrooms also lightly brown. Remove the bacon, onions, and mushrooms from the pan with a slotted spoon and place into a large pot.

Take the sauté pan used for cooking the bacon, onions, and mushrooms, add the remaining butter and oil, and return to the heat. Season and seal the chicken pieces, keeping the dark and white meat separate. It may be necessary to do this in several batches to prevent the chicken from steaming rather than sealing. When sealed and lightly browned, add the leg meat to the pot containing the bacon mixture and set the white meat aside. Add the flour to the sauté pan and whisk to combine. Add more butter if necessary to make a roux. Cook the flour lightly for 2 minutes. Slowly add the wine, whisking constantly. Add the warm chicken stock and bring the ingredients to a boil, season, and strain through a fine mesh sieve over the leg meat and mush-room mixture. Add the garlic, cover the pot, and let simmer for 20 minutes. Add the white meat and cook until the juices run clear. To serve, remove the chicken breasts from the pot and remove the breast bone. Place the de-boned breast meat back into the pot.

Serve the coq au vin family-style in a soup terrine or plate it in rimmed bowls, ensuring each person receives both a piece of leg and some breast meat.

Serve the coq au vin with crusty bread or on top of a buttery pomme purée. Garnish with chopped parsley.

CHEF'S TIP

Red wine like Pinot Noir can be substituted for the white wine called for in the recipe. If red wine is substituted, use 2 cups (500 mL) red wine plus 2 cups (500 mL) reduced dark veal stock.

SUGGESTED WINE PAIRING IF WHITE WINE IS USED IN COOKING

BC: Cedar Creek Platinum Chardonnay, Kelowna
International: The Bret Brothers/Domaine de la Soufrandiere "La Verchére" Viré-Clessé, Burgundy, France

SUGGESTED WINE PAIRING IF RED WINE IS USED IN COOKING

BC: La Frenz "Reserve" Pinot Noir
International: Cameron "Clos Electrique" Pinot Noir, Dundee, Oregon

POACHED FREE-RANGE SPRING CHICKEN BREAST WITH FIDDLEHEADS AND OKANAGAN MOUNTAIN FIRE MORELS

Serves 4

FOR THE CHICKEN

1 lb (500 g) fiddleheads, washed and
    dried
4 cups (1 L) chicken stock
4 large free-range chicken breasts,
    boneless and skinless

FOR THE SAUCE

1 Tbsp (15 mL) unsalted butter
1 shallot, minced
2 cups (500 mL) fresh morels, cleaned
    (larger one cut in half or into rounds,
    tiny ones left whole) or rehydrated
    dried morels (save the rehydrating
    liquid and strain it into your poaching
    liquid for extra flavor)
1 cup (250 mL) white wine, like
    Chardonnay
1 cup (250 mL) whipping (35%) cream
1 tsp (5 mL) salt
½ tsp (2 mL) freshly ground white
    pepper

butter to warm the fiddleheads

This is a delicious spring recipe adapted from Rob Feenie's *Lumière* cookbook. I love poached chicken and this is a classic Burgundian preparation, especially in Bresse, home of the magnificent Bresse chicken. I don't have access to Bresse chickens, alas, but I do get wonderful chickens in the late spring from my dear friend Rebecca Kneen in Sorrento. I make this recipe once a year when the morel mushrooms are at their peak. This recipe saw heavy rotation during the spring of 2004, after the fire in Okanagan Mountain Park, which resulted in incredible morel foraging just 15 minutes from our house. Poaching the chicken breasts keeps a tender cut of meat moist, and the reduction cream sauce from the poaching juices is a far cry from a stodgy traditional roux-based cream sauce or velouté.

Prepare a bowl of ice water. Bring a large pot of salted water to a boil. Add the fiddleheads and simmer, uncovered, for 2 minutes. Drain the fiddleheads and immediately plunge them into ice water to stop them cooking and shock in their green color. Reserve until needed.

Bring the stock just to a boil in a pot set over medium heat and season with salt. Poach the chicken breasts in the stock, uncovered, for about 10 minutes at a gentle simmer. Remove the chicken from the stock and reserve, tented with aluminum foil. Reheat the stock over medium heat and reduce by half.

To make the sauce, melt the butter over medium heat in another pot and sweat the shallot. Add the morels and cook for 2–3 minutes. Add the wine and reduce by half. Add the reduced stock and reduce by half again. Add the cream and reduce by one-third. Season with the salt and pepper. Keep the sauce warm over low heat until ready to serve.

Just before serving, sauté the blanched fiddleheads in a bit of butter until they are warmed through. Season to taste with more salt and pepper.

To serve, place some fiddleheads and morel mushrooms on warmed plates. Slice the warm, poached

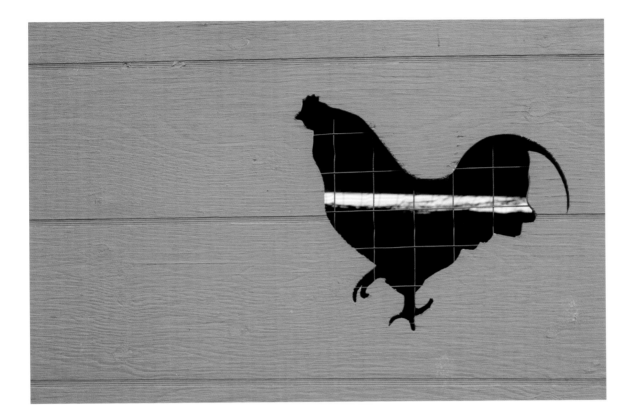

chicken breasts on the bias. Arrange the chicken slices over the fiddleheads and morels. Drizzle the top of the chicken with enough sauce to cover the meat and pool slightly on the bottom of the plate.

SUGGESTED WINE PAIRING
BC: Joie "Un-oaked" Chardonnay, Naramata
International: Domaine Guillemot-Michel Macon-Clessé, Burgundy, France

WENTZLE DUCK TWO WAYS: CONFITED LEGS AND SOY AND MAPLE MARINATED BREASTS

Serves 4 larger, or 8 smaller portions

FOR THE DUCK CONFIT

1 clove garlic, peeled and roughly
  chopped
1 bay leaf
4 sprigs fresh thyme
¼ cup (60 mL) coarse sea salt
1 tsp (5 mL) black peppercorns
4 duck legs, thighs attached
3–4 cups (750 mL–1 L) rendered duck
  fat or lard

FOR THE DUCK BREASTS

1 cup (250 mL) soy sauce
½ cup (125 mL) maple syrup
3 sprigs thyme
4 duck breasts, bone out, skin scored
  with Xs
2 Tbsp (30 mL) vegetable oil

FOR THE SAUCE

1 cup (250 mL) duck stock, reduced
reserved marinade from the breasts

Guest chef John Schubert made this dish for one of our Orchard Dinners. I loved the marinade for the duck breasts—it was perfectly salty and sweet at the same time. The dish was full of textural contrasts as well, with the sumptuous confited leg, crispy skin, and juicy, tender breast. I think we paired the dish with buttered cabbage that evening. Note that you have to begin preparing this dish at least 1 day before you plan to serve it.

For the duck confit, mix the garlic, bay leaf, thyme, coarse sea salt, and peppercorns in a roasting pan or large casserole dish. Rub the seasonings into the duck legs and arrange them in 1 layer in the same pan. Cover and refrigerate overnight.

For the dusk breasts, combine the soy sauce, maple syrup, and thyme in a bowl and submerge the scored duck breasts in the marinade. Cover the bowl with plastic wrap and refrigerate overnight.

Preheat oven to 275°F (140°C).

Remove the duck from the refrigerator. Rinse off the spice mixture from the duck legs under cold running water and pat dry. Arrange the duck legs in 1 layer in a roasting pan or deep casserole.

Melt the duck fat (or lard) in a saucepan over medium heat and pour over the duck legs, covering them completely. Cover the roasting pan with a lid or aluminum foil. Bake for 3–4 hours, or until the meat

falls off the bone. Remove from the oven and allow the duck to cool in the fat. Place the duck legs in an airtight container and cover with more duck fat strained through a fine mesh sieve. At this point you can continue the recipe, or refrigerate for up to 2 weeks or freeze for up to 3 months.

Preheat oven to 350°F (180°C).

Remove the duck legs from the fat, wiping off any excess with a paper towel, and place on a baking sheet. Place in the oven for 10–15 minutes to heat through and to crisp the skin. Remove from the oven and keep warm until needed.

While the confit is crisping, prepare the sauce. Heat a frying pan over medium-high heat. When hot, add about 2 Tbsp (30 mL) vegetable oil, or enough to coat the hot pan. Remove the breasts from their marinade and pat dry. Add the marinade to the pot with the warmed, reduced duck stock. Bring to a boil and reduce further, until the stock is a little sticky when rubbed between your thumb and forefinger.

Place the duck breast scored-skin side down in the hot pan to sear and cook for about 3 minutes. When the cooked edges start to creep around the sides of the meat, flip the breasts over to quickly sear the other side (about 1 minute) and remove from the heat. Duck breast should be served fairly rare. Let the duck breasts rest for 3 minutes in a warm place before slic-

ing them on the bias. Ensure that the confited legs are crisped at this point, your sauce has been reduced, and your cabbage or other garnish is warm.

To serve, place a spoonful of cabbage or starch of your choice in the middle of a warm dinner plate. Place a crisp confited leg to 1 side and a fan of duck breast slices beside it. Spoon a little of the duck sauce over the breast and onto the plate. Serve immediately while the confit is hot and crispy.

SUGGESTED WINE PAIRING
BC: Blue Mountain "Striped Label" Pinot Noir, Okanagan Falls
International: Méo-Camezet Fixin, Burgundy, France

SEARED HALIBUT CHEEKS
WITH ROSÉ BEURRE BLANC

Serves 4

FOR THE ROSÉ BEURRE BLANC

2 shallots, finely diced
1 cup (250 mL) cold unsalted butter,
    cut into small cubes
½ cup (125 mL) quality rosé wine
    (no white Zinfandel, please!)
½ cup (125 mL) rice wine vinegar
1 Tbsp (15 mL) whipping (35%) cream
1 tsp (5 mL) cornstarch, optional
salt
freshly ground white pepper
zest of 1 lemon

FOR THE HALIBUT CHEEKS

12 halibut cheeks (small to
    medium-sized)
1 tsp (5 mL) salt
½ tsp (2 mL) freshly ground pepper
1 Tbsp (15 mL) olive oil

This is a pretty dish that allows the seasonal treat of halibut cheeks in early summer to shine through. It's also an excuse to eat a butter sauce, which I love. Just for kicks one day I decided to make a classic beurre blanc with our Joie rosé. It was a tasty and colorful experiment.

To make the rosé beurre blanc, heat a saucepan or shallow frying pan over medium heat and soften the shallots in 1 Tbsp (15 mL) of the butter. When translucent, add the rosé and vinegar and reduce until the shallots are almost glazed. The wine will form a thick syrup around the shallots. This syrup will help the butter bind and emulsify into a sauce without splitting. Over very low heat, whisk in the remaining butter, 1 cube at a time. As the emulsification begins you can start to add more than 1 cube at a time. When a sauce begins to form add the whipping cream with the cornstarch, if using, mixed into it. Cornstarch will help stabilize your emulsion, as long as you don't allow the sauce to get too hot while you're preparing it. Whisk the beurre blanc constantly until all the butter cubes are incorporated.

Make the sauce as close to serving time as you can so you lessen the risk of destabilizing it. A tepid water bath is a good way to keep it warm until needed. If your sauce does break, put it into the blender, and with the motor running, add a little hot water to help it re-emulsify. Right before serving, season the sauce with salt and white pepper and add the lemon zest.

Preheat oven to 400°F (200 °C).

Place the halibut cheeks on a plate and season with salt and pepper. Heat a cast-iron frying pan or non-stick pan over medium-high heat, add a few drops of olive oil to coat the bottom of the pan, and sauté the cheeks for about 1 minute until golden and then turn them. Place the pan in the oven for 4 minutes (for small cheeks) to cook through. Do not overcook the cheeks as they become stringy when overcooked.

To serve, place 3 seared halibut cheeks in the center of a warmed dinner plate and drizzle the rosé beurre blanc over the cheek in a circle.

SUGGESTED WINE PAIRING

BC: Joie Rosé, Naramata
International: Chateau de Fesles Rosé d'Anjou,
Loire Valley, France

CHEF'S TIP

To be really fancy and play with the coral-colored beurre blanc, garnish the plate with a bit of tobiko (Japanese fish roe) and finely chopped chives.

JOIE

Year One

We made this wine because, quite simply, we love drinking rosé — good rosé. In the tradition of Southern France, the Loire Valley, Spain, Portugal and Italy, enjoy this wine from the "whites of the red," as an aperitif or as the ultimate summer food wine. We have used premium Pinot Noir, harvested October 20 at 24.3 brix from Little Straw Vineyard in Westbank. It has been made in an off-dry style to emphasize the lush fruit

PANCETTA-WRAPPED KOOTENAY TROUT WITH ROASTED TOMATO SAUCE

Serves 4

FOR THE TOMATO SAUCE

olive oil for brushing the pans
1 head garlic
4 lb (2 kg) vine-ripened red tomatoes
    (about 10 medium), cut into ½-inch
    (1-cm) slices
1 Tbsp (15 mL) fresh rosemary leaves
1 Tbsp (15 mL) fresh thyme leaves
salt
freshly ground pepper
3 Tbsp (45 mL) fresh orange juice
zest of 1 orange
1 Tbsp (15 mL) sherry vinegar

FOR THE TROUT

4 6-oz (150-g) pieces of trout (or wild BC
    spring salmon, halibut, or arctic char
    in season)
salt
freshly ground pepper
4 thyme branches, leaves de-stemmed
    and coarsely chopped
3½ oz (100 g) (about 8 slices) pancetta
1 Tbsp (15 mL) olive oil

This recipe combines the rich, end-of-summer flavor of roasted tomatoes with the bright kick of sherry vinegar and orange juice.

Preheat oven to 425°F (220°C). Line 2 baking sheets with parchment paper and lightly brush with oil.

Separate the garlic head into cloves, discarding the loose papery outer skin but keeping the inside skin intact, and wrap in aluminum foil, sealing the edges tightly. Arrange the tomatoes in one layer on the prepared baking sheets. Sprinkle them evenly with 2 tsp (10 mL) each of rosemary and thyme and season with salt and pepper. Put the foil-wrapped garlic with the tomatoes into one of the baking pans and place the pans in the upper and lower thirds of oven. Switch the position of pans halfway through roasting, about 35 minutes total, or until the garlic is tender and the tomatoes are slightly charred. Unwrap the garlic and let cool slightly. Peel the skins from each clove and force the garlic pulp with the warm tomatoes and herbs through a food mill fitted with small disk.

Finely chop the remaining rosemary and thyme

and stir into the sauce with the orange juice and zest. Season to taste with salt, pepper, and sherry vinegar.

When the sauce is complete, begin preparing the fish. Season with the salt, pepper, and thyme leaves. Wrap the pancetta slices around the fish pieces and use waxed paper to tightly roll like sushi.

Heat the 1 Tbsp (15 mL) olive oil in a large oven-proof cast-iron frying pan over medium heat. Add the fish and fry for 2 minutes per side, until the pancetta is golden and crispy. Place the pan in the oven, which is still hot from roasting the tomatoes, and roast for about 10 minutes, until the fish is just cooked through.

Reheat the sauce over low heat and adjust seasoning to taste with more orange juice, salt, and pepper. Place fish on a serving plate and serve with roasted tomato sauce or sage brown butter (see page 240).

SUGGESTED WINE PAIRING

BC: Le Vieux Pin Rosé, Oliver
International: Lafond Roc Epine Tavel, Rhone Valley, France

CONSOMMÉ

Serves 8

FOR THE CONSOMMÉ

5 egg whites

20 cups (5 L) dark chicken, pheasant, or
   duck stock, cold, and de-greased

1¼ lb (575 g) ground meat (a mix of
   chicken, pheasant, or even veal)

1 carrot, finely diced

1 rib celery, finely diced

1 medium onion, finely diced

½ cup (125 mL) tomato paste

½ cup (125 mL) chopped fresh parsley,
   stalks included

1 bay leaf, crushed

1 sprig thyme

mushroom stems and peelings

4 whole black peppercorns

TO FINISH

salt

freshly ground white pepper

2½ cup (625 mL) dry sherry

1 Tbsp (15 mL) soy sauce

various garnishes: fresh filled pasta,
   thinly sliced root vegetables, or tomato
   concassé (see page 141)

I enjoy using consommé as a broth around a main course like a seared piece of fish or a filled pasta like an agnolloti or a mezzaluna filled with a meat farce. "Brothy" main courses are a perfect way to eat protein when it is hot in the summer time and you don't want any sauce or jus.

In a cold heavy pot whip the egg whites until frothy and add the cold strained stock. Mix well to dissolve the egg whites. The egg whites are used to clarify at a ratio of 1 large egg white per 4 cups (1 L) stock. Add the ground meat, and stir well with a wooden spoon, so that the meat is broken up and well distributed through the stock. The ground meat clarifies the albumen and contributes a deep flavor. Add the carrot, celery, onion, tomato paste, parsley, bay leaf, thyme, mushrooms, and peppercorns and stir well.

Note: for a chicken or duck consommé, you can grind the poultry thighs, bones and all. For a fish consommé, no meat is used, only bones.

The carrots, onion, and celery are added for background flavor, the tomato paste is added for a richer brown color, and the aromatics and mushroom stems are for complementary flavor. Once all the ingredients are added to the pot, your consommé is ready to go on the stove.

Place the pot over high heat. You can stir it while it is heating, making sure no crust forms on the bottom of the pot. The egg whites will begin to coagulate at about 120–130°F (49–54°C). You can see this happening at the sides of the pot where whitish strands will begin to appear. Lower the heat to medium. As the egg whites coagulate, they capture the ground meat and vegetable matter, along with minute impurities. This makes what is called the "cap," a mat of cooked egg whites, meat, and vegetables. The meat is lighter than the stock, and so it rises to the surface, clarifying as it rises. Be sure not to let the stock boil though. Keep the consommé at a gentle simmer so you don't break the cap.

After the cap has risen and simmered for 45 minutes, drain off the clear consommé without breaking the raft (cap), as it may release cloudy particles when disturbed. The best way to do this is to do nothing! Let the soup cool and the raft will sink to the bottom of the pot, further filtering the liquid. If you want to use the consommé right away, use a metal spoon to cut a hole in the side of the raft so that you can ladle out the soup. When this becomes difficult, set up a fresh container with a sieve overtop, and carefully pour off the remainder. It may not be as clear as the first batch, but straining the consommé through cheesecloth may help. The consommé now needs to be degreased. If you have the time, cover it with plastic wrap and refrigerate it. Any fat will become hard and easy to skim. If you must use it right away, paper towels laid gently over the top will skim the grease. Consommé should be completely free of any fat.

(continued next page)

(continued from previous page)

To finish the consommé, bring it to a boil and add salt to taste. Add white pepper very sparingly. Add the sherry at about ½ cup per 4 cups (125 mL per L) of consommé. To intensify the color, you can add a touch of soy sauce. Garnish the consommé delicately if serving it as a soup or use it as a broth around a main course for seared fish or filled pastas.

SUGGESTED WINE PAIRING
BC: Blue Mountain Brut, Okanagan Falls
International: Pastrana Manzanilla Pastrana Sherry, Jerez, Spain

PASTA DOUGH

Makes enough pasta for 8 servings

1⅔ cups (250 g) all-purpose flour
1⅔ cups (250 g) semolina flour

3 large eggs
8 egg yolks

Making pasta is extremely rewarding and not all that difficult. It does make a bit of a mess, though! The quality of the eggs is paramount to the quality of the pasta so use the best, freshest eggs you can buy. We are lucky at our farm as we keep a flock of 12 hens that supply us with fabulous eggs. The other key to excellent pasta is the quality of the "hard" flour (see page 309). Use high-gluten or hard durum semolina flour.

Place both flours on a clean surface. Make a well in the center and add the eggs and yolks. Use a fork to break up the eggs as you bring in the flour. Stir with the fork or your fingers until the dough resembles a shaggy mass and is firm but still soft.

It is at this point that you must decide whether or not to add water. If the dough is not soft, add cold water 1 Tbsp (15 mL) at a time. Once you have started to knead the dough, it is impossible to add more water as the gluten in the flour will have started to form an elastic sheath that water cannot penetrate. The dough must be malleable, but not too dry. If the dough is too dry, it will tear when you are rolling it through the

pasta machine. If the dough is too wet, the pasta will have a mushy texture when cooked. If you can work the dough into a ball with your hands, you have added enough water.

When the dough is together, form a ball and knead well until you have smooth, silky, and elastic dough and a clean work surface, about 5 minutes. The dough will have picked up all of the flour from the work surface and should feel like a baby's soft cheek. Wrap the dough in plastic and rest it in the refrigerator to let the gluten relax for a least 1 hour.

After the dough is rested, divide it into 4 pieces and flatten them into rectangles so that they will easily fit into the widest setting on your pasta machine. To use the pasta machine to roll out the pasta, liberally dust the machine and pasta with all-purpose flour. Run the flattened dough through each setting on the pasta

machine twice. Start with the widest setting and work your way down.

If you do not have a pasta machine and are feeling brave, you can roll the dough by hand with a rolling pin, but you will have to flex your muscles!

As the sheets of dough come out of the pasta machine, dust them with semolina flour and keep them under layers of parchment paper or plastic wrap, covered with a slightly damp towel. Do not let the pasta sheets dry out or they will crack and become unusable.

Fresh pasta will keep in the refrigerator for 1 day, wrapped in plastic, or it can be cut into noodles and dried on a rack or on the back of a chair until the dough is completely hard. If using fresh, then shape, cut, or fill the pasta as desired into spaghetti, tagliatelli (wide noodles), ravioli, cappelletti (shaped like tortellini), and so on.

MINT, SORREL, AND RICOTTA-FILLED RAVIOLI WITH SAGE BROWN BUTTER

Makes 8 servings of ravioli (3 per person)

FOR THE FILLING

1 shallot, minced

1 tsp (5 mL) butter

1 cup (250 mL) ricotta cheese,
    mascarpone, or fresh goat cheese

4 mint sprigs, leaves de-stemmed,
    rolled, and cut into a chiffonade
    (see page 250)

1 cup (250 mL) sorrel, finely chopped

zest of 1 lemon

1 tsp (5 mL) salt

1 tsp (5 mL) freshly ground pepper

FOR THE RAVIOLI

1 recipe of pasta dough (see page 258)

1 egg white for the egg wash

FOR THE SAGE BROWN BUTTER

1 lb (500 g) unsalted butter

fresh sage leaves and blossoms, about
    1 handful

This is my favorite filled pasta recipe to make in the early spring when the first mint and sorrel are poking up in the garden.

Prepare the filling by sautéing the shallot in the butter until soft. When cool, blend the shallots with the ricotta, mint, and sorrel in the food processor until smooth. Season the mixture with lemon zest, salt, and pepper. Reserve and set aside at room temperature until the pasta dough is rolled out.

Roll out the pasta dough to the second-last setting on your pasta machine. Liberally dust the pasta sheets with semolina flour and reserve under slightly damp kitchen towels.

To form the ravioli, lay out a sheet of pasta dough. You can either leave the pasta as a sheet or cut out rounds with a round, sharp, 3-inch (7.5-cm) stainless-steel cutter. Place 1 tsp (5 mL) filling on top of the rounds or pasta sheet at about 3-inch (1.5-cm) intervals (depending on how large you want the ravioli to be). Use a pastry brush to brush round the filling with egg white or water. Lay out another sheet of pasta dough, or another batch of rounds, overtop the first, draping the dough over the filling mounds. Gently seal the second layer on top of the first, tapping down the pasta dough over the filling to create a pouch. Be certain to press out any air pockets as they will cause your ravioli to blow-out when they are cooked. Cut in between the pouches to form square envelopes around the filling. Reserve the finished ravioli on a dry, semolina-dusted baking sheet lined with parchment paper. Do not stack the finished ravioli layers. Cover with plastic wrap so the ravioli do not dry out.

For the sage brown butter, slowly melt the unsalted butter in a heavy-bottomed pot. Leave the butter at a bare simmer until it turns golden brown as all the milk solids slowly caramelize, about 45 minutes. Add the sage leaves and blossoms and let simmer for about 10 minutes. Right before serving, turn up the heat to crisp the sage leaves, being careful not to burn the butter. Remove the crispy sage leaves from the butter with a slotted spoon and drain on a paper towel.

To serve, bring a pot of heavily salted water to a boil. Plunge in the ravioli and cook for about 2–3 minutes until they float to the surface and are warmed through.

Serve the ravioli right out of the water into warmed bowls, drizzle with sage brown butter, and sprinkle with fresh sage leaves and blossoms.

CHEF'S TIP

For variations on the pasta filling, use different soft cheeses like mascarpone, goat cheese, or quark cheese instead of ricotta.

For other seasonal fillings, try roasted root vegetables. Cut the vegetables into 2-inch (1-cm) pieces and toss in oil, salt, and pepper until coated. Roast the vegetables on a baking sheet covered with foil at 400°F (200°C) until fork-tender. Process the roasted vegetables while still warm in the food processor until very smooth and combine with the soft cheese, softened shallot, and seasonings. Try delicious combinations such as Roasted Carrot with Fresh Ginger Mascarpone Cheese, Goat Cheese with Fine Herbs and Lemon Zest, Roasted Beets and Caramelized Onion, Roasted Squash and Chestnut with Mascarpone Cheese, and Roasted Pumpkin with Orange Blossom Water Mascarpone.

Also try filling fresh pasta with shredded, braised meats like shank or cheek meat. Softened wild mushroom mixes also are delicious in ravioli.

SUGGESTED WINE PAIRING
BC: Herder "Twin Benches" Chardonnay
International: Aldo Conterno "Bussiador" Chardonnay, Piedmont, Italy

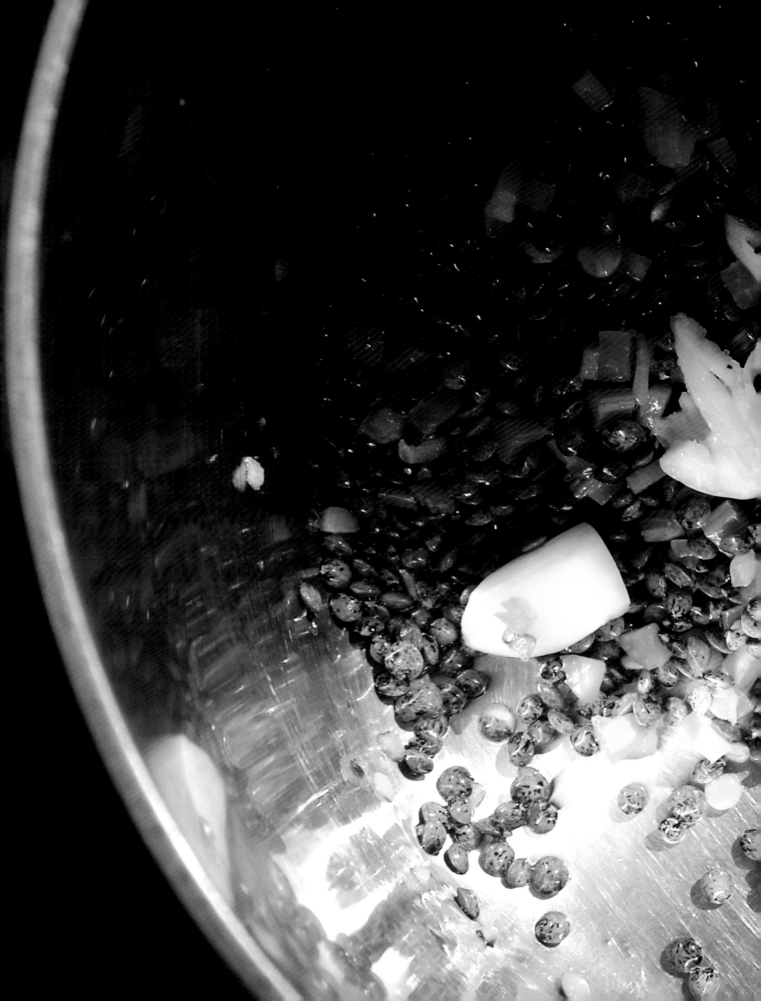

SIDES

THE ART OF THE GREEN SALAD

Serves 10

FOR THE DRESSING
1 shallot, minced
¼ cup (60 mL) red wine vinegar
¼ cup (60 mL) extra virgin olive oil
1 tsp (5 mL) salt
1 tsp (5 mL) freshly ground black pepper
juice and zest of 1 lemon

FOR THE LEAVES
1 large head red leaf lettuce
1 bunch baby spinach
1 bunch young arugula leaves (rocket)
beet tops
lamb's lettuce or mâche
watercress
curly endive or frisée
radicchio, pulled away from its core and
   torn up

FOR THE FINE HERBS, PICKED INTO
SPRIGS AND GENTLY WASHED
flat-leaf parsley
chervil
tarragon
basil
chives
edible flower petals (like pansies,
   nasturtiums, chive blossoms, borage,
   and calendula)

It is no overstatement to say that a cook is only as good as his or her green salad. A green salad is an exercise in elegant simplicity. A good one will showcase a bounty of carefully selected greens and perfectly snipped herbs. Its beauty lies in careful details and its organic natural state. The nuances of salad making are important and greens must be treated with respect. You should choose an appropriate mix of young greens, washing the leaves gently in enough cold water so as not to crowd and bruise them, and then drying them and wrapping them in clean kitchen towels until they're ready to be used.

Dressing salad greens is an exercise in balance. Their flavor should be heightened by the dressing, not overwhelmed by it. The dressing should lightly coat the leaves, not have them swimming in it. Salad dressings should always be freshly made and greens dressed right before they are to be served.

For the dressing, place the shallot in the red wine vinegar and let sit for 10 minutes. Combine the oil, salt, pepper, and lemon juice and zest with a whisk in a small bowl. Combine the acidulated shallots with this right before tossing the salad.

Prepare the greens and herbs. Gently wash the salad greens, dry with a salad spinner, and reserve between damp towels. Pick the herbs into sprigs, and reserve in water until ready to serve.

To assemble the salad, use your hands to gently toss together the leaves and the greens in a large stainless-steel bowl. Add half of the dressing and toss gently. Add the dressing to the greens right before serving or the salad will wilt from the vinegar! To serve the salad, transfer to a serving bowl with serving spoons if serving family style, or serve right on to individual salad plates or bowls if serving individually. Drizzle another 1 tsp (5 mL) of dressing over the already lightly dressed greens.

CREAMED AND BAKED CIPPOLINI ONIONS

Serves 4

4 large-sized cippolini onions, peeled
1 Tbsp (15 mL) olive oil
2 cloves garlic, peeled and finely
  chopped
4 sprigs fresh rosemary, lower leaves
  picked and chopped
½ cup (125 mL) heavy cream, like Devon
  cream, not whipping (35%) cream

1 cup (250 mL) grated Parmigiano
  Reggiano cheese or other hard,
  salty cheese
salt
freshly ground pepper
4 slices pancetta or bacon

This is adapted from a recipe in Jamie Oliver's *Happy Days* book. It's a fantastic recipe for baked onions that I just had to include. I get fabulous fresh cippolini onions from the Penticton farmer's market and when I go up north in the Okanagan Valley I stop at Gourt's Dairy in Salmon Arm and pick up a pint of their heavy cream, which is thick like Devon cream or crème fraîche. That cream makes these onions heavenly.

Boil the onions in a large pot of salted water for 15 minutes until fork-tender. Remove from the pot with a slotted spoon and allow to cool. Use a sharp knife to remove the top 1 inch (2.5 cm) of each onion, and then finely chop and place to one side. Trim the stalk end of the onions so that they'll sit flat on a roasting tray. Use a melon-baller to scoop out or cut about 1 Tbsp (15 mL) from the inside of each onion, keeping the outside intact.

Finely chop and add to the rest of the chopped onion.

Preheat oven to 400°F (200°C).

Heat a frying pan over medium-high heat and add olive oil. Add the chopped onion, garlic, and a few chopped rosemary leaves. Fry for a couple of minutes until softened, and then turn the heat down, add the cream, and remove from the heat. Stir in the cheese and season to taste with salt and pepper.

Wrap a thin slice of pancetta around the outside of each onion and spike it in place with a sharpened twig of rosemary or a wooden toothpick. Place the onions in a roasting tray and spoon some of the chopped onion mixture inside each onion. Bake until soft and tender, about 25 minutes depending on the size of the onions. The creamed onion part should be golden brown on the top and the pancetta should be crispy.

BRAISED PURPLE CABBAGE

Serves 6

1 Tbsp (15 mL) unsalted butter
1 large yellow onion, chopped in small dice
1 large head purple cabbage, cored and thinly sliced
1 firm cooking apple (like Granny Smith, Spartan), peeled, cored, and finely diced
1 tsp (5 mL) salt, or to taste

1 clove garlic, finely minced
1 bay leaf
3 whole cloves
1 Tbsp (15 mL) grainy mustard
1½ cups (375 mL) dry red wine
¼ cup (125 mL) red wine vinegar
½ cup (125 mL) maple syrup
1 cup (250 mL) peeled chestnuts (optional)

Braised cabbage is an excellent accompaniment to duck confit or any fatty pork dish. The acidic vinegar and wine in this dish keep the cabbage a beautiful purple color. Without the acid, the cabbage will turn blue.

Heat the butter in a large pot. Add the onion and sauté over medium heat until translucent. Add the cabbage and apple, mix well, and then add salt to taste, the garlic, bay leaf, cloves, mustard, wine, vinegar, and maple syrup. Bring to a simmer, cover, and cook for about 1 hour until the cabbage is tender. Remove the bay leaf and adjust the seasoning to taste. If you're using chestnuts, add them to the pot with the cabbage and apple.

MELTED SAVOY CABBAGE WITH BACON

Serves 6

1 lb (450 g) smoked bacon, thick cut, cut
   into ½-inch (1-cm) strips or lardons
1 large head Savoy cabbage
¼ cup (60 mL) unsalted butter

salt
freshly ground pepper
juice and zest of 1 lemon
1 Tbsp (15 mL) rice wine vinegar

My husband, Michael, is a cabbage fanatic (I attribute this to a genetic predisposition as his heritage is Newfie and Ukrainian). We eat it often and I'm always thinking up new ways to cook it with love. One of my favorite produce growers in the Similkameen Valley, Gabi and Dave Cursons of Dumplingdale Farm in Cawston, grow incredibly beautiful cabbages that I can never resist buying at the market. Savoy cabbage is the beautiful one with the loose, crinkled leaves. This recipe often accompanied our recipes during our Saturday Morning Market Classes.

Render the bacon at a medium-low heat until it is fairly crispy.

While the bacon is frying, remove whole leaves from the tight cabbage head. Stack the leaves one on top of the other, roll up, and cut into a chiffonade (see page 250). When the bacon is crispy, add the butter to the pan with the bacon and its fat, add all the shredded cabbage, and begin to let it wilt. Fold the cabbage into the bacon fat and butter until it is coated. Slowly cook the cabbage until it's "melted" and soft. Before serving, check the cabbage for seasoning. Add some salt and pepper if necessary, and the lemon juice and zest and rice wine vinegar.

Serve with crispy skinned pheasant or duck confit and spaetzle (see pages 224 and 265).

ROASTED GREEN BEANS
WITH MINT AND CUMIN

Serves 6

2 lb (1 kg) green beans, preferably
    haricot verts
1 Tbsp (15 mL) extra virgin olive oil
½ tsp (2 mL) salt

½ tsp (2 mL) freshly ground pepper
2 Tbsp (30 mL) whole cumin seed
½ cup (125 mL) fresh mint leaves

I made up this recipe in the summer of 2006 to demonstrate the Moorish influence on the flavors of regional Spanish cooking for a cooking class. We had a guest chef that weekend, John Taboada from Portland's Navarre Restaurant, and he suggested that we roast the beans as he does in his restaurant, serving them as small plates. Roasted beans are now my new favorite thing!

Preheat oven to 400°F (200°C).

Put on a large pot of salted water to blanch the beans. Set up an ice-water bath for refreshing the beans. While the water in the blanching pot is heat-

ing, wash the beans and remove the tip-end, leaving their little "tails" on. When the water comes to a rolling boil, plunge the beans into the pot and cook for about 1 minute, until they're bright green and float. Remove the beans from the boiling water with a slotted spoon and plunge into the ice-water bath. This will shock their green color into them (preserving the color during roasting) and stop them from cooking further. Remove the beans from the water and pat dry. Toss the beans in a large bowl in the olive oil, salt, and pepper. Place the coated beans on a large baking sheet (do not crowd them or they will steam) and put them in the oven to roast for about 30–40 minutes, until they're very crispy at their tips.

While the beans are roasting, toast the whole cumin seeds in a dry frying pan on the stovetop. Move them around a little while they are toasting and toast them only until you can smell them. Do not toast the cumin too much (i.e., until it starts to smoke!) or it will be acrid and have a bitter flavor. Let the cumin seeds cool and then grind them slightly with a mortar and pestle or spice grinder. Pile the mint leaves on top of one another and roll them into a log. Thinly slice the log to make a thin chiffonade (see page 250).

When you're happy with the level of crispiness (John prefers his roasted beans to be well done, almost burnt), remove the beans from the oven. They'll have withered a bit and become puckered. Toss them in a large bowl with the toasted cumin and the shredded mint. Serve warm or at room temperature.

SWISS CHARD WITH PINE NUTS AND CURRANTS

Serves 4

1 lb (500 g) Swiss chard
2 Tbsp (30 mL) extra virgin olive oil
2 cloves garlic, finely slivered
½ cup (125 mL) pine nuts, lightly toasted
pinch of chili flakes
½ cup (125 mL) currants or other dark
  dried fruit (I use diced dried pears
  rehydrated in 2 cups/500 mL of
  warm wine)

½ tsp (2 mL) salt
½ tsp (2 mL) freshly ground black
  pepper
juice and zest of 1 lemon

I had this dish recently at Chris MacDonald's Cava Restaurant in Toronto and enjoyed it so much I made up a version for our Spanish cooking class this past summer. I love the meaty texture of Swiss chard as a vegetable.

Bring a large pot of salted water to a rolling bowl. Set up an ice-water bath beside the stove. While the water is boiling, wash and dry the Swiss chard and then de-stem it. Reserve the stems and chop them up finely. Take the leaves and pile about 6 on top of each other. Roll the leaves tightly and cut into 1-inch (2.5-cm) pieces to chiffonade (see page 250). Plunge the shredded Swiss chard leaves into the pot and let cook, uncovered, until the leaves turn bright green, about 1 minute. Using a slotted spoon, take the chard out of the pot and plunge the leaves into the ice water to stop the cooking. Once the chard is cooled, remove it from the ice-water bath and pat dry.

Heat the olive oil in a frying pan over medium heat. Add the garlic slivers and pine nuts and sauté quickly to make sure neither burns. When the pine nuts are slightly golden, add the chili flakes and then the Swiss chard. Coat the Swiss chard in the flavored ol-

ive oil, add the plumped currants, and warm the chard through. Season with salt and pepper to taste and add the lemon juice and zest. Serve warm or at room temperature.

CARAMELIZED APPLE AND SAGE COMPOTE

Serves 4

juice of 1 lemon
2 large Spartan or other firm cooking
    apples, like Golden Delicious or Gala,
    peeled, cored, and each cut into
    12 wedges
2 Tbsp (30 mL) vegetable oil

1 Tbsp (15 mL) unsalted butter
1 Tbsp (15 mL) honey
6 fresh sage leaves, cut into a chiffonade
    (see below)
1 Tbsp (15 mL) sherry vinegar

This compote is an excellent addition to any fall pork dish.

Squeeze the lemon juice over the apples to keep the flesh from oxidizing and turning brown.

Heat the vegetable oil and butter in a frying pan over medium heat. Add the apple wedges and cook on both sides. Increase the heat to medium-high and add the honey. Continue to cook until the apples are dark golden brown and can easily be pierced with a knife. Add the sage leaves and vinegar and continue to cook the apples until they begin to break down slightly. Remove from the heat and set aside. This compote will keep for 1 week in the refrigerator and also makes an excellent condiment for canning.

CHIFFONADE is a technique in which herbs or leafy green vegetables (such as lettuce, cabbage, or basil) are cut into long, thin strips. The leaves are stacked, rolled tightly, and then cut across with a sharp knife to produce fine ribbons. The term is a French word meaning "made of rags."

SPRING VEGETABLE RAGOUT

Serves 6

24 small asparagus spears
1 lb (500 g) thin French green beans, tips
   removed, tails left on
1 cup (250 mL) green peas, shelled
1 cup (250 mL) fava beans, shelled

24 pearl onions or baby garlic
1 Tbsp (15 mL) unsalted butter
2 Tbsp (30 mL) fresh chives, finely
   minced
few drops truffle oil, optional

This mixture of vibrant green vegetables epitomizes late spring to me, when the last asparagus, the first green beans and peas and fresh Fava beans are in season all at the same time.

Blanch each of the vegetables separately, uncovered, in a large pot of boiling salted water. Prepare an ice-water bath. Cook the vegetables only until they float and turn bright green, about 1–2 minutes. They'll cook more in the frying pan, so leave them al dente. You're blanching to keep their color rather than actually to cook them at this stage. Plunge the vegetables into the ice-water bath to stop them cooking and preserve their color. Peel the onions or garlic after blanching. You'll also need to peel the fava beans after blanching. They have their obvious outer pod, but also a jacket that must be removed to reveal a bean that can be pinched into 2 bright green lobes. Reserve the vegetables in a bowl until ready to serve.

Sauté the vegetables together in the butter and top with chives and truffle oil, if you desire.

MOORISH PILAF

Serves 4

2 cups (500 mL) basmati rice, well rinsed
2½ cups (375 mL) chicken stock
2 Tbsp (30 mL) unsalted butter
pinch of salt

pinch of saffron
zest of 1 orange
½ cup (125 mL) toasted pine nuts
   or pistachios

This is a delicious accompaniment to roasted lamb or pork. It's also a great side dish to make with leftover rice, which is how this recipe was created! If you're not a fan of couscous, try this instead. Chicken stock makes the pilaf very flavorful.

Cook the rice in the stock in a rice cooker or a pot. Add 1 Tbsp (15 mL) of the butter and the salt and saffron as the rice cooks.

When the rice is fluffy and still warm, stir in the remaining butter and sprinkle with the orange zest. Place the scented rice in a serving dish and sprinkle with the toasted nuts.

CHEF'S TIP
Adding some dried fruit, like currants or figs, with the rice in the pot or rice cooker, is delicious as well.

RATATOUILLE

Serves 8

3 Tbsp (45 mL) olive oil
2 cups (500 mL) chopped onion
4 cloves garlic
1 bay leaf
2 tsp (10 mL) dried basil
1 tsp (5 mL) dried oregano
1 medium eggplant, cut into 1-inch
   (2.5-cm) cubes
2 tsp (10 mL) salt
freshly ground pepper
1 tsp (5 mL) fresh rosemary
1 tsp (5 mL) fresh thyme
1 medium zucchini, cut into
   1-inch (2.5-cm) cubes

2 medium bell peppers, cut into
   1-inch (2.5-cm) cubes
1 28-oz (796-mL) can plum tomatoes,
   broken up slightly, seeds removed, or
   use 2 lb (1 kg) fresh plum tomatoes if
   they're in season, skins off
2 Tbsp (30 mL) red wine vinegar
juice and zest of 1 lemon
½ cup (125 mL) roughly chopped fresh
   parsley
1 cup (250 mL) black sun-dried or
   kalamata olives, pitted and halved

Ratatouille is a traditional southern French vegetable stew. It can be eaten on its own as a summer vegetable stew or as an accompaniment to roasted meats like a lamb leg rubbed with *herbes de Provence*. I often make ratatouille in Naramata in the summer as the hot climate here encourages the growth of our eggplants, peppers, and tomatoes. You can leave the vegetables in this recipe super chunky if you're making a rustic stew or you can *brunoise* (chop) them finely if you require a more delicate side dish to accompany a piece of grilled fish, for example.

Heat the olive oil in a deep skillet or large flame-proof casserole. Add the onion, garlic, bay leaf, basil, and oregano and sauté over medium heat for about 5 minutes until the onion is translucent.

While the onion is cooking, salt the eggplant to draw out the bitterness. Let sit for 10 minutes and then rinse off the salt and pat the eggplant dry. Add the eggplant, 2 tsp (10 mL) salt, pepper to taste, rosemary, and thyme and stir. Cover and cook over medium heat, stirring occasionally, for 15–20 minutes or until the eggplant is really soft, almost breaking down. Add the zucchini and cook for a further 10 minutes. Add the bell peppers and break up the plum tomatoes with the back of a spoon and add to the pot. Cover and simmer for about 10 more minutes or until the zucchini and bell peppers are tender. Season the stew with more salt and pepper to taste and stir in the red wine vinegar and the lemon juice and zest.

Serve on a warmed platter if serving the stew family style or on individual plates if serving as an accompaniment. Serve the ratatouille hot, warm, or at room temperature, topped with parsley and olives.

GRILLED SUMMER VEGETABLES

Serves 6

SUITABLE VEGETABLES FOR GRILLING

5 lb (2.5 kg) mixed vegetables such as eggplant (salt to draw out bitterness first, then rinse and pat dry), zucchini, asparagus, green beans, red onions, fennel bulb, peppers, carrots, and corn on the cob

FOR THE MARINADE

1 cup (250 mL) extra virgin olive oil
1 cup (250 mL) red wine vinegar
2 cloves garlic, minced
1 large handful fresh oregano leaves
juice and zest of 2 lemons
2 tsp (10 mL) sea salt
2 tsp (10 mL) freshly ground pepper

adjust quantities depending on volume of vegetable being grilled

Grilled vegetables are a classic accompaniment to summer barbecues and are tasty with grilled fish and meat or salty cheese like goat feta. They also make excellent condiments for sandwiches. I am very particular about the way that I grill them. I put the dry vegetables on an oiled grill and only throw them into a marinade once they're cooked. When you put something warm into a marinade, it sucks it up like crazy. This is an excellent method to avoid a burnt mess on your barbecue, and results in exceptionally flavorful grilled vegetables.

Prepare the vegetables and cut into uniformly sized pieces.

Combine the oil, vinegar, garlic, oregano, lemon juice and zest, salt, and pepper and reserve until the vegetables are grilled.

Begin to grill the vegetables on an oiled grill, starting with the thickest ones first (eggplant, zucchini). Definitely put the green beans and asparagus on last if you are using them. Do not oil the vegetables or they will smoke and burn!

Plunge the hot vegetables into the marinade right off the grill while they are still warm. Leave the grilled vegetables in the marinade for 5 minutes to deeply flavor them. Serve the grilled vegetables at room temperature.

CHEF'S TIP

Try layering grilled vegetables in a small gratin dish with some excellent melting cheese like fontina or friulano, a simple tomato and basil sauce, and a topping of a hard grated goat cheese for a flavorful, vegetarian meal.

POTATO, CHÈVRE, AND THYME GRATIN

Serves 8

2 cups (500 mL) whipping (35%) cream
2 sprigs thyme
1 bay leaf
1 whole garlic clove, peeled
1 tsp (5 mL) salt

1 tsp (5 mL) freshly ground white pepper
6 oz (175 g) soft, unripened goat cheese
  (unflavored)
10 yellow-fleshed potatoes (like Yukon
  Gold), peeled

This dish is the perfect accompaniment to roasted meats. It will add a creamy element to the crispy textured protein on your plate and the goat cheese makes the gratin extra creamy and a bit tangy.

Preheat oven to 350°F (180°C).

Infuse the cream in a pot with the thyme sprigs, bay leaf, garlic, salt, and pepper. Bring the cream to a gentle boil and then turn off the heat and cover with a lid. Let the cream infuse for 10 minutes and then add the goat cheese. Whisk until any lumps are gone and the cream is smooth.

While the cream is infusing, slice the potatoes very thinly with a mandoline or Japanese vegetable slicer. If you don't have a slicer, slice the potatoes as thinly as you can by hand. Do this quickly so the potatoes don't oxidize. Don't put the potatoes into water to prevent oxidation as this will leach out the starch, and we want to keep the starch to thicken the cream mixture while the potatoes cook. Pour some of the cream into your sliced potato bowl instead.

To build the gratin, grease a 13- × 9-inch (3.5 L) porcelain casserole dish with butter. Layer the dish with overlapping circles of potato. Complete 1 layer of potato, season with a pinch of salt, and then top with cream. Repeat until the dish is full, ending with a layer of cream. Press the mixture down with your hands to compact the potato layers.

Cover the dish with aluminum foil or a round of parchment paper and put into the oven. Bake for 20 minutes, lift the cover, and press the gratin down with a spatula again, as you did before putting it into the oven. Pressing down will leach the starch from the potatoes and thicken the cream. Do this every 15 minutes. Total baking time for the gratin should be about 1 hour. Check the doneness of the gratin by piercing the potatoes with the tip of a knife. When done, the potatoes should be tender to the tip of the knife.

Right before serving, gratinée (or brown) the top of the gratin under the broiler.

CHEF'S TIP

If you're not keen on goat cheese, you have the option of omitting it.

ROOT VEGETABLES EN PAPILLOTTE

Serves 6

1 lb (500 g) baby carrots, cleaned and cut in half lengthwise

1 lb (500 g) celery root, peeled and cut into ½-inch (1-cm) cubes

16 pearl onions, peeled

¼ cup (60 mL) unsalted butter, cut into small cubes

3 sprigs thyme

½ tsp (2 mL) salt

½ tsp (2 mL) freshly ground white pepper

For a more delicate root vegetable dish, if you don't want the heavy caramelized flavors of roasted root vegetables, try cooking them in a foil or parchment paper envelope (en papillotte).

Preheat oven to 400°F (200°C).

Cut 3 large squares of aluminum foil or parchment paper and evenly divide the vegetables among the 3 squares. Dot with the butter, add a sprig of thyme, and season with salt and pepper. Tightly seal the packages and place on a baking sheet. Bake for 30–45 minutes or until the vegetables are tender. Remove from the oven, and carefully open the packages to let the steam escape. Set aside until needed.

POMME PURÉE

Serves 4

1½ lb (750 g) yellow-fleshed potatoes, like Yukon Gold, skins on

1 bay leaf

1 sprig thyme

1 Tbsp (15 mL) salt

2 peppercorns

¼ cup (60 mL) whipping (35%) cream, warm

¼ cup (60 mL) buttermilk

¼ cup (60 mL) unsalted butter, cut into ½-inch (1-cm) cubes, softened

freshly ground white pepper

Pomme purée is the fancy version of the unfailingly comforting mashed potato. It is silky, rich, and addictive. Instead of mashing the potatoes, put them through a food mill or potato ricer as this recipe specifies. The ricer will keep the potatoes light, fluffy, and lump free. I add buttermilk for an extra tang. Leaving the skin on the potatoes prevents them from absorbing excess water, which would make the purée too moist.

Place the potatoes in a pot with the bay leaf, thyme, salt, and peppercorns. Add enough salted water to cover and bring to a boil on high heat. Lower the heat to medium and simmer for 15–20 minutes, or until fork-tender. Drain.

Peel the potatoes while they're still slightly warm and pass them through a ricer or fine mesh sieve into a clean pot over medium-low heat. Slowly fold in the warm cream and buttermilk, and then gently fold in the butter, one piece at a time. Be careful not to mix the potatoes too much when adding the cream and butter as the mixture will become gluey. Season to taste with more salt and white pepper.

POTATOES LYONNAISE

Serves 8

2 lb (1 kg) yellow-fleshed potatoes, like
   Yukon Gold (about 4 large), peeled
   and halved
2 Tbsp (30 mL) unsalted butter
½ tsp (2 mL) salt

¼ tsp (1 mL) freshly ground pepper
1½ cups (375 mL) sliced onion
1 Tbsp (15 mL) olive oil
¼ cup (60 mL) chopped parsley

This is the perfect bistro accompaniment to a rich duck dish.

Steam or boil the potatoes until tender and then cut into ¼-inch (0.5-cm) thick slices. Melt the butter in a large skillet on medium heat. Add the potato slices and cook for 15 minutes, shaking the pan periodically. After 10 minutes, add the salt and pepper and then turn the potatoes. In a small skillet, sauté the onion in the olive oil until almost caramelized. Add the onion and parsley to the potatoes and cook for 5 more minutes.

ROASTED POTATOES

Serves 4

2 Tbsp (30 mL) vegetable oil
2 Tbsp (30 mL) olive oil
1 Tbsp (15 mL) fresh rosemary, roughly
   chopped

1 tsp (5 mL) paprika
1 Tbsp (15 mL) coarse sea salt
freshly ground pepper
2 lb (1 kg) nugget potatoes, cut in half

Roasted potatoes are the perfect accompaniment to a simple roasted chicken or lamb leg. They also make a nice addition to a warm salad.

Preheat oven to 400°F (200°C).

Combine the vegetable and olive oil with the rosemary, paprika, salt, and pepper. Toss the potatoes in this mixture and spread out on a baking sheet. Do not crowd the potatoes or they will steam and not get crispy. You may have to use 2 baking sheets.

Roast the potatoes for 15 minutes, and then lower the oven temperature to 350°F (180°C) for about half an hour until the potatoes are golden and crisp on the outside and tender in the middle. Turn the potatoes only once during cooking—this ensures crispiness. Give the roasted potatoes an extra drizzling of good extra virgin olive oil after you remove them from the oven and serve hot.

POTATO BOULANGER

Serves 8–12

½ cup (125 mL) unsalted butter
1 cup (250 mL) sliced onion
1 cup (250 mL) sliced button mushrooms
½ oz (15 g) dried porcini or cep
    mushrooms, rehydrated and squeezed
    dry

1 tsp (5 mL) salt
1 tsp (5 mL) freshly ground pepper
2 large yellow-fleshed potatoes like
    Yukon Gold, peeled
2 cups (500 mL) well-flavored chicken
    stock

This is a classic potato dish that you can buy at any boulangerie in France. It's usually put in the window of French country bakeries along with the tarte Tatin and composed salads. This potato dish is much like a gratin, but it's not creamy as it's cooked in flavorful stock and butter rather than cream. This is a side dish that slices well and is fantastic to serve when you have lots of people coming for dinner and you need a sturdy starch that can be pre-portioned.

Preheat oven to 450°F (230°C). Butter a round 9-inch (1.5 L) cake pan.

Melt 3 Tbsp (45 mL) of the butter in a sauté pan over medium heat. When hot, add the sliced onion, button mushrooms, and porcini mushrooms. Lightly season and cook over medium heat until the onions and mushrooms are soft and lightly golden.

Using a mandoline, cut the potatoes into thin slices, about ¼ inch (0.5 cm) thick. Cover the bottom of the cake pan with slices of potato. Spread half the mushroom-onion mixture on top. Lightly season and top with another layer of potato. Continue layering in the same manner. When finished, there should be 3 layers of potatoes and 2 layers of the mushroom-onion mixture. Pour the chicken stock into the cake pan. Dot the top of the boulanger with the remaining butter. Season lightly and bake, uncovered, for 45 minutes. Every 10 minutes during baking, press down on

the top of the boulanger with a spatula to ensure that the finished boulanger is compact. Test for doneness by inserting a knife into the potatoes. The boulanger is ready when the potatoes are tender and the top has formed a golden crust. Remove from the oven and keep warm until needed.

RISOTTO

Serves 6–8

8–12 cups (2–3 L) chicken stock
2 Tbsp (30 mL) olive oil
1 Tbsp (15 mL) unsalted butter
½ cup (125 mL) finely chopped onion
1 clove garlic, finely chopped
2 cups (500 mL) Arborio rice, superfino
1 cup (250 mL) white wine
2 large slices dried porcini mushroom

1 tsp (5 mL) salt
½ cup (125 mL) grated Parmigiano
 Reggiano cheese, or other hard, salty
 cheese
¼ cup (60 mL) whipping (35%) cream or
 mascarpone
¼ cup (60 mL) unsalted butter
5 drops white truffle oil, optional

Arborio rice is a short-grained rice, which means it has a high starch content that is released by slowly braising the kernels in stock. This starch in combination with the stock creates a binding sauce for the rice. Risotto can be eaten on its own, or as a vehicle for braised meat or a ragù. When a few threads of saffron are added to the cooking broth, it's called risotto Milanese and is the classic accompaniment to Osso Bucco. I like to add morel mushrooms, peas, and mint in the spring and Swiss chard in the summer. The combinations for risotto are endless, and whether you serve it as a starch or as a quick meal, it's always satisfying.

Bring the chicken stock to a boil in a pot, and lower the heat to a simmer. The stock must be warm when added to the risotto.

Warm the olive oil and butter in a large, heavy pot. Add the onion and sauté over medium-high heat until the onion softens slightly and begins to color lightly. Add the garlic and sauté for another minute. Add the rice and cook for another 3 minutes, stirring often to prevent the rice from sticking to the bottom. Ensure the rice is well coated with the fat. The rice will begin to toast and pop, adding a lovely nutty flavor to the risotto. Deglaze the rice by pouring the wine over and stirring with a wooden spoon to dislodge any kernels or caramelized bits that have stuck to the bottom of the pan. Add the porcini mushroom, salt, and about 1½ cups (325 mL) of warm stock, enough to just barely cover the rice. Stir well to combine all the ingredients, lower the heat, and simmer gently. At this point, the rice should be surrounded by stock so that it absorbs the liquid evenly.

As the rice absorbs the stock, continue to add more stock in 1-cup (250-mL) amounts, keeping the heat at a constant simmer. Stir often and continue to add the stock, keeping the level just above the rice. After 15 minutes, the rice will lose most of its hard-kernel quality, but will still be firm in the middle. In the next 3–5 minutes it will finish cooking. If you're adding any garnish like shredded braised meats or greens like chard or spinach, add them now to heat them up.

Taste the rice for texture and seasoning. If it still feels firm but has absorbed most of the liquid in the pot, add a little more stock. If too much stock has been added in the last few minutes, the rice and stock will separate. If too little stock is added, the rice will become heavy and sticky. The risotto should be cooked so that the rice is bound together by sauce and doesn't resemble a rice pudding or goopy porridge.

Properly cooked risotto is all about timing. Prepare risotto right before serving it. If you're cooking risotto for a dinner party you can cook the risotto through halfway and then pour it onto a baking sheet to stop the cooking and reserve it until serving time. You can then finish cooking the risotto by putting it back into the pot, surrounded by liquid, and commence the stirring and hydration process.

Just before serving, stir in half the cheese, the cream, and butter. This will cause the risotto to thicken to the consistency of a sauce. Finish the risotto with a slight drizzle of truffle oil. Sprinkle the remaining cheese over each portion.

Serve immediately before it gets stodgy.

TRUFFLE OIL is created when truffles are soaked in olive oil. Before commercial truffle oil was introduced in the 1980s, chefs in Italy and France traditionally made their own by steeping tiny bits of fresh truffles in high-quality olive oil. This delicate and expensive oil loses its characteristic aroma quickly, so store in the refrigerator. The oil will cloud up and solidify, but that dissipates once you bring it back to room temperature.

SOFT AND CRISPY POLENTA

Serves 12

8 cups (2 L) water

1 Tbsp (15 mL) salt

1 cup (250 mL) stone-ground Italian
   yellow cornmeal, fine grind

1 cup (250 mL) white cornmeal

½ cup (125 mL) unsalted butter

½ cup (125 mL) Parmigiano Reggiano,
   grated

1 baked potato, crumbled, for crispy
   polenta

1 Tbsp (15 mL) salted butter

1 Tbsp (15 mL) olive oil or duck fat

I adore a bowl of soft, creamy polenta with a braise or a stew, especially when the polenta is drizzled with sage brown butter (see page 240). It is also delicious topped with crispy salami and a poached egg like chef Peter Zambri makes for lunch at Victoria's Zambri's restaurant. When making soft polenta it's important to stir constantly and to serve it immediately. I don't recommend serving soft polenta that has been made ahead of time. Like risotto, make the soft polenta to order.

For a different polenta experience try making crispy polenta. My mom makes the best crispy polenta in the world. This is my version of hers, but I never seem to make it quite as well as she does. We traditionally have polenta for Christmas Eve with seafood stewed in tomatoes. We had northern Italian neighbors when I was growing up and this recipe was passed on to our family. It has the traditional crumbled potato in it to make the polenta a little less dense.

Bring the water to a boil in a medium-heavy pot. Add the salt and gradually whisk in the cornmeal. Continue to whisk until the polenta starts to thicken. Reduce the heat to low, switch to a wooden spoon, and continue to simmer gently for 30–40 minutes. Be careful not to burn yourself as the polenta sputters away. Stir frequently so that the polenta doesn't stick to the bottom of the pot and burn. If it becomes too thick, add a ladle or 2 of water. Once the polenta has absorbed all the water and is smooth, stir in the butter and cheese. If you're eating the polenta soft, serve immediately.

If you're going to make crispy polenta, crumble in the flesh of the baked potato (no skin) after the butter and cheese have been added. On a baking sheet lined with waxed or parchment paper, form the polenta into a roll (or spread flat in a baking sheet) and refrigerate until set.

Once the polenta is firm, remove it from the refrigerator and cut the roll into 2-inch (5-cm) rounds. Melt butter and olive oil or duck fat in a cast-iron frying pan over medium-low heat and fry the polenta pieces slowly. Cook three-quarters of the way on one side. Turn only once. Don't fiddle with the polenta pieces or they'll fall apart. Cook until golden brown and crispy on both sides. Serve immediately while the pieces are hot and crispy.

ROASTED ROOT VEGETABLES

Serves 8

4 beets, scrubbed
2 yams, scrubbed
4 carrots, peeled
4 parsnips, peeled
¼ cup (60 mL) vegetable oil

½ tsp (2 mL) salt
½ tsp (2 mL) freshly ground black
  pepper
2 Tbsp (30 mL) chopped fresh thyme
  leaves

Roasted root vegetables are the perfect accompaniment to roasted meats in the winter months. Full of vitamins and fiber, they are also full of caramelized flavor and can be further flavored with savory herbs like rosemary, thyme, or savory. The key to perfect roasted vegetables is to start them at a high temperature and then finish them off at a lower temperature. They must be roasted in a pan large enough to accommodate all of the pieces without steaming them!

Preheat oven to 425°F (220°C).

Cut the vegetables into uniform pieces to ensure even roasting times. If the beets are small, leave them whole. When roasting, keep the beets separate from the other vegetables, either in a foil pouch or on a separate roasting pan, so that their color does not bleed on to the other vegetables, turning everything pink.

Toss the vegetables in the vegetable oil (do the beets separately) and season with salt and pepper. Place in a roasting pan or on a large baking sheet. Roast for 20 minutes and then lower the oven temperature to 350°F (180°C) and roast for another 20 minutes until all the vegetables are slightly caramelized on the outside.

CHEF'S TIP

Only turn the vegetables once during cooking to ensure they become golden. If you keep moving them as they cook, they will not have an opportunity to caramelize on the bottom of the pan and you will keep letting the heat escape from the oven, thus extending the roasting time. If the root vegetables are old and woody, they may require longer roasting times.

SAUTÉED WHITE BEANS
WITH ROSEMARY AND LEMON

Serves 8

2 19-oz (540-mL) cans white beans
    (or 1 cup/250 mL dried white or
    cannellini beans soaked overnight
    and simmered)
2 garlic cloves, roughly chopped
1 Tbsp (15 mL) unsalted butter
1 Tbsp (15 mL) olive oil
large handful fresh rosemary, taken off
    its stems and chopped

2 tsp (10 mL) salt
½ tsp (2 mL) chili flakes or crumbled dry
    peperoncino
juice and zest of 1 lemon

FOR GARNISH
4 oz (125 g) (about 6 slices) pancetta,
    thinly sliced and crisped, to garnish

These beans are a delicious accompaniment to any roasted pork dish or roasted chicken stuffed with lemons and rosemary. I like them because they get little nubby crispy bits on the outside that give textural interest.

To prepare the beans, rinse and pat dry the canned white beans. Heat a frying pan and sauté the beans with the garlic in the butter and oil over medium heat, being careful not to burn the garlic. Add the rosemary and season with salt and pepper. After coating the white beans in the salt and rosemary, leave them mainly on one side to get crispy, before continuing to sauté. As the beans begin to cook they will soften slightly and the inner mush will stick to the outside of the beans and get crispy. These little crispy bits are the best part. You can encourage the crispiness by crushing the beans slightly as they cook. Finish the crispy white beans by drizzling them with the lemon juice and a fresh grating of the lemon zest. Garnish the beans with crumbled crisped pancetta slices.

DU PUY LENTILS COOKED IN ROSÉ WINE

Serves 8

1 shallot, finely diced
1 carrot, finely diced
1 celery rib, finely diced
2 Tbsp (30 mL) olive oil
2 cups (500 mL) du Puy lentils (small French lentils) or Lenticchie di Castelluccio

1 sprig thyme
1 bay leaf
1 clove garlic, peeled and left whole
1 bottle (750 mL) rosé wine (no white Zinfandel, please!)
4 cups (1 L) warm chicken stock

Du Puy lentils are those tiny spotted French lentils. They have their own appellation in the south of France, in Puy, and are much more delicious, I think, than a regular large green lentil. When cooked, a du Puy lentil has much more integrity than a green lentil. They hold their form and are less mushy when cooked properly. I like to cook mine with a mirepoix (see page 133) in rosé wine in the spirit of the south of France!

Sauté the diced shallot, carrot, and celery in the olive oil. Add the lentils, lightly toasting them until you can hear them start to crackle a little bit (about 2 minutes). Toasting gives them a nutty flavor. Add the thyme, bay leaf, and garlic clove. Do not add salt to legumes when they are cooking as salt will toughen their skins. Deglaze the lentils and vegetables with the wine. Add enough warm stock to the pot to generously cover the lentils. Bring the lentils, wine, and stock to a boil and then turn the heat down to a bare simmer. Cook the lentils gently until they're cooked through and tender, but still firm. Add more stock to the pot if necessary. Don't cook the lentils until mushy, though! They should still have some integrity when they're cooked.

Lentils are an excellent accompaniment to roasted game meat, small game birds, and robust, oily fish like salmon or ling cod.

PANISSE

Serves 6

2 tsp (10 mL) vegetable oil	freshly ground pepper
1½ cups (375 mL) chickpea flour	1 clove crushed garlic, finely minced
3 cups (750 mL) cold water	1½ Tbsp (22 mL) olive oil
2 tsp (10 mL) salt	8 cups (2 L) peanut oil for frying

These southern French chickpea "french fries" are a delicious snack on their own or as an accompaniment to roasted lamb, when dipped in anchovy aioli.

Prepare a baking sheet to set the batter by lining it with plastic wrap and oiling the wrap with the vegetable oil.

Put the chickpea flour in a large bowl, stir in the cold water, and beat with a wire whisk for 1–2 minutes, or until you have a smooth paste. Stir in the salt, pepper, garlic, and olive oil.

Pour the paste into a heavy-bottomed pot and place over medium heat, stirring constantly with a wooden spoon. After 5–10 minutes, the mixture will thicken, then become lumpy, and finally form a thick mass. It's important to fully cook the batter for it to set properly. Remove from the heat and beat until the dough is very smooth.

Spoon into the prepared baking sheet and allow to cool in the refrigerator for at least 1 hour. You can also put the panisse into the freezer to solidify. When the panisse dough is cool, cut it into little sticks (½ inch/1 cm wide and about 2 inches/5 cm long).

Heat the peanut oil in a heavy pot until very hot, and then fry the little sticks in the same manner as you would french fries, not cooking too many at one time to avoid crowding the pan and lowering the temperature of the oil. When they're crisp and golden, turn them very carefully with a slotted spoon. They'll be done in about 4 minutes. Remove and drain on paper towels. Put them on trays in a slow oven (250°F/120°C) to stay warm while you fry the remaining panisse.

Sprinkle with salt while still warm and serve immediately.

SCHUBERT'S GRAINY MUSTARD SPAETZLE

Serves 6

5 large eggs, slightly beaten
1 cup (250 mL) whole (3.25%) milk
2 Tbsp (30 mL) grainy mustard
2½–3 cups (625–750 mL) all-purpose
   flour
2 tsp (10 mL) salt

2 Tbsp (30 mL) vegetable oil
½ lb (250 g) smoky bacon, cut into very
   thin strips
butter for frying
2 Tbsp (30 mL) each of finely chopped
   chives, parsley, and tarragon

This recipe was given to me by my chef friend Jason Schubert. These little German dumplings are the perfect accompaniment to any braised dish with a creamy sauce or wine-laced jus. Note that you will need a spaetzle maker for this recipe.

Put a large pot of salted water on the stove to boil. Prepare an ice-water bath. Mix together the eggs, milk, and mustard until blended. Gradually add the flour and salt, stirring with a whisk, until the flour is incorporated. The batter should be smooth and not lumpy and will begin to become "glutinous," i.e., you can judge when the batter has had enough flour incorporated into it by how quickly it falls off the whisk when it is held up above the bowl. When the batter is ready, hold a spaetzle maker above the boiling water, and ladle batter into its holding compartment. Slide the box over the grater and the spaetzle will fall in tear-drop shapes into the water below. Cook the spaetzle in the boiling water until they float and are tender. Remove the spaetzle from the water into a fine mesh sieve and plunge them into the ice-water bath. Strain and cool. Toss with 1 Tbsp (15 mL) of the vegetable oil so that they won't stick together. While the spaetzle are cooling, render the bacon in the remaining oil until crispy. Remove the bacon with a slotted spoon onto a paper towel and reserve the bacon fat.

To serve, reheat the spaetzle by heating them in a frying pan with the reserved bacon fat and a knob of butter. Fry the spaetzle in the bacon fat and sauté until golden. Season to taste with more salt if necessary. Right before serving, toss the spaetzle in the pan with the crispy bacon. Add the fresh herbs, toss the spaetzle until coated, and serve immediately.

DESSERTS

BITTERSWEET CHOCOLATE TART

Serves 12

FOR THE PÂTE SABLÉE (TART CRUST)

1¾ cup (425 mL) pastry flour

1 cup (250 mL) confectioner's sugar

pinch of salt

14 Tbsp (210 mL) unsalted butter, chilled
and cut into small cubes

seeds from ¼ vanilla bean pod

½ tsp (1 mL) lemon zest, optional

2 large egg yolks

CHOCOLATE FILLING

¾ cup (175 mL) whipping (35%) cream

⅓ cup (75 mL) half-and-half (10%)
cream

7 oz (200 g) bittersweet chocolate, such
as Valrhona, Scharffen Berger, or
Green and Black's

1 large egg, slightly beaten

This is probably the tart I served most frequently for our Orchard Dinners. It's a classic, barely set chocolate ganache tart. Its distinction comes from the delicate tart crust and the quality of dark chocolate you use. You can also flavor the ganache with orange zest or oil and stud the tart with dried or fresh cherries.

For the tart crust, place the flour, confectioner's sugar, and salt in the bowl of a food processor. Add the butter and process lightly until the ingredients form a fine crumb. Mix the vanilla seeds and lemon zest, if using, into the egg yolks. Add the yolks to the dry ingredients while the machine is running and pulse until the ingredients hold together. Remove from the food processor and bring the dough together gently. Divide into 2 disks, wrap the dough in plastic wrap, and refrigerate for 2 hours before using. Freeze the second disk to use later.

Preheat oven to 375°F (190°C).

Roll out 1 disk of the pastry, line a 9-inch (1.5-L) removable-bottom tart pan, and chill the shell for 1 hour before baking. Once the shell is chilled, prick the pastry with a fork, and then blind-bake (see page 270) the shell for 15 minutes. Remove the beans from the tart and bake for another 15 minutes without the beans. When the tart is fully baked, dry in the middle, and slightly golden, remove from the oven and let cool slightly.

Lower the oven temperature to 275°F (140°C).

While the pastry is cooling, make the filling. Combine both creams in a saucepan and bring to a simmer over moderate heat. Remove the pan from the heat, add the chocolate, and stir until the chocolate is thoroughly melted and the mixture is well blended.

Let cool slightly and add the egg, whisking until thoroughly blended. Pour the filling into the cooled tart shell. Bake in the center of the oven until the filling is slightly firm but still trembling in the center, 12–15 minutes. Watch carefully as oven temperatures can vary. Remove from the oven and place on a rack to cool. When the tart is cool, remove the sides of the tart pan. Cut the tart into 12 wedges. Place a wedge into the center of a plate. Garnish with candied orange peel (see page 303) and serve.

SUGGESTED WINE PAIRING
BC: Elephant Island Stellaport, Naramata
International: Domaine du Mas Blanc Banyuls Rimage
La Coume, Languedoc-Roussillon, France

ALMOND AND APRICOT TART
PERFUMED WITH LAVENDER

Serves 12

FOR THE CRUST

1½ cups (375 mL) all-purpose flour
½ cup (125 mL) confectioner's sugar
zest of 1 lemon
pinch of salt
6½ Tbsp (97 mL) unsalted butter, cut
   into small cubes
seeds from ¼ vanilla bean pot
4 egg yolks

FOR THE ALMOND CREAM OR
FRANGIPANE

6 Tbsp (90 mL) unsalted butter
1 cup (250 mL) ground almonds
⅔ cup (150 mL) confectioner's sugar
2 large eggs
1 Tbsp (15 mL) almond extract or vanilla
zest of 1 orange
1 Tbsp (15 mL) culinary lavender
   (see page 271)
2 Tbsp (30 mL) pastry flour

12 fresh apricots (not too ripe) cut in half
   with pits removed, or 12 figs plumped
   in warm wine

BLIND-BAKING a tart will ensure that the tart pastry is mostly cooked before the filling goes into the shell. The shell is lined with aluminum foil or parchment paper and weighted down with dried beans or pastry weights and then baked for 20 minutes or until the foil and weights lift away easily from the pastry. This will prevent an unevenly baked tart. I like to cook the shell for another 3–5 minutes after the weights have been lifted away, just to ensure the middle is cooked through.

CULINARY LAVENDER is a delicious addition to desserts and petits fours. All lavender is edible, but usually buds of the English Lavender or True Lavender (*Lavandula angustifolia*) or the 'Provence' or 'Vera' hybrids (*Lavandula intermedia*) are used in cooking. I suggest 'Provence' as the most appealing culinary lavender as it has a lower camphor and resin content than English Lavender does.

This tart is a classic from the south of France. It's a flexible recipe that can be perfumed with other aromatics and studded with fruit such as figs, apricots, or plums.

To prepare the pastry, place the flour, confectioner's sugar, lemon zest, and salt into the bowl of a food processor. Add the butter and process lightly until the ingredients form a fine crumb. In a separate bowl, mix the vanilla seeds into the egg yolks. Add this yolk mixture to the dry ingredients while the machine is running and process until the ingredients hold together. Remove from the food processor, bring the dough together gently, and press into a disk. Wrap the dough in plastic wrap and refrigerate for 2 hours before using.

For the almond cream, cream the butter in a standing mixer until very soft. Combine the ground almonds and confectioner's sugar in a separate bowl and add to the butter. Add the eggs very slowly, 1 at a time, beating well after each addition. Stir in the almond extract, zest, lavender, and flour.

Preheat oven to 375°F (190°C).

Roll out the pastry between 2 layers of plastic wrap or parchment paper. Line a 9-inch (1.5 L) removable-bottom tart pan with the pastry, and then chill the shell for 1 hour before baking. Once the shell is chilled, cover with aluminum foil and add dried beans to weigh down the pastry. Blind-bake the shell for 20 minutes or until the foil and weights lift away easily from the pastry. Remove the beans from the tart and bake for another 15 minutes without the beans. Once fully baked, dry in the middle, and slightly golden, remove from the oven and let cool slightly.

Once the tart is cool, spread the almond cream on the bottom of the tart crust. Place the apricots in concentric circles, hump side up, around the tart in the almond cream. Bake for about 25 minutes or until a skewer comes out clean from the center of the tart. The frangipane will puff up around the apricots and the almond cream should be a deep golden brown color.

Cool tart slightly before eating.

SUGGESTED WINE PAIRING
BC: Elephant Island Apricot Dessert Wine
International: Royal Tokaji Company Tokaji Aszu "Birsalmas" 5 puttonyos, Hungary

CHÈVRE AND DRIED FRUIT TART

Serves 8

FOR THE PASTRY

1½ cups (375 mL) all-purpose flour

½ cup (125 mL) confectioner's sugar

pinch of salt

½ cup (125 mL) unsalted butter, chilled
and cut into small cubes

1 large egg yolk

2 Tbsp (30 mL) water

FOR THE GOAT CHEESE FILLING

1 lb (500 g) fresh goat cheese, softened
(labane, quark cheese, mascarpone, or
cream cheese – use all of 1 kind or a
combination of a few)

¾ cup (175 mL) granulated sugar

4 eggs, separated

zest of 1 lemon

½ cup (125 mL) unsalted butter, melted,
cooled, and skimmed (clarified butter)
(see page 172)

½ cup (125 mL) all-purpose flour

pinch of salt

½ cup (125 mL) raisins or chopped dried
fruit like cherries, soaked in warm
rum, brandy, or wine

This is a lighter, more European-style of cheese tart compared to our dense, North American–style cheesecake. This recipe is ideal for the wonderful local goat cheese yogurt or "labane" from Carmelis Artisan Goat cheese dairy, which is full of flavor and short on calories and fat.

For the pastry, combine the flour, sugar, and salt in a food processor. Add the butter and pulse just until the ingredients form a fine crumb. Add the egg yolk and water while the machine is running and continue to process until the dough forms a ball. Pour out onto a counter, bring the dough together, shape into a ball, wrap with plastic wrap, and chill in the refrigerator for 1 hour before using.

Roll the pastry out into a circle ¼ inch (0.5 cm) thick and 2 inches (5 cm) wider in diameter than a 9-inch (1.5-L) removable bottom tart pan. Line the pan with the pastry, cutting off any excess, and chill for half an hour in the freezer. Prick the pastry with a fork.

Preheat oven to 375°F (190°C).

Line the chilled pastry shell with parchment paper, fill with dried bean or weights, and blind-bake (see page 270) for 30 minutes or until the crust is set in the center.

Lower oven temperature to 325°F (160°C).

For the filling, combine the cheese and ¼ cup (60 mL) of the sugar in a bowl. Add the egg yolks to the cheese and mix in until light and fluffy. Add the lemon zest and butter and continue to combine. Sift the flour and salt together in a separate bowl and fold into the cheese mixture. Add the raisins and gently mix in. Do not overwork at this point.

Whisk the egg whites with the remaining sugar until the whites hold stiff peaks. Stir one-quarter of the egg whites into the cheese filling. Gently fold in the remaining egg whites until thoroughly combined. Pour the filling gently into the blind-baked tart shell, and using a palette knife, spread the filling to the edges of the tart and smooth the top. Bake for 45 minutes. When finished baking, let cool and remove the ring from the tart pan to slice and serve.

SUGGESTED WINE PAIRING

BC: Gray Monk Ehrenfelser Ice Wine, Winfield
International: Château de Fesles Bonnezeaux,
Loire Valley, France

CARAMELIZED TARTE AU CITRON

Serves 8–12

FOR THE PÂTE SUCRÉE

1¾ cups (425 mL) all-purpose flour

1 cup (250 mL) confectioner's sugar, sifted

pinch of salt

7 Tbsp (105 mL) unsalted butter

2 large eggs, at room temperature

FOR THE FILLING

6 large eggs

1½ cups (375 mL) whipping (35%) cream

½ cup (125 mL) granulated sugar

juice and zest of 6 lemons

confectioner's sugar for dusting

Visiting chef Jason Schubert and I loved serving this lemon tart, which is inspired by the classic recipes of the Roux brothers from Le Gavroche Restaurant in London, UK. A lemon tart is the classic way to end a rich meal and lemon is a perfect flavor accompaniment to all seasonal soft fruits. The crunchy caramelized lemon custard adds an extra textural pleasure.

For the pastry dough, place the flour, sugar, salt, and butter into the bowl of the food processor. Process until the ingredients form a fine crumb. Add the eggs through the feed tube while the machine is running and pulse just until the ingredients come together. Remove the dough from the bowl and form it into a ball. Chill in the refrigerator for at least 1 hour before using.

Roll the pastry out ⅛ inch (0.3 cm) thick into a circle slightly larger than a 9-inch (1.5-L) removable-bottom tart pan. Line the pan with the pastry dough, pressing it into the sides of the pan. Place the pan on a baking sheet. Prick the pastry with a fork and refrigerate for half an hour.

Preheat oven to 400°F (200°C).

Blind-bake (see page 270) the pastry shell for 20 minutes until the parchment paper with the beans on it pulls away from the cooked pastry beneath. Finish baking the tart shell by removing the baking beans and baking for another 5–10 minutes until the shell is golden brown and fully cooked through.

To make the filling, beat the eggs, cream, and sugar together in a large stainless-steel bowl. Add the lemon juice and zest and whisk to incorporate thoroughly. Strain the filling through a fine mesh sieve into a clean container. This filling can be stored in the refrigerator for up to 1 week before using.

Preheat oven to 300°F (150°C).

Fill the tart shell to the rim with the lemon filling. It's important to fill the shell as full as possible to cre-

ate a level surface for you to caramelize and to prevent the pastry crust from burning. Bake for 15–20 minutes. The tart must cook gently to prevent the filling from bubbling or rising. The tart is cooked when the filling is firm around the edges and the center jiggles slightly. It will continue to cook during cooling. Remove from the oven and cool on a wire rack.

Dust the top of the tart lightly with confectioner's sugar. Glaze the top of the tart by using a blow torch or put it under a preheated broiler. Cut the tart into wedges and place a wedge on each plate. Garnish with fresh fruit, compote, or coulis and serve.

SUGGESTED WINE PAIRING

BC: Lang Late Harvest Riesling, Naramata

International: Michele Chiarlo "Nivole" Moscato d'Asti, Piedmont, Italy

ORANGE AND GINGER TART

Serves 8

FOR THE PÂTE SUCRÉE

1¾ cup (425 mL) all-purpose flour

1 cup (250 mL) confectioner's sugar, sifted

pinch of salt

½ cup (125 mL) finely diced candied ginger

7 Tbsp (105 mL) unsalted butter, cold and cut into cubes

2 large eggs, at room temperature

FOR THE FILLING

6 large eggs

1½ cups (375 mL) whipping (35%) cream

½ cup (125 mL) granulated sugar

¼ cup (60 mL) finely grated fresh ginger, about a 2-inch (5-cm) piece, peeled (see page 289)

juice and zest of 6 oranges

confectioner's sugar for dusting

Orange and ginger are a fresh way to end a meal. I love candied ginger and adding it to the tart dough gives extra texture.

To make the pastry, place the flour, sugar, salt, and candied ginger into the bowl of a food processor. Pulse until combined. Add the cold butter and pulse until the ingredients form a fine crumb. Add the eggs through the feed tube while the machine is running and process just until the ingredients come together. Remove the dough from the bowl and form it into a ball. Chill in the refrigerator for at least 1 hour before using.

Roll the pastry out into a circle ⅛ inch (0.3 cm) thick and slightly larger than a 9-inch (1.5-L) removable-bottom tart pan. Line the tart pan with the pastry, pressing the dough into the sides of the pan. Place the shell onto a baking sheet. Prick the pastry with a fork and refrigerate for half an hour.

Preheat oven to 400°F (200°C).

Place the baking sheet with the tart shell into the oven. Blind-bake (see page 270) the shell for 20 minutes until the parchment paper with the beans on it pulls away from the cooked pastry beneath. Remove the baking beans and bake for another 5–10 minutes until the shell is golden brown and fully cooked through.

To make the filling, beat the eggs, cream, and sugar together in a large stainless-steel bowl. Add the grated ginger, orange juice, and zest and whisk to incorporate thoroughly. Strain the filling through a fine mesh sieve into a clean container. This filling can be stored for up to 1 week before use.

Lower oven temperature to 300°F (150°C).

Fill the tart shell to the rim with the orange filling. It's important to fill the shell as full as possible to create a level surface for you to caramelize and to prevent the pastry crust from burning. Bake for 15–20 minutes. The tart must cook gently to prevent the filling from bubbling or rising. The tart is cooked when the filling is firm around the edges and the center jiggles slightly. The tart will continue to cook during cooling. Remove from the oven and cool. Once cool, dust the top of the tart lightly with confectioner's sugar. Glaze the top of the tart using a blow torch or put it under a preheated broiler. Cut the tart into wedges and place a wedge on each plate. Garnish with fresh fruit, compote, or coulis and serve.

SUGGESTED WINE PAIRING

BC: Wild Goose "TBA" Riesling, Okanagan Falls
International: Dr Pauly Bergweiler Bernkasteler alte Badstube am Docterberg Riesling Beerenauslese, Mosel, Germany

NECTARINE AND BLUEBERRY CROSTATA

Makes enough for one large 13-inch (32.5-cm) or two 6-inch (15-cm) tarts

FOR THE PASTRY
1½ cups (375 mL) all-purpose flour
½ cup (125 mL) cornmeal
½ tsp (2 mL) salt
½ tsp (2 mL) granulated sugar
¼ cup (60 mL) salted butter
¾ cup (175 mL) unsalted butter
3 Tbsp (45 mL) ice water

FOR THE TART
1 Tbsp (15 mL) cornmeal
4 nectarines (about 2 lb/1 kg), sliced, skins on
3 Tbsp (45 mL) granulated sugar
zest of 1 lemon
2 cups (500 mL) blueberries

FOR THE EGG WASH
1 large egg yolk
1 Tbsp (15 mL) whole (3.25%) milk

A crostata is a rustic, open-faced tart with a crunchy pastry. You can add any seasonal fruit to the top of this tart. Berries like gooseberries or currants are particularly pretty when mixed with other fruits.

MAKING THE PASTRY BY HAND

Mix the flour, cornmeal, salt, and sugar in a bowl big enough to play around in without spilling ingredients over the side. Cut the salted butter into ½-inch (1-cm) cubes and the unsalted butter into ¼-inch (0.5-cm) cubes. Using a pastry cutter, blend the butter into the dry mixture until the dough resembles coarse meal. Sprinkle in the ice water, tossing lightly with your hands or a fork. Press the dough into a solid mass, divide in half, and wrap tightly in plastic wrap. Shape into ½-inch (1-cm) flattened discs (this will make rolling the dough later a much easier task) and refrigerate or freeze. The dough can be frozen indefinitely if well wrapped.

MAKING THE PASTRY IN FOOD PROCESSOR

Combine the flour, cornmeal, sugar, and salt in a food processor fitted with a steel blade and pulse until combined. Cube both butters into ¼-inch (1-cm) cubes, keeping it very cold. Put the butter into the mixer and pulse a few times until the mixture looks like coarse meal. Drizzle in the water while continuing to pulse. Dump the dough into a bowl and lightly push it together by hand and wrap in plastic wrap. Shape the dough into a ½-inch (1-cm) flattened disc (this will make rolling the dough later, a much easier task) and refrigerate or freeze. The dough can be frozen indefinitely if well wrapped.

For best results, refrigerate the dough for at least 2 hours, although overnight is best. Roll the dough to ¼ inch (0.5 cm) in thickness to use for a crostata, and chill again for at least 2 hours before baking.

Preheat oven to 375°F (190°C).

To make the tart, remove the rolled dough from the refrigerator. Place on an inverted baking sheet lined with parchment paper or a pizza stone sprinkled with the 1 Tbsp (15 mL) cornmeal. Toss the sliced nectarines in 2 Tbsp (30 mL) of the sugar and the lemon zest and arrange evenly in the tart shell, leaving 2 inches (5 cm) around the edge of the tart. Scatter the blueberries over the nectarines. Sprinkle the fruit with the remaining sugar. Crimp or fold over the edges of the tart shell to form a rustic crust around the fruit, rotating the tart and folding the border of the exposed dough up and over itself at regular intervals. Make an egg wash with the egg yolk and milk by whisking with a fork to combine. Brush the egg wash over the tart crust. For extra crunch, sprinkle the crust with sugar.

Bake the crostata for 30–45 minutes, until the tart shell is fully cooked and a deep golden brown. Cool the tart for 5 minutes on the inverted baking sheet it was baked on and then transfer to a wire rack to finish cooling. Cut the crostata into wedges or 2-inch (5-cm) slices and serve with crème fraîche or ice cream.

SUGGESTED WINE PAIRING
BC: Elephant Island Apricot Dessert Wine, Naramata
International: Pellegrino Moscato Passito di Pantelleria, Italy

PLUM AND PISTACHIO GALETTE

Makes one 12-inch (30-cm) tart, enough to serve 8 people

FOR THE GALETTE DOUGH
(MAKES ABOUT 20 OZ (550 G) OF
DOUGH, ENOUGH FOR 2 OPEN-FACED,
12-INCH (30-CM) GALETTES OR
1 COVERED GALETTE)

2 cups (500 mL) unbleached all-purpose
   flour, organic if possible
1 tsp (5 mL) granulated sugar
¼ tsp (1 mL) salt
¾ cup (175 mL) butter, chilled and cut
   into ½-inch (1-cm) cubes
7 Tbsp (105 mL) ice water

FOR EACH OPEN TART

one ½ recipe galette dough (about
   10 oz/275 g)
¼ cup (60 mL) crushed amaretti biscuits
1½ lb (750 g) plums (I like the beautiful
   Elephant Heart plums)
¼ cup (60 mL) granulated sugar
½ cup (125 mL) pistachio nuts, lightly
   toasted and left whole
¼ cup (60 mL) chopped candied orange
   peel (see page 303)
1 tsp (5 mL) orange blossom water

1 Tbsp (15 mL) unsalted butter, melted,
   for brushing the crust
2 tsp (10 mL) granulated sugar, optional
3 Tbsp (45 mL) apricot or red currant
   jam, warmed for glazing
1 tsp (5 mL) orange blossom water, to
   infuse the glazing jam

This galette has an exotic feel to it, with the pistachios and orange blossom water adding a Middle Eastern bent that is perfect for the hot weather.

I've always used the *Chez Panisse Fruit* book's recipe for galette dough. It's a no-fail recipe that you must make by hand, and it yields a crunchy crust. The idea of using ground-up amaretti biscuits to soak up all the juices from the plums is brilliant. They provide a sweet, almond flavor to the tart that complements the apricots and plums. Try making a similar tart with apricots and red currants or cherries in season. The combinations for a fruit galette are as endless as the Okanagan summer is long.

To prepare the dough, combine the flour, sugar, and salt in a large mixing bowl. Cut 4 Tbsp (60 mL) of the butter into the flour mixture with a pastry cutter, mixing until the dough resembles coarse meal. This dispersion of butter throughout the pastry will make it tender. Cut in the remaining butter with the pastry cutter, just until the biggest pieces of butter are the size of large peas. These larger pieces of butter will make the pastry flaky. Dribble the ice water into the flour

mixture in several stages, tossing and mixing between each addition, until the dough just comes together. Do not pinch or squeeze the dough or you'll overwork it, making it tough. Keep tossing the dough until it comes together. Add more water if the dough is too dry. Divide the dough in half, and firmly press each half into a ball and wrap tightly in plastic wrap. Press each ball down into a 4-inch (10-cm) disc. Refrigerate for at least 1 hour before rolling the dough out.

When you're ready to roll the dough, take 1 disc at a time from the refrigerator and let it soften slightly so that you can roll it, but it's still cold. Between 2 pieces of parchment paper or on a clean, floured work surface, roll out the disc into a 14-inch (35-cm) circle about ⅛ inch (0.3 cm) thick. Transfer the dough to a parchment-lined baking sheet and refrigerate for at least 1 hour before baking. This will prevent the tart from shrinking.

Preheat oven to 400°F (200°C).

Remove the rolled dough from the refrigerator and sprinkle it with the crushed amaretti biscuits, leaving a 2-inch (5-cm) border unsprinkled. Cut the plums in half, or quarters if they're large, and remove the pits. Arrange the fruit snuggly, purple skin side up, in concentric circles on the dough over the amaretti, leaving the border bare. Sprinkle the sugar over the fruit with the pistachios, candied peel, and orange blossom water.

Fold the border up around the fruit and crimp the edges, pushing the dough toward the fruit to make a rim that resembles a braided rope. Crimp this rim if you like, but remember that it must act like a dam, preventing the plum juices from escaping. Be careful to avoid cracks or wrinkles. Brush this border with melted butter and sprinkle it with some sugar, if you like.

Bake the tart for about 45 minutes until the crust is a dark golden brown and slightly caramelized. As soon as the galette is out of the oven, remove it from its baking sheet by sliding it off the parchment paper onto a cooling rack. This will keep the bottom of the tart crisp and not soggy from any steam trapped under the tart. Let cool for at least 20 minutes before slicing. You can glaze the tart by brushing it with a little warmed apricot or currant jam, also infused with orange blossom water.

SUGGESTED WINE PAIRING
BC: Quails' Gate Riesling Icewine, Westbank
International: Domaine Zind-Humbrecht Pinot Gris "Clos Windsbuhl," Alsace, France

CHEF'S TIP
Orange blossom water can be bought at Indian or Middle Eastern groceries.

PATI'S PRUNE JEWEL

Serves 8–10

½ cup (125 mL) soft unsalted butter
1 cup (250 mL) granulated sugar
2 large eggs, beaten
3 tsp (45 mL) pure vanilla extract
1 cup (250 mL) unbleached flour
1 tsp (5 mL) baking powder

pinch of salt
20 Italian prunes, halved and pitted
4 tsp (20 mL) freshly squeezed lemon
  juice
1 tsp (5 mL) granulated sugar
cinnamon

My friend Pati Hill has the most beautiful Italian prune plum tree. Prune plums are the gorgeous blue-pewter colored plums with the green flesh that are ripe right at the end of August or early September. You can see the iridescent silvery blue of a prune plum tree from far away. Pati game me this recipe to accompany the prunes we get from her tree every year. I wait all year to enjoy this treat.

Preheat oven to 350°F (180°C). Grease and flour a 9-inch (2.5-L) springform pan.

Cream the butter and sugar and then add the eggs and vanilla. In a separate bowl, whisk together the flour, baking powder, and salt. Add to the creamed mixture and then beat well. Spoon the batter into the prepared pan. Stand the prune halves on their long sides in a circle next to, but not touching, the edges of the pan. Push them down into the batter. Make another circle inside, and then add a few prune halves to the center of the cake, pushing all the prune halves into the batter. Sprinkle with the lemon juice, sugar, and finally

cinnamon to taste. You can tart it up even more if you like by scattering fresh culinary lavender buds (see page 271) over the top before baking.

Bake in the middle of the oven for about an hour or until a toothpick inserted in the center of the cake comes out clean. Cool on a rack until the cake shrinks away from the springform ring. Run a knife around the outer edge before removing from the ring and cutting your prune jewel.

Pati always doubles this recipe and puts 1 in the freezer. Thaw at room temperature, warm briefly in the oven at 250°F (120°C), and dazzle winter guests with it. Whipped cream or crème fraîche simply "gild the lily," as Pati says.

SUGGESTED WINE PAIRING
BC: Okanagan Spirits Old Italian Prune Eau de Vie, Vernon
International: Stara Slivovitz "Old Plum Brandy," Zadar, Croatia

TARTE TATIN

Serves 12

FOR THE PÂTE BRISÉE

1⅔ cups (400 mL) all-purpose flour
6½ Tbsp (98 mL) cold unsalted butter,
    cut into pieces
2 tsp (10 mL) granulated sugar
½ tsp (2 mL) salt
1 large egg yolk
3 Tbsp (45 mL) water

FOR THE FILLING

6 lb (2.7 kg) firm apples like Spartan,
    Spy, Granny Smith, or Golden
    Delicious, peeled, halved, and cored,
    kept in acidulated water
¾ cup (175 mL) unsalted butter
2 cups (500 mL) granulated sugar

FOR GARNISH

crème fraîche or vanilla ice cream

This upside-down apple tart is known around the world as "La tarte des Demoiselles Tatin," after two sisters from the small Loire town of Lamotte-Beuvron, who invented it. The sisters ran the Hôtel de la Gare, where it's still possible to see their cooking stove and eat genuine tarte Tatin. Sugar caramelizes on the bottom of the pan to form a rich topping when the tart is unmolded with the succulent apples lying underneath on the pastry base.

    We make quite a bit of tarte Tatin in the fall, and it's equally delicious when made with Bartlett pears.

To make the pastry, combine the flour, butter, sugar, and salt to form a meal-like consistency, either in a bowl with a pastry cutter or in the bowl of a food processor fitted with the steel blade attachment. Add the egg yolk and water to the dry ingredients and mix well until coarse crumbs are formed. Gather this dough into a neat ball and knead it slightly, until it forms a cohesive mass. Do not overwork the pastry or it will be tough. Shape the dough into a ball and then pat down into a disk shape (this will help when rolling the pastry dough later). Wrap in plastic wrap and chill for half an hour or until firm. You may also choose to use puff pastry (see page 286) for this recipe.

    Roll out the dough on a floured surface or between 2 sheets of plastic wrap into a disk shape, roughly 12 inches (30 cm) in diameter, a little larger than the 10-inch (25-cm) cast-iron pan it will be baked in. Rest and chill this rolled dough again. The longer it rests, the less it will shrink in the pan, but it must rest for a minimum of 1 hour. If you can prepare the pastry a day ahead that would be ideal! If you're baking the Tatin that same day, rest the pastry in the freezer.

    Preheat oven to 425°F (220°C).

    Prepare the caramel by melting the butter in a cast-iron pan over medium heat and sprinkle with the sugar. Let the sugar dissolve into the butter to form a caramel. Do not stir the sugar or the caramel will crystallize. Once a golden caramel has formed, remove the apples from the acidulated water and arrange them, cored side up, in concentric circles on top of the sugar. They should fill the pan completely and be tightly packed. Now warm the apples on the stovetop to ensure that they will cook at the same rate as the pastry and be soft and caramelized. Cook the apples on medium heat, until a deep golden caramel is formed, about 15–20 minutes. Note: the apples will produce juice that must evaporate before the fruit will caramelize. Let the apples cool slightly. Set the pastry round on top of the apples so that they're completely covered, tucking it in at the edges. Work fast so that the dough isn't softened by the heat of the apples.

Bake the tart for about 30–35 minutes, until the pastry is golden, puffy, and cooked through. Once out of the oven, let the tart sit for about 10 minutes to let the caramel and apples set up slightly. If there is extra caramel and juices in the bottom of the pan, drain out and reduce this juicy caramel slightly so that it can be drizzled on top of the tart once it has been flipped out.

Arm yourself with oven mitts and kitchen towels for your arms and then flip the tart out onto a large plate by placing the plate on top of the pastry and the pan, holding onto both sides of the plate, and quickly flipping over the whole works. Serve slightly warm or cold with a dollop of Chantilly cream, crème fraîche, or cinnamon ice cream (see page 295).

SUGGESTED WINE PAIRING FOR APPLE TARTE TATIN
BC: Elephant Island Fuji "Lee" Ice Wine, Naramata
International: Cristian Drouin "Coeur de Lion" Pommeau de Normandie, Normandy, France

CHEF'S TIP
Substitute a firm Bartlett pear (not a grainy Bosc pear) for the apples to make pear tarte Tatin.

DARK CHOCOLATE MOUSSE

Makes 12 small ramekins

½ cup (125 mL) granulated sugar
¼ cup (60 mL) water
12 oz (350 g) chopped dark chocolate
    with 65–77% cocoa solids

6 Tbsp (90 mL) unsalted butter
2 cups (500 mL) whipping (35%) cream
5 large eggs, separated
1 Tbsp (15 mL) espresso

Dark chocolate mousse is a favorite of mine to serve in ramekins with slices of poached pears and a petits fours–style biscuit like a langue du chat (see page 309).

Simmer the sugar and water together in a small pot to make a sugar syrup. Set aside to cool. Melt the chocolate and butter together in a double boiler or bain-marie. Whip the cream to soft peaks and refrigerate until needed.

Whip the egg yolks until very light and fluffy and then gradually add the cooled sugar syrup. Do not add it too quickly or the yolks will fall. Fold the melted

chocolate mixture into the egg yolks and then fold the whipped cream into the chocolate-egg yolk mixture. Whip the egg whites and fold those in too. Pour into small ramekins or glasses and chill for at least 2 hours to set the mousse.

SUGGESTED WINE PAIRING
BC: La Frenz Tawny, Naramata
International: Seppelt DP 90 Rare Barossa Valley Tawny, South Australia, Australia

ROASTED RHUBARB WITH LAVENDER SUGAR

Serves 12 as an accompaniment

FOR THE LAVENDER SUGAR
²/₃ cup (150 mL) granulated sugar
¹/₃ cup (75 mL) dried culinary lavender
   buds (see page 271)

FOR THE ROASTED RHUBARB
3 cups (750 mL) rhubarb, cut into 1-inch
   (2.5-cm) pieces
juice and zest of 1 orange

This recipe was a spontaneous creation one day during a cooking class. We needed an accompaniment to go with our goat cheese tart for a Provençal meal. Some lavender sugar I had made was just sitting on the ingredient shelf, so we decided to take the still abundant rhubarb (at the end of June!) and toss it in lavender sugar and roast it until the rhubarb was still tender, with a slight sauce around it.

Preheat oven to 375°F (190°C).

To make the lavender sugar, put the sugar and lavender buds into the bowl of a food processor fitted with the metal blade attachment and process for up to 1 minute, until the lavender is ground up with the sugar. This sugar can be made in a larger quantity and stored in an airtight container for up to a year. The flavor just keeps on getting better. I keep both lavender sugar and vanilla sugar in my kitchen and use them all summer long to toss with the procession of summer fruits.

Toss the rhubarb with the lavender sugar, orange juice, and zest. Place the rhubarb into a greased deep 11- × 7-inch (2-L) casserole dish and roast for about 40 minutes, until the pieces of rhubarb start to soften and break down only slightly. When the rhubarb is tender, but not cooked into a stew, remove from the oven and let cool. The rhubarb will continue to cook even after it has been removed from the oven. If you have some extra strawberries around, cut a few up and stir them in now. The residual heat will cook them slightly. I like to serve this compote-like creation slightly warm. Its sweet astringency is a nice complement to anything made with goat cheese.

SUGGESTED WINE PAIRING
BC: Elephant Island Apricot Dessert Wine, Naramata
International: Bava Malvasia di Castelnuovo Don Bosco, Piedmont, Italy

SOUR CHERRY CLAFOUTIS

Serves 6

2 Tbsp (30 mL) unsalted butter
1 lb (500 g) sour cherries, washed, stemmed, and de-pitted
⅓ cup (75 mL) granulated sugar for sweet cherries or ½ cup (125 mL) for sour cherries, plus 3 Tbsp (45 mL)
pinch of ground cinnamon
½ tsp (2 mL) grated lemon zest

2 large eggs, separated
3 Tbsp (45 mL) all-purpose flour
1 tsp (5 mL) vanilla extract
1 tsp (5 mL) almond extract
⅓ cup (75 mL) whipping (35%) cream
pinch of salt
confectioner's sugar for dusting

A clafoutis is a simple baked dessert, half pudding, half sponge, and often served in the south of France. This clafoutis recipe is adapted from the *Chez Panisse Fruit* book. I refer to that book frequently in the summer as the Okanagan is full of fruit. I used this recipe a lot during our cooking classes, as it was a simple way to use some of the "ripe fruit of the week" from our trip to the farmer's market on Saturday mornings.

Preheat oven to 375°F (190°C). Grease a 9-inch (1.5-L) baking dish.

Melt the butter in a sauté pan over medium heat. When the butter is foaming but hasn't begun to brown, add the cherries, ⅓ cup (75 mL) of sugar, cinnamon, and lemon zest. Cook for 7–10 minutes, stirring occasionally, or until the cherries are tender when pierced with the point of a knife and the juices have begun to thicken. Omit this step if using fresh berries or other soft fruits.

Arrange the fruit in the bottom of the prepared baking dish or shallow individual ramekins or gratin dishes.

Beat the egg yolks and the remaining sugar together for several minutes, until light and creamy. Beat in the flour, vanilla, almond extract, and cream. In a separate bowl, beat the egg whites with a pinch of salt until they form soft peaks. Fold the whites into the batter just until blended, and pour the batter over the fruit.

Bake in the top one-third of the oven for about 20 minutes, until the batter is puffed and well browned. Let the clafoutis cool slightly, dust with confectioner's sugar, and serve.

CHEF'S TIP

Clafoutis is also very nice made with peaches, nectarines, plums, blackberries, blueberries, raspberries, poached pears, or a mixture of summer berries. If you're using soft fruits, they don't need the initial cooking but should be tossed in a big bowl with sugar and lemon zest and several tablespoons of flour, and then arranged in a generously buttered baking dish or individual gratin dishes.

SUGGESTED WINE PAIRING

BC: Okanagan Spirits Kirsch Eau de Vie, Vernon
International: Domaine Jean Sipp Kirsch Eau de Vie, Alsace, France

POACHED PEARS

Makes 6 poached pears

FOR THE PEARS
6 pears
freshly squeezed lemon juice

BASIC SIMPLE SYRUP FOR POACHING
2 cups (500 mL) granulated sugar
2 cups (500 mL) water
1 cup (250 mL) wine or tea
1 Tbsp (15 mL) one or a combination
   of sweet/savory spices – choose from
   the following list

Add the following in ¼ tsp (1 mL)
   additions (add just 1 or any
   combination to equal a spice
   addition of 1 Tbsp/15 mL)

SWEET SPICES
cinnamon, vanilla bean, cloves, ginger,
   nutmeg, cardamom, orange zest,
   lemon zest

SAVORY SPICES
juniper berries, black peppercorns, bay
   leaves, coriander

Poached pears are beautiful served with vanilla ice cream, crème fraîche, chocolate sauce, or some of their poaching liquid that has been reduced and had some butter whisked into it. Poached pears are an elegant dessert served on their own, or they can be used to garnish French toast or roasted meat dishes when they've been cut up.

Begin to prepare the pears by neatly peeling and coring them. Use a Swiss swivel peeler for best results when peeling the pears. Use a melon baller to core the pears from the bottom, scooping out the seeds and the hard core. Leave the stem for a pretty presentation and to give you something to grab on to when pulling the pears out of the poaching liquid. Be careful when peeling the pears to be neat and tidy with the peeler or knife, as every mark that you make on the pear's flesh will show up and become magnified once the pear is poached. Put the peeled and cored pears into a bowl with lemon juice and water to prevent them from oxidizing and turning brown.

To prepare the simple syrup, bring the sugar and water to a boil, let simmer for 2 minutes, and then turn down to a bare simmer. Add wine or tea and your flavoring spices. Add the peeled and cored pears to this poaching liquid. Simmer the pears in the syrup for about half an hour, until they're tender (check with the point of a paring knife). You can keep the pears submerged in the syrup by making a parchment paper lid,

placing it over the pears, and weighing it down with some cutlery. This will ensure the pears poach evenly.

Eat the pears immediately after poaching or keep them submerged in their poaching liquid in the refrigerator for up to 2 days. If canning the poached pears, place them in sterilized wide-mouthed Mason jars and pour the hot poaching liquid overtop.

SUGGESTED WINE PAIRING
BC: La Frenz Tawny, Naramata
International: Broadbent Vintage Boal Madeira, Portugal

CHEF'S TIP
Heavy simple syrup, which is a 1:1 ratio of water to granulated sugar, is the poaching liquid for the pears. Make enough simple syrup to accommodate the number of pears you want to poach. Make sure you also choose a large enough pot. You can create an infinite combination of flavors for the syrup. My favorites are white wine, ginger, vanilla bean, lemon zest, and cardamom pods. For a darker, more flavorful pear I add a mixture of red wine, black peppercorns, juniper berries, clove, vanilla bean, and orange zest to the simple syrup.

CHEF'S TIP
Syrup flavorings: red wine and black tea will make for a dark, bold-flavoured syrup and green tea and/or white wine will make for a more delicately flavored syrup.

QUICK PUFF PASTRY

Makes 2.2 lb (1 kg)

3 cups (750 mL) hard flour (see page 309)
1 cup (250 mL) soft flour (see page 309)
2 cups (500 mL) unsalted butter, cut into
¼-inch (0.5-cm) cubes

2 cups (500 mL) whipping (35%) cream
½ tsp (2 mL) salt

It is not always necessary to go through the process of making puff pastry the traditional way. Most chefs use a shortcut method known as "rough puff pastry" that takes only a fraction of the time. Though the results are not quite as spectacular in terms of height, quick puff pastry is just as irresistibly flaky, buttery, and tender as traditional puff pastry. Use quick puff pastry to make millefeuilles, turnovers, and cheese straws, or use it as a crust for tarts, quiches, and pot pies.

Sift the flours and salt into a bowl. Add the butter and toss to coat. Pour in the cream and toss again. On a lightly floured surface roll the dough away from you into a 6 × 18-inch (15 × 45-cm) rectangle. Brush the surface free of excess flour and fold in three, like a business letter. Turn the dough 90° and roll it out again to a 6- × 18-inch (15- × 45-cm) rectangle and fold as before. Wrap well and refrigerate for 1 hour.

Remove from the refrigerator and repeat the 2 turns and folds. Refrigerate again for 1 hour. Remove from the refrigerator for a second time and repeat the 2 turns and folds. Refrigerate again for 1 hour. Roll to the desired thickness and refrigerate or freeze for 1 hour. Bake at 400°F (200°C) until evenly golden, but the darker the better.

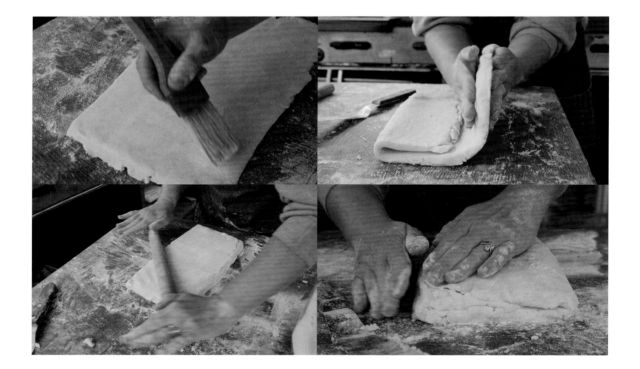

PUFF PASTRY is a light, flaky pastry created by repeatedly folding and turning dough and butter together. Unlike short pastry, which incorporates butter into the dough, in puff pastry butter is folded into the layers. Classic puff pastry begins with a basic dough called a *détrempe* (pronounced 'day-TRAHMP'), which is rolled out and wrapped around a slab of butter. The dough is then repeatedly rolled, folded, and turned. The goal is to distribute the butter evenly in sheets throughout the dough. When the pastry bakes, the moisture in the butter creates steam, causing the dough to puff and separate into many layers. Making classic puff pastry takes a lot of time because the dough needs lengthy rests after the initial *détrempe* stage and between its many "turns" (each series of rolling, folding, and turning).

SPRING MILLEFEUILLE WITH GINGER PASTRY CREAM, FRAISES DU BOIS, AND ROASTED RHUBARB COMPOTE

Serves 6

FOR THE GINGER PASTRY CREAM
(MAKES 1 CUP/250 ML)
1 cup (250 mL) whole (3.25%) milk
¼ cup (60 mL) granulated sugar
½ vanilla bean pod, split and scraped
1 large egg
1 large egg yolk
2 Tbsp (30 mL) cornstarch
1 tsp (5 mL) powdered ginger
½ cup (125 mL) whipping (35%) cream, whipped to stiff peaks

¼ cup (60 mL) candied ginger, finely chopped
1 pint (500 mL) fraises du bois or tiny strawberries (try a fruit farm if you don't have any growing nearby)

FOR THE PASTRY
2.2 lb (1 kg) puff pastry (see page 286)

FOR THE GARNISH
mint leaves

I make this dessert in the spring when strawberries and rhubarb are in season at the same time. Mille-feuille means "a thousand layers" and refers to the classic preparation of buttery puff pastry. If you're feeling ambitious, you can make puff pastry by the classic or "long" method. If you're not feeling ambitious, make a quick puff pastry (see page 286). If you must, you can buy some puff pastry.

Mix together all the milk, 2 Tbsp (30 mL) of the sugar, and the vanilla pod and its seeds in a pot and bring to a boil. In a bowl, beat together the egg and egg yolk and the remaining sugar. Add the cornstarch, powdered ginger, and a little of the warmed milk to temper the eggs, stirring well. Add the remaining warm milk. Once the eggs are tempered, slowly add the rest of the warmed milk to the bowl, whisking constantly. Once all the ingredients are combined put the mixture back into the pot on low heat and stir constantly for 3 minutes, until the mixture coats the back of the spoon. Remove the vanilla pod and strain the custard through a fine mesh sieve into a cold bowl.

Chill the custard. When it's cold, beat the whipping cream to stiff peaks and fold it into the custard with the small chunks of candied ginger. Wash the strawberries and cut them in half if tiny or into slices if bigger and add to the custard.

Preheat oven to 350°F (180°C).

Roll out the pastry to about ⅛ inch (0.3 cm) in thickness, and cut into 12 rectangles. Score the rectangles with cross hatches (X) and bake for 35 minutes on a baking tray lined with parchment paper. The scores will help the pastry to rise evenly and puff up tall. Once cooked, remove from the oven, and cool. When cool, cut the millefeuilles in half with a serrated knife.

To build the millefeuille, place a layer of pastry on the bottom of a plate. Spoon over a generous scoop of custard and strawberries and then top with a scored pastry lid. Serve the millefeuille with a roasted rhubarb compote (see page 282) and decorate with a few strawberries and fresh mint leaves.

SUGGESTED WINE PAIRING
BC: Elephant Island "Little King" Sparkling, Naramata
International: Marchesi di Gresy "La Serra" Moscato d'Asti, Piedmont, Italy

GINGER POUND CAKE

Serves 12

2 cups (500 mL) unsalted butter, cut into cubes
3 cups (750 mL) granulated sugar
6 large eggs
½ cup (125 mL) minced fresh ginger, about a 3-inch (7.5-cm) piece, peeled
4 cups (1 L) all-purpose flour

1 tsp (5 mL) baking powder
1½ tsp (7 mL) ground ginger
¼ tsp (1 mL) mace
½ tsp (2 mL) salt
zest of 1 orange
¾ cup (175 mL) milk

This pound cake is a tremendous accompaniment to fresh fruit and even better when cut into fingers and toasted. Serve these alongside a crème fraîche panna-cotta (see page 292) and some fresh berries or peaches. This cake is also tremendous for breakfast! Over the years it has become my mom's favorite and I bake it for her a number of times a year when she visits Joie.

Preheat oven to 300°F (150°C). Grease and flour a 10-inch (4-L) tube pan or mini loaf baking pan.

Cream the butter and then add the sugar 2 Tbsp (30 mL) at a time. Add the eggs 1 at a time, beating after each addition. Add the fresh ginger and mix until combined.

Mix together the flour, baking powder, ground ginger, mace, salt, and orange zest in a separate bowl and then fold into the butter mixture in batches, alternating with the milk. Fold the batter together gently, being careful not to overmix (or your cake will be tough).

Bake for 1¾–2 hours until a skewer inserted in the center of the cake comes out clean. Cool the cake on a rack for 20 minutes and then invert it onto another wire rack to unmold. Allow to cool completely before slicing.

CHEF'S TIP

Try grating ginger on a rasp. It goes much more quickly than mincing by hand with a knife and gets out all the stringy bits of the ginger root.

SUGGESTED WINE PAIRING

BC: La Frenz Liqueur Muscat, Naramata
International: Paul Jaboulet Muscat de Beaumes-de-Venise, Rhone, France

DARK CHOCOLATE PAVLOVA WITH BALATON SOUR CHERRY COMPOTE

Serves 8–10

FOR THE CHOCOLATE MERINGUE BASE
6 egg whites
1½ cups (375 mL) granulated sugar
3 Tbsp (45 mL) high-quality cocoa
    powder, sieved
1 tsp (5 mL) balsamic vinegar
2 oz (50 g) finely chopped dark chocolate
    with 65–77% cocoa solids

FOR THE SOUR CHERRY COMPOTE
1 lb (500 g) sour cherries, pitted
juice and zest of 1 large orange
1 cup (250 mL) honey
½ cup (125 mL) red wine
juice and zest of 1 lemon

FOR THE TOPPING
2 cups (500 mL) whipping (35%) cream
dark chocolate shavings, made with a
    vegetable peeler

This pavlova is adapted from Nigella Lawson's recipe in her *Endless Summer* cookbook. Experiencing the endless summers in the Okanagan, I gave a nod to her comments about pavlova being the ultimate summer dessert. This dessert is not heavy with pastry and instead has a crisp and chewy chocolate meringue base studded with melting dark chocolate and astringent cocoa. It provides the perfect end to a summer's meal. I made mine into individual pavlovas (as one large pavlova was too difficult to cut for 20 people!), topped them with a sour cherry compote, and served them with Elephant Island's Stella Cherry Port. This dessert is a delicious chocolate and cherry combination.

Preheat oven to 350°F (180°C). Line a baking tray with parchment paper.

To make the meringue base, beat the egg whites until soft peaks form and then beat in the sugar, a spoonful at a time, until the meringue is stiff and shiny. Sprinkle over the cocoa, vinegar, and chopped chocolate. Gently fold everything until the cocoa is thoroughly mixed in. Mound onto the prepared baking sheet in small individual circles about 3 inches (8 cm) in diameter, or 1 large circle about 9 inches (23 cm) in diameter, smoothing the sides and top. Place in the oven, then immediately lower the temperature to 300°F (150°C) and cook for about 1–1¼ hours. The individual pavlovas will cook faster than the single large one. When ready, pavlova should look crisp around the edges and on the sides and be dry on top, but when you prod the

center you should feel a slight give under your fingers, as the center should still be chewy. Turn off the oven, open the door slightly and let the chocolate meringue discs cool completely.

For the compote, put the cherries into a saucepan with the red wine and orange juice and zest and bring to a slow simmer. The cherries will begin to release their juice. Let the cherries simmer, uncovered, for half an hour. After the cherries have softened, remove them from the saucepan with a slotted spoon and reserve. Add the honey to the sour cherry juice and reduce slightly until the sauce is somewhat glossy. Return the sour cherries to the saucepan and coat with the sauce to glaze them. Adjust the sweetness with a little more honey if necessary and add the lemon juice and zest. Let the compote cool before topping the pavlova.

When you're ready to serve, invert the meringue onto a big, flat-bottomed plate for a large pavlova or onto small individual plates. Whip the cream until thick but still soft, pile it on top of the meringue, and then spoon over the compote, leaving a rim of white cream around the edges. Sprinkle the chocolate shavings haphazardly over the top, letting some fall onto the plate.

SUGGESTED WINE PAIRING
BC: Elephant Island Stellaport, Naramata
International: Chapoutier Rivesaltes,
Languedoc-Rousillon, France

PETITS POTS DE CRÈME

Makes 6 ramekins

¾ cup (175 mL) whole (3.25%) milk
¼ cup (60 mL) whipping (35%) cream
¼ vanilla bean pod
1 large egg
2 large egg yolks
3 Tbsp (45 mL) granulated sugar

FLAVOR VARIATIONS

Try adding 1 tsp (5 mL) orange or lemon zest, a cardamom pod, a cinnamon stick, 1 Tbsp (15 mL) reduced espresso or 2 tsp (10 mL) coarsely ground espresso beans, or 1 Tbsp (15 mL) brandy or rum to infuse the custard

I love pots de crème. They're a lighter custard alternative to crème brûlée. I like to make them in smaller ramekins and serve several flavors at one time. Maybe I prefer pots de crème to crème brûlée because I have made one too many crème brûlée in restaurants! Pots de crème are definitely the new crème brûlée.

Preheat oven to 350°F (180°C).

Combine the milk, cream, and vanilla bean in a saucepan. Scald the cream (heat it until it starts to form a skin), turn off the heat, and cover, letting the cream infuse for 10 minutes with the lid on the pot. If you're adding other flavors to be infused into the cream, now is the time to add them.

In a bowl whisk together the egg, egg yolks, and sugar. Stir in the hot cream and strain the mixture through a fine mesh sieve into a bowl. Skim any froth from the surface of the mixture with a ladle. Place 6 ramekins in a shallow baking dish and fill each ramekin three-quarters full with the custard. Place the baking dish with the full ramekins in the oven. Gently pour enough hot water into the baking dish to come halfway up the sides of the ramekins. By doing this in the oven, you lessen the chance of splashing water into the ramekins while walking to the oven, thus diluting the custard. The water bath around the ramekins will provide a gentle, even heat to cook the ramekins. This will give you your best chance of not "splitting" or scrambling the custard while baking it.

Bake the ramekins in the water bath for 20 minutes or until the custard is set and the surface feels elastic when lightly pressed and they wobble slightly when jiggled. Remove the custard from the water bath and cool before serving.

SUGGESTED WINE PAIRING
BC: La Frenz Tawny, Naramata
International: Lustau East India Solera Sherry, Jerez, Spain

CRÈME FRAÎCHE PANNACOTTA

Makes 12 small ramekins

6 sheets of gelatin, or 2 packets (30 mL) powdered gelatin
1 cup (250 mL) buttermilk
1 cup (250 mL) whipping (35%) cream

1 cup (250 mL) crème fraîche or sour cream
½ cup (125 mL) granulated sugar
juice and zest of 1 lemon

Pannacotta translates literally as "cooked cream." This recipe was passed on to me by a chef friend, Jason Schubert. Pannacotta is a light dessert for hot summer days and less "eggy" than ice cream or crème brûlée. It's a fresh accompaniment to seasonal fruit, especially when made with tangy buttermilk and crème fraîche.

Soak the gelatin in cold water in a bowl to soften. While the gelatin is softening, grease 12 small ramekins with butter and place on a baking sheet. Combine the buttermilk, cream, crème fraîche, and sugar in a saucepan and stir over medium heat until warm and smooth. Add the dissolved gelatin to the saucepan and stir until combined. Pour the pannacotta liquid into the greased ramekins, cover with plastic wrap, and refrigerate until set.

To serve, warm the outside of the ramekins with a torch to unmold easily. If you don't have a torch, dunk the ramekins into a warm water bath, being careful not to get water inside them. Run a paring knife along the rim of the ramekin when warm. Unmold the pannacotta onto a small plate by flipping the warmed ramekin upside down and giving it a few good shakes while holding onto both the plate and inverted ramekin until the pannacotta falls out.

SUGGESTED WINE PAIRING
BC: Elephant Island Crabapple Dessert Wine
International: La Spinetta Moscato d'Asti Bricco Quaglia, Piedmont, Italy

LEMON CURD

Serves 8

4 large egg yolks
2 large whole eggs
¼ cup (60 mL) granulated sugar
½ cup (125 mL) freshly squeezed lemon
   juice

zest of 2 lemons
4 Tbsp (60 mL) unsalted butter, cut into
   cubes

This recipe can also be prepared with lime and orange citrus. Lemon curd is delicious served for breakfast or set in a ramekin and served with a biscuit and fresh fruit.

Whisk together the egg yolks and whole eggs in a medium bowl and reserve. Combine the sugar and lemon juice and zest in a small, heavy-bottomed saucepan. Bring to a gentle simmer and stir until the sugar is dissolved. Once hot, pour a tiny bit of the lemon juice and sugar into the egg mixture to temper the eggs. This means that you're attempting to raise the temperature of the cold egg yolks a little bit a time, to prevent the eggs from scrambling. Continue to add the hot liquid a little bit a time, until it is all combined.

Once combined, transfer the curd mixture back into the saucepan in which you heated the lemon juice. Cook the curd mixture over low heat, stirring constantly with a wooden spoon, until the mixture coats the back of the spoon, about 5 minutes. Do not let the mixture curdle or cook on the bottom of the saucepan.

Remove the saucepan from the heat and stir to cool slightly. Strain through a fine mesh sieve into a medium bowl and add the butter, a piece at a time, stirring until smooth. To stop the lemon curd from cooking any further, let the mixture cool in a bowl floating in an ice-water bath.

Transfer to a serving dish or ramekins to set, and cover with plastic wrap to prevent a skin from forming. Let cool completely in the refrigerator before using. Curd may be refrigerated for up to 4 days.

SUGGESTED WINE PAIRING
BC: Mission Hill SLC Riesling Icewine, Westbank
International: Prinz von Hessen Johannisberger Klaus Riesling Eiswein, Rheingau, Germany

LAVENDER HONEY ICE CREAM

Serves 12

¾ cup (175 mL) local honey
1 sprig fresh lavender or 1 tsp (5 mL)
    dried culinary lavender (see page 271),
    crushed

1 cup (250 mL) half-and-half (10%)
    cream
2 cups (500 mL) whipping (35%) cream
6 large egg yolks

This recipe yields a wonderful, silky ice cream. Both the honey and the lavender lend a spicy quality to the dessert. Be careful when adding the lavender to the honey. Don't add too much or your ice cream will taste like soap! Less is more when baking with lavender.

Warm the honey with the lavender in a pot over low heat. Remove from the heat and infuse the honey to taste, about 5 minutes. Let the honey cool with the lavender in it.

In another pot, heat both creams to scald. While the creams are heating, whisk the egg yolks in a bowl until broken. When the cream is scalded, whisk some hot cream into the egg yolks to temper them. This will raise the temperature of the eggs slowly and ensure that the hot cream will not scramble them. Once all the cream has been added to the eggs, return the cream and egg mixture to the pot.

Prepare an ice-water bath.

Cook the egg mixture over low heat, stirring constantly, until the mixture coats the back of the spoon. Remove from the heat immediately and chill the pot in the ice-water bath. Stir in the cooled honey-lavender infusion. Once cold, freeze the mixture in an ice cream maker (see page 295) and then transfer to small ramekins to set for individual servings.

CINNAMON ICE CREAM

Serves 12

1 cup (250 mL) half-and-half (10%) cream	1 cinnamon stick
2 cups (500 mL) whipping (35%) cream	¼ tsp (1 mL) freshly grated cinnamon or cassia bark
¾ cup (175 mL) granulated sugar	6 large egg yolks

Cinnamon ice cream is a comforting accompaniment to a pear or apple tarte Tatin (see page 280) or a rustic apple pie. The warm spice of the freshly grated cinnamon is a nice counterpoint to caramelized fruit.

Warm both creams, the sugar, cinnamon stick, and grated cinnamon in a pot. Steep, covered, off the heat, for about 10 minutes. Taste toward the end of the steeping process to ensure that the cinnamon flavor is not becoming too overpowering.

Prepare an ice-water bath.

Whisk the egg yolks just enough to break them up and pour in some of the hot cream to temper the eggs, stirring constantly after the hot liquid has been added. Add the hot cream ladle by ladle, slowly raising the temperature of the egg mixture. Return the egg and cream mixture to the pan and cook over low heat, stirring constantly, until the custard coats the spoon. Strain the ice cream through a fine mesh sieve into a bowl that is sitting in the ice-water bath. This will prevent the custard mixture from cooking any further and will cool the mixture so that it can be frozen. While the mixture is cooling, remove the cinnamon stick and then chill thoroughly. Freeze in an ice cream maker, according to the manufacturer's instructions.

AN ICE CREAM MAKER (either manual or electric) allows you to make homemade ice cream. It has to do two things: first, cool the mixture while constantly churning to break up any ice crystals that form and, second, introduce air into the mixture so that the resulting ice cream will have a smooth, creamy texture. Most ice cream machines usually have a chilled bowl that spins on a motor with a paddle that locks into place and churns the mixture. Some machines, such as certain low-priced counter-top models, require that the resulting mixture be frozen for an extra 4 hours or more (or overnight), depending on the recipe, for the ice cream to harden to the desired consistency.

COCONUT ICE CREAM

Serves 8

1 ½ cups (375 mL) half-and-half (10%)
   cream
½ cup (125 mL) premium coconut milk
1 cup (250 mL) freshly grated coconut,
   or unsweetened dessicated coconut

6 large egg yolks
1 cup (250 mL) granulated sugar
1 cup (250 mL) whipping (35%) cream

This is a book of regional ingredients for the most part. However the Okanagan is the land of extremes when it comes to weather and calls for some outside relief occasionally. So, when it's really hot, sometimes coconut ice cream suits the mood of the heat. When it's hot out, this treat transports you to somewhere tropical.

   Bring the cream and coconut milk to a simmer in a saucepan, remove from the heat, and add the coconut. Allow to infuse for 10 minutes.

   Whisk together the egg yolks and sugar in a bowl. Pour the steeping milk mixture over the egg yolks, stir well, and pour into a heavy saucepan.

   Before you start to cook the ice cream, have ready the following: the whipping cream, a bowl, and a fine mesh strainer. These items are very important for finishing off the ice cream.

   Place the saucepan with the coconut mixture over medium heat. Stir well and let thicken until the mixture coats the back of a spoon. Remove from the heat and stir for 1–2 minutes to make sure that the cream has thickened. Add the whipping cream and pour the mixture through the fine mesh sieve into the prepared bowl. Allow the mixture to really cool and then freeze in an ice cream maker (see page 295).

COCONUT MILK is a sweet, milky white cooking liquid derived from the meat of a mature coconut. The color and rich taste of the milk can be attributed to its high oil content and sugars. Coconut milk usually can be found in the Asian food section of supermarkets, either frozen or canned. Depending on the brand and age of the milk itself, a thicker, more paste-like consistency floats to the top of the can. This part is sometimes separated and used in recipes that require coconut cream rather than coconut milk. Shaking the can before opening will even the contents to a cream-like thickness.

DANA'S SOUR CREAM ICE CREAM

Serves 12

2 cups (500 mL) sour cream, organic if
    possible
¾ cup (175 mL) granulated sugar

¼ cup (60 mL) whipping (35%) cream
juice and zest of 1 lemon

My friend chef Dana Ewart gave me this recipe when she came to us on her second visit. It's a wonderful ice cream creation to make in a pinch as it doesn't involve making a custard. Use the best sour cream you can buy from a local dairy. The less weird gummy things the sour cream has in it, the nicer the texture and flavor of the ice cream. I particularly like to serve this tangy ice cream with rich apple or pear desserts like Tatin (see page 280). Try it instead of vanilla ice cream.

Combine the sour cream, sugar, whipping cream, and lemon juice and zest over a double boiler, and stir until the sugar is dissolved. Cool the mixture and put into an ice cream maker (see page 295) and freeze until thick. Transfer the ice cream to a flat-bottom dish or to individual ramekins and freeze until needed.

HONEY AND LIME FROZEN YOGURT

Serves 12

2 cups (500 mL) full-fat natural yogurt,
    organic and unhomogenized if
    possible

½ cup (125 mL) local honey
¼ cup (60 mL) whipping (35%) cream
juice and zest of 1 lime

I like to make this frozen treat when it's really hot in the Okanagan in August and I couldn't possibly imagine eating anything rich for dessert.

Combine the yogurt, honey, cream, and lime juice and zest in a bowl and whisk until combined. Put the mixture into an ice cream maker (see page 295) and freeze until thick. Transfer the ice cream to a flat-bottomed dish or to individual ramekins and freeze until needed.

Serve on its own with a toasted coconut macaroons (see page 308) or with fresh white peaches. Try serving it with something tropical in the winter months, when mangoes and pineapples are in season.

PEACH AND PURPLE BASIL SORBET

Makes 12 small servings

2 lb (1 kg) Redhaven peaches
1 cup (250 mL) purple basil leaves, left
    whole

2½ cups (625 mL) granulated sugar
juice of 2 lemons

This sorbet captures the pure essence of summer—ripe peaches right off the tree and fragrant basil.

Prepare an ice-water bath.

Score the bottoms of the peaches. Bring a pot of water to a boil, blanch the peaches quickly, and then plunge them into the ice-water bath to remove the skins. Cut the peaches in half, remove the pit, and cut the peach into slices. Toss the whole purple basil leaves with the peach slices in a large bowl. Cover the peaches with the sugar and toss until completely coated.

Macerate the peach and basil overnight in the sugar. In the morning the peaches should have released their juice. Blend with a hand-held immersion blender or in a stand-up blender until the peaches are puréed. Add the lemon juice to balance the sweetness of the purée. Pass the purée through a fine mesh sieve into the bowl of an ice cream machine.

Freeze the sorbet in an ice cream maker (see page 295) until the purée is slushy and then transfer into small ramekins or a casserole dish. Freeze until hard.

ORANGE SORBET

Makes 12 small servings

1 cup (250 mL) water
1 cup (250 mL) granulated sugar
2 cups (500 mL) freshly squeezed orange
    juice

juice of 1 lemon
zest from 2 of the oranges used for the
    juice

Orange sorbet is a refreshing treat and a nice alternative to lemon sorbet. Try substituting the juice from blood oranges or grapefruit for regular oranges. You could also try adding sorbet to cocktails for a refreshing summer drink.

Heat the water and sugar in a pot until dissolved to make a simple syrup. Bring to a boil, simmer for 2 minutes, and let cool.

Add the orange and lemon juices and the zest to the cold syrup and strain, if necessary, through a fine mesh strainer. Chill. Freeze the sorbet in an ice cream maker (see page 295). Transfer to small dishes and freeze until hard.

MASCARPONE SORBET

Makes 8 large servings or 16 smaller scoops to accompany a tart

1 cup (250 mL) water
1 cup (250 mL) granulated sugar
2 cups (500 mL) mascarpone, softened

zest of 1 lemon
seeds from ½ vanilla bean pod

Mascarpone certainly doesn't need to be made into an egg-rich ice cream as it's already so decadent. I like this sorbet as a rich accompaniment to a tangy currant tart or plum galettes.

Heat the water and sugar in a pot until dissolved to make a simple syrup. Bring to a boil, simmer for 2 minutes, and let cool.

Whisk the cold simple syrup into the softened mascarpone. Do not overwhip; mix only until just combined. Add the lemon zest and vanilla seeds. Freeze in an ice cream maker (see page 295). Transfer to small dishes and freeze until hard.

LEMON BALM SORBET

Serves 12

1¼ cups (310 mL) freshly squeezed
    lemon juice (about 7–8 lemons)
zest of 3 lemons
handful of lemon balm leaves, left whole

1 cup (250 mL) water
1 cup (250 mL) granulated sugar
2 egg whites

This sorbet is a fresh variation on the enduring favorite lemon sorbetto. Adding lemon balm leaves gives a nice herbal note with a clean citrus flavor.

Heat the water and sugar in a pot until dissolved to make a simple syrup. Bring to a boil, simmer for 2 minutes, and let cool.

Combine the lemon juice, zest, lemon balm leaves, and cold simple syrup in a bowl to make a sorbet.

IF YOU'RE USING AN ICE CREAM MAKER
Whisk the egg whites until they form stiff peaks, fold them into the sorbet mixture, and then put the mix-ture into an ice cream maker (see page 295). Turn the machine until the mixture is very slushy. Place in a cold flat-bottomed dish, ramekins, or a container and freeze for at least 2–3 hours before serving.

IF YOU'RE FREEZING THE SORBET
IN A DISH IN THE FREEZER
Cover the sorbet mixture and freeze for 2–3 hours, stir-ring occasionally until you have a thick slush. Whisk the egg whites to stiff peaks and fold into the sorbet mixture when it is slushy. Return to the freezer for 2–3 hours.

PETITS FOURS

CLAYBANK FARM LAVENDER BISCUITS

Makes 48 small biscuits

2 cups (500 mL) all-purpose flour
½ tsp (2 mL) baking powder
½ tsp (2 mL) salt
¾ cup (175 mL) unsalted butter, softened
   (use the best organic butter you can
   buy!)
1 cup (250 mL) granulated sugar
1 large egg

½ tsp (2 mL) pure vanilla extract
zest of 1 orange
zest of ½ lemon
1 tsp (5 mL) dried culinary lavender,
   crumbled (see page 271)
½ cup (125 mL) sanding sugar or cane
   sugar

A recipe created by Joie for Pati Hill of Claybank Farm Lavender on the Naramata Bench. Pair them with seasonal fruit, lemon curd (see page 293) or homemade ice cream or sorbet (see pages 294–299).

Whisk together the flour, baking powder, and salt in a bowl.

Beat together the butter and sugar in a separate large bowl with an electric mixer at medium-high

speed until pale and fluffy, about 3 minutes, or in a standing mixer with a paddle attachment. Beat in the egg and vanilla, zests, and crumbled lavender. It's very important not to use too much lavender, or your cookies will taste like a bar of soap! Less is more, when cooking with lavender. Reduce the speed to low and add the flour mixture, mixing it until just combined and being careful not to overwork the dough.

Form the dough into a 12-inch (30-cm) log, 2 inches (5 cm) in diameter, on a sheet of plastic wrap and roll in plastic wrap. Chill the dough on a baking sheet until firm, at least 4 hours.

Preheat oven to 375°F (190°C). Line a baking sheet with parchment paper.

Take the sanding sugar, spread it out on a baking sheet and roll the cold log to coat the outside. Cut the log into ¼-inch (0.5-cm) thick slices with a heavy knife. Arrange the slices 1 inch (2.5 cm) apart on the prepared baking sheet and bake for about 10–12 minute until slightly golden around the edges.

Cool the cookies slightly before transferring them onto a cooling rack to cool completely.

CHEF'S TIP
Demerara and turbinado sugar make good sanding sugars.

CANDIED PEEL AND PAMELA

Makes 3 cups (750 mL) candied peel or 24 Pamela

4–6 thick-skinned pink grapefruit (about 4 lb/2 kg) or other citrus fruits like oranges or limes

2¾ cups (675 mL) granulated sugar
1¾ cups (425 mL) granulated sugar, for rolling the finished peel

Candied citrus is one of my favorite dessert garnishes. It's handy to have around all the time to eat on its own, dip in chocolate, or garnish a tart. Sometimes I'll finely chop it and add it to the ganache of a chocolate tart or add it to biscotti dough. Wide strips of candied grapefruit peel are known as "Pamela" and are a classic petit four. They make an elegant end to a meal.

Cut the 2 ends off the grapefruit and then divide into quarters lengthwise. Using a sharp knife, make a clean sweep, removing the peel but leaving one-third of the pulp attached to the rind. Cut each of the quarters of peel lengthwise into 4 equal strips. Each fruit should yield 16 strips about 3 inches (7.5 cm) long and ¾ inch (2 cm) wide. If you're using oranges or limes, cut the strips into a julienne.

Place the peel in a large saucepan. Cover with cold water and slowly bring to a boil, uncovered. Boil rapidly for 5 minutes and then drain the peel. Repeat this procedure 4 or more times, beginning with fresh cold water each time. The peel has been blanched enough when the skin can be broken by squeezing it with your fingers. This blanching removes all but a pleasing trace of bitterness from the peel.

Return the peel to the saucepan, add the 2¾ cups (675 mL) sugar and cook, uncovered, over very low heat. Turn the peel frequently with a wooden spoon during cooking. It's important to cook the peel very slowly; if the liquid evaporates too fast, the peel will be insufficiently cooked. It will take 1–2 hours to cook and glaze the peel.

Arrange the candied citrus on racks set over waxed paper, so that the excess syrup can drain away. When cool enough to handle, take the peel, 1 piece at a time, and roll it in the remaining sugar.

Candied citrus lasts a long time when packed in sugar and put into an airtight container or jar.

CARDAMOM AND ESPRESSO
CHOCOLATE BUTTER COOKIES

Makes 48 cookies

2 cups (500 mL) all-purpose flour
½ cup (125 mL) unsweetened
    Dutch-process cocoa powder
    (I like to use Valrhona cocoa powder)
½ tsp (2 mL) baking powder
½ tsp (2 mL) baking soda
½ tsp (2 mL) salt
2 Tbsp (30 mL) finely ground espresso
    beans
2 cardamom pods, finely ground
¾ cup (175 mL) unsalted butter, softened
    (use the best organic butter you can
    buy!)

1 cup (250 mL) granulated sugar
1 large egg
½ tsp (2 mL) pure vanilla extract
11 oz (315 g) best quality bittersweet
    chocolate you can afford (I like to use
    Valrhona organic "Manjari" 67%
    cocoa solids), melted and cooled
½ cup (125 mL) finely ground, salted,
    roasted pistachios
½ cup (125 mL) demerara sugar with the
    zest of 1 orange grated in

These butter-rich biscuits are a beautiful way to end a meal when paired with strong Arabic coffee and an orange pot de crème (see page 291).

Whisk together the flour, cocoa powder, baking powder, baking soda, salt, espresso, and cardamom in a bowl.

Beat together the butter and sugar in a separate large bowl with an electric mixer at medium-high speed until pale and fluffy, about 3 minutes, or in a standing mixer with a paddle attachment. Beat in the egg and vanilla. Reduce the speed to low and add the flour and cocoa mixture, mixing until just combined and being careful not to overwork the dough.

Add the cooled melted chocolate to the dough in a continuous stream, with the mixer running on medium-low. This will make the dough quite stiff.

On a sheet of plastic wrap, form the dough into a 12-inch (30-cm) log (2 inches/5 cm in diameter), or 2 6-inch (15-cm) logs for smaller cookies. Garnish by rolling the log(s) in the ground pistachios and then the demerara sugar and orange zest. Roll up the dough in plastic wrap and chill on a baking sheet in the refrigerator until firm, at least 4 hours.

Preheat oven to 375°F (190°C). Line a baking sheet with parchment paper.

Cut the log into ¼-inch (0.5-cm) thick slices with a heavy knife. Arrange the slices 1 inch (2.5 cm) apart on the prepared baking sheet and bake for about 10–12 minutes until the cookies are set, but not rock hard.

Cool the cookies slightly before transferring them onto a cooling rack.

CHOCOLATE is made from the fermented, roasted, and ground beans taken from the pod of the tropical *Theobroma cacao* tree, which was native to Central America and Mexico, but is now cultivated throughout the tropics. Cacao beans have an intensely flavored bitter taste. Cacao products are known as chocolate or, in some parts of the world, as cocoa. It's the solid and fat combination, sweetened with sugar and other ingredients, that's made into chocolate. Chocolate is very sensitive to temperature and humidity. Ideal storage temperatures are 59–62°F (15–17°C), preferably in a dark place, as sunlight can warm the surface of the chocolate and cause it to "bloom" as cocoa butter crystals form on its surface.

>> Unsweetened or baking chocolate is simply cooled, hardened chocolate liquor and generally of low quality. I don't use baking chocolate.

>> Semi-sweet chocolate has extra cocoa butter and sugar added. A nice option for chocolate chips.

>> Milk chocolate is chocolate liquor with extra cocoa butter, sugar, milk, and vanilla added. This is the most popular form of chocolate and it's primarily an eating chocolate.

>> Dark chocolate has a higher grade of cocoa solids than semi-sweet chocolate. Generally, quality dark chocolate starts at 65% cocoa solids and goes up as high as 77%. The darker the chocolate, the deeper and more bitter the flavor.

>> White chocolate is actually not chocolate at all. It's a confection made from cocoa butter, milk, sugar, and flavorings. You either love it or hate it.

>> Chocolate liquor is a thick paste of crushed cocoa nibs (the inner part of the cocoa bean) mixed with the bean's inner cocoa butter.

JOIE BISCOTTI

Makes 48 small biscotti

2 cups (500 mL) all-purpose flour
1 cup (250 mL) granulated sugar
1 tsp (5 mL) baking powder
1 tsp (5 mL) ground anise seeds
¼ tsp (1 mL) salt

3 large eggs
1 Tbsp (15 mL) marsala
¾ cup (175 mL) toasted whole
   almonds, hazelnuts, or walnut pieces
¼ cup (60 mL) chopped dried fruit

Biscotti are the perfect accompaniment to ice cream, sorbet, or fresh fruit. I like eating them for breakfast with my coffee. This is a traditional biscotti recipe that contains very little fat, yielding quite hard biscuits, which are best for dipping. You can put together any combination of fruit and nuts that you like. My favorites are currant and hazelnut, and at Christmas time, cranberry and pistachio for a festive color scheme. Try making a more savory biscotti by halving the sugar, adding a bit more salt, and adding a savory herb like rosemary or thyme. Walnut and rosemary biscotti make a nice addition to a cheese plate.

Preheat oven to 300°F (150°C). Line a baking sheet with parchment paper.

Combine the flour, sugar, baking powder, anise, and salt in a medium bowl and mix together thoroughly with a whisk. Set aside.

Whisk the eggs and marsala together in a large bowl until well blended. Stir in the flour mixture and then the nuts and dried fruit. The dough will be thick and sticky. Do not work the dough too much or the biscotti will be tough. Scrape the dough into a long log shape lengthwise on the prepared baking sheet. Flour your hands and shape the dough into a long flat loaf, about 10 inches (25 cm) long and 5 inches (12.5 cm) wide (you can make smaller biscotti, if you prefer).

Bake until firm and dry, about 50 minutes. Remove from the oven and let cool for about 10 minutes. Carefully transfer the loaf to a cutting board. Using a long serrated knife, cut the loaf on the diagonal into slices ½ inch (1 cm) wide. Lay the slices, cut side down, on the cookie sheet. Bake for 20 minutes; turn each cookie over and bake for 15–20 minutes more, or until the biscotti are just starting to turn golden brown. Place the cookie sheet on a rack to cool. Cool the biscotti completely before storing. They'll keep in an airtight container for several weeks.

HONEY MADELEINES

Makes 14 large or 40 small madeleines

2 eggs
5 Tbsp (75 mL) granulated sugar
1 Tbsp (15 mL) soft dark brown sugar
pinch of salt
⅔ cup (150 mL) all-purpose flour
1 tsp (5 mL) baking powder

1 tsp (5 mL) pure vanilla extract
6 Tbsp (90 mL) melted unsalted butter,
  browned slightly and cooled
1 Tbsp (15 mL) clear honey
2 Tbsp (30 mL) melted unsalted butter,
  cooled, for greasing the pans

This recipe was created to showcase the fabulous honey from Similkameen Apiary in Cawston, which I buy at the Penticton Farmer's Market. You'll need a special madeleine tray to make this recipe.

To prepare the batter, combine the eggs, both sugars, and the salt in the bowl of a standing mixer. Using the whisk attachment, beat on medium speed until the mixture begins to turn light in color. This will take about 3–5 minutes. Sift together the flour and baking powder and fold them gently into the mixture with the vanilla. Do not overwork the mixture or the madeleines will be chewy. Pour in the cooled melted butter and honey and mix until completely combined. Cover the bowl with plastic wrap and leave to rest in a cool place for half an hour, or longer if necessary.

Preheat oven to 425°F (220°C).

Brush the madeleine tray thoroughly with melted butter. Pipe the mixture into the cavities in the tray, using a piping bag fitted with a ½-inch (1-cm) plain-tipped nozzle (or a ziplock bag with a corner cut off), forming the mixture into evenly shaped domes. Bake for about 5 minutes for small madeleines and 10 min-

utes for larger ones. Do not overcook them or they will not be moist. As soon as they are cooked, invert the tray directly onto a wire rack to cool. My preference is to serve the madeleines warm.

TOASTED COCONUT MACAROONS

Makes about 3 dozen large macaroons

1½ cups (375 mL) sweetened shredded
  coconut
4 large egg whites

pinch of salt
½ cup (125 mL) granulated sugar

My husband, Michael, adores macaroons and co-conut, so when I want to do something nice for him I make him these cookies. These are a nice petit four with a tropical bent perfect for hot weather if you make them tiny.

Preheat oven to 350°F (180°C). Line a baking sheet with parchment paper.

Toast the shredded coconut in a dry frying pan on medium heat until it begins to smell toasty and turns a light golden brown. In a standing mixer fitted with a whisk attachment, or by hand, whip the egg whites and salt until they become very white and begin to stiffen. Add the sugar in 3 additions, beating after each addition. Continue to whip until the egg whites are very stiff, but not dry. Using a spatula, fold in the toasted coconut. Drop the mixture 1 tsp (5 mL) at a time onto the prepared baking sheet, leaving 1–2 inches (2.5–5 cm) around each cookie. Bake for 15–20 minutes. The outside should be golden brown but the insides should still be moist and chewy when eaten. Store in an airtight container—although at my house they never make it that far!

BRANDY SNAPS

Makes 24 large snaps

⅔ cup (150 mL) unsalted butter,
  softened or melted
¾ cup (175 mL) granulated sugar

1¼ cups (310 mL) all-purpose flour
⅔ cup (150 mL) corn syrup
1 Tbsp (15 mL) brandy

Brandy snaps are always a beautiful, lacy accompaniment to ice cream or sorbet (see pages 294–99) or lemon curd (see page 293) with a garnish of fresh berries.

Combine the butter, sugar, flour, corn syrup, and brandy. Chill the dough until it sets, about 1 hour.

Preheat oven to 375°F (190°C). Grease a baking sheet.

Roll the dough into small balls, press down onto the prepared baking sheet, and bake for 5 minutes. While still warm, but not molten, remove the brandy snaps from the baking sheet with a spatula or off-set palette knife and shape into your preferred form. Shape them over a rolling pin for a tuille-shape or over a cup to form a "nest." You can also leave them flat as cookies.

LANGUES DE CHAT

Makes 2 dozen cookies

½ cup (125 mL) unsalted butter

½ cup (125 mL) granulated sugar

3 egg whites

1 cup (250 mL) pastry flour

These classic petits fours are a light and elegant accompaniment to ice cream or sorbet (see pages 294–99), mousse, or crème brûlée.

Preheat oven to 400°F (200°C).

Cream the butter and sugar until light and fluffy. Beat in the egg whites. Add the flour gradually, mixing after each addition, and continue to beat until the batter is smooth. Do not overbeat as this will create a tough batter.

Place the batter into a piping bag with a round tip and pipe out your preferred shapes. The classic shape for langues de chat is a long oval or a long S-shape. Allow sufficient space between each biscuit on the tray as they spread during baking. Bake until golden around the edges, about 5 minutes. Remove the biscuits from the tray while they're still warm. Shape them by lifting them off the baking sheet with a spatula and hanging them over a rolling pin. The biscuits will now harden into a curled or twisted shape (like a cat's tongue, in fact!). Let the biscuits cool on the rolling pin and store in an airtight container.

TYPES OF FLOUR are generally differentiated by their protein (or gluten) content. When hydrated and then agitated, gluten is what forms the elastic quality and "chewy" texture in good bread and pasta. When making finer pastry, lower-gluten–content flour is therefore desired.

>> All-purpose flour is a blend of hard and soft wheat; it may be bleached or unbleached. It is commonly known as "plain flour."

>> Semolina flour is used in making pasta and Italian puddings. It's made from durum wheat, the hardest type of wheat grown. This flour has the highest gluten of all.

>> Whole-wheat flour is made from the whole kernel of wheat and is higher in dietary fiber and overall nutrient content than white flours. It doesn't have as high a gluten level, so it's often mixed with all-purpose or bread flour when making yeast breads.

>> Bread flour is white flour made from hard, high-protein wheat. It has more gluten strength and protein content than all-purpose flour. It's unbleached and sometimes conditioned with ascorbic acid, which increases volume and creates better texture. This is the best choice for yeast products.

>> Pastry flour is also made with soft wheat and falls somewhere between all-purpose and cake flour in terms of protein content and baking properties. Use it for making biscuits, pie crusts, brownies, cookies, and quick breads. Pastry flour makes a tender but crumbly pastry. Do not use it for yeast breads.

WALNUT COOKIES

Makes 36 cookies

1 cup (250 mL) fresh chopped walnuts
¾ cup (175 mL) unsalted butter
1½ cups (375 mL) brown sugar
2 large eggs
1 tsp (5 mL) pure vanilla extract

3 cups (750 mL) all-purpose flour
1 tsp (5 mL) baking soda
1 tsp (5 mL) baking powder
1 tsp (5 mL) salt
nuts, halved and toasted, for garnish

We have a huge black walnut tree at the top of our driveway. I make these cookies in the late fall when the walnuts are ready to be harvested. The key to these cookies is using the freshest walnuts you can find (rancid nuts are why many people don't like walnuts, I think) and using the best unsalted organic butter you can buy. If you don't have your own walnut tree, buy your nuts from a store with a high turnover of its dry goods and spices.

Preheat oven to 350°F (180°C). Line a baking sheet with parchment paper.

Toast the walnuts in a dry pan, until they're just warm. This will awaken their oils and make them more aromatic.

Cream together the butter and sugar until pale and fluffy. Add the eggs, 1 at a time, beating after each addition. Add the vanilla. Mix together the flour, baking soda, baking powder, and salt in a separate bowl and fold into the creamed butter by hand until just combined. Add the chopped, toasted walnuts.

Form the dough into 1-inch (2.5-cm) balls and flatten. Garnish each cookie with a whole walnut half.

Bake for 10–12 minutes, until just golden.

DARK CHOCOLATE TRUFFLES

Makes 20 truffles

2 Tbsp (30 mL) unsalted butter, chopped
3 Tbsp (45 mL) whipping (35%) cream
3½ oz (85 g) dark chocolate with
    65–77% cocoa solids) (see page 305)

1 small egg yolk
high-quality cocoa to finish

Truffles are a classic way to end a large meal without having something too heavy and voluminous. I prefer mine made with straight-up ganache with the best chocolate you can afford, simply rolled in high-quality astringent cocoa. This literally makes them look like truffles from the ground—hence the name and mis-formed shape.

Combine the butter and cream in a small saucepan. Cook over low heat until the butter melts and the cream bubbles around the edge. Remove from the heat. Put the chocolate in a small bowl and add the butter and cream. Let stand until the chocolate melts, stirring until smooth.

Stir in the egg yolk and any flavorings you have chosen to add (see Chef's tip). Chill the ganache until firm and then form into 20 balls. Roll in cocoa and then refrigerate in an airtight container for up to 2 weeks.

CHEF'S TIP
Try the following variations as additions to the ganache: ½ tsp (2 mL) grated orange zest, 1 Tbsp (15 mL) rum or brandy, 1 Tbsp (15 mL) mint extract, 1 Tbsp (15 mL) chopped soft citrus peel or dried cherries, or 1 Tbsp (15 mL) crushed praline.

CHEF'S TIP
Brands of chocolate I enjoy: Valrhona, Green and Black's, Scharffen Berger.

ACKNOWLEDGEMENTS

To my publisher Robert McCullough at Whitecap who kept asking me to do this project until I said, yes! Thank you for your friendship, kindred spirit, and good taste.

To my fabulous editor, Lesley Cameron, and proofreader, Ann-Marie Metten, who drove this book toward clarity like "personal trainers for words." *Menus from an Orchard Table* is 10 times the book with their input.

With gratitude I would like to thank all the chefs who have pushed my boundaries as a cook. Cam and Dana, not only was I happy to see you the day you drove down our driveway, but thank goodness you have stayed to keep us company . . . and Schubert, thank you for a summer of inspiration. I value your friendships and opinions dearly. Best of luck to all of you with your own new ventures.

To my producers, without you I would have no inspiration.

My endless gratitude goes out to my brother Craig for his boundless energy for farm projects that I never seemed to have the time to get to, such as our incredible hand-built smoker, raised irrigation in our garden beds, the indulgent outdoor shower, and the coolest chicken coop in the Okanagan, the *Coop de Luxe*. I hope someday you have a farm of your own and a patron for your amazing film projects like *Tableland*. Your portraits bring to life the producers featured in this book.

To my other brother Alex, whose patience and hard work went into our fabulous deck overlooking Okanagan Lake and the thousands of litres of wine he helped to get into the finished bottle despite consuming several of them along the way . . .

To my Mom and Dad, Peigi and Terry Noble, who took all of us kids around the world on culinary adventures, sat us up to the table like adults, and fed us marinated octopus after school. Thank you for your confidence and support with our Joie project from the beginning.

I also thank my Dad for teaching me that "cashflow will never lie . . . "

To PoPo and her love of the farm. Thank you for all your hard work in our first years.

To Pati I give thanks for all of your infinite country know-how, friendship, and eagle-eye editing.

To John Archer and Douglas Bertz for being an oasis of style, class, and domestic skill; providing a respite in the middle of nowhere and preserving the art of true hospitality. You are also the most handsome professional dinner guests in the whole valley.

To Paul Gardner for being "The Captain"—our friend and winemaking mentor. Making wine with you was like making wine with MacGyver.

To Dwight Sick for your calm patience and taking the time during the chaos to pass down your invaluable cellar and lab skills.

To Franca Mooijer for keeping my house in order for both me and my guests. Your help was and still is an invaluable part of my life.

To Misha who was with me at my side through two summers of crazy times at that orchard table. 2004 would not have happened without you (and yes, I still love you Miss Mish).

To Kali and Chloe, who are the hardest working teenagers you'll ever meet. Thank you for your all-purpose help in the fourth season of the cooking school and for your invaluable typing skills with the book. With your smiles and drive you both are going places.

To my favorite (fearless) eating friends in the entire world: Graham and Jenny Peers. Here's to cross-border adventure eating. We miss you.

To Sinclair Philip for his wise advice at the beginning of our project and for his leadership of local food movements in BC and throughout Canada.

To Mara Jernigan for being a culinary soul-sister and powerhouse inspiration.

To Chris Stearns for his friendship and delicious libations. Your stunning photography made this book.

To dng23 and his graphic design for putting a classy face on Joie from Day One. Our website has always been our best tool. Thanks, Dale!

To Kelly Reid of Tourism Penticton for tirelessly promoting our project with class and dignity to only the best media. Your efforts have drawn the eyes of the world to the Okanagan Valley.

To the Stratford Chefs School for forging "the field to table" early in my formative cooking days and giving me the entrepreneurial foundations for a dynamic career!

To Jack Segal for hiring me out of one stage of my life and pushing me forward into the next. The wine business is so much more civilized than the kitchen . . . Thank you for all the wonderful producers and families you have shared with me, for the opportunity to travel, and for being yet another entrepreneurial influence in my life.

To the wine trade and the restaurant community of British Columbia and beyond who believed in our project from the beginning and have supported our wines from our first release.

Most of all, I would like to thank our Joie clients from the past four years who have made our project a resounding success. I look forward to sharing the new changes on our farm with you in the years to come.

INDEX